Public Indians, Private Cherokees

CONTEMPORARY AMERICAN INDIAN STUDIES

J. Anthony Paredes, *Series Editor*

Public Indians, Private Cherokees

Tourism and Tradition on Tribal Ground

CHRISTINA TAYLOR BEARD-MOOSE

THE UNIVERSITY OF ALABAMA PRESS
Tuscaloosa

Typeface: ACaslon

∞

The paper on which this book is printed meets the minimum requirements of American
National Standard for Information Sciences-Permanence of Paper for Printed Library
Materials, ANSI Z39.48-1984.

Library of Congress Cataloging-in-Publication Data

Beard-Moose, Christina Taylor.
    Public Indians, private Cherokees : tourism and tradition on tribal ground / Christina Taylor
Beard-Moose.
        p.   cm. — (Contemporary American Indian studies)
    Includes bibliographical references and index.
    ISBN 978-0-8173-1634-1 (cloth : alk. paper) — ISBN 978-0-8173-5513-5 (pbk. : alk. paper) —
ISBN 978-0-8173-8115-8 (electronic) 1. Eastern Band of Cherokee Indians of North Carolina—
History. 2. Cherokee Indians—Industries. 3. Cherokee Indians—Economic conditions.
4. Cherokee Indians—Attitudes. 5. Heritage tourism—Economic aspects—North Carolina.
6. Culture and tourism—North Carolina. I. Title.
    E99.C5B37 2009
    306.4′81909756—dc22

                                                                            2008021836

Contents

Illustrations

Public Indians, Private Cherokees

1
Researching the Obvious
Tourism and the Eastern Cherokee

It was the summer of 2006, and I was standing in the very same geographical spot that I had ten years earlier. In 1996, when I tentatively began my fieldwork in Cherokee, North Carolina, I would never have predicted that in a decade the Boundary of the Eastern Band of the Cherokee Nation would be so different. After all, the town and most of its environs had been much the same since I first came to the place in the 1950s as a young child, a tourist with my family. In 1996 my focus was working with Cherokee women and collecting and creating an ethnographic package about Cherokee women's identity at the end of the twentieth century in America. Prior to that I had made numerous summer excursions as another among millions of tourists who travel annually to consume the commodities that are the Great Smoky Mountains and the tourist strip through Cherokee. I then came as a parent myself, and as such I was always an eager participant in the tour. I had brought my son to Cherokee on numerous occasions when he was in preschool and kindergarten. When I arrived to begin my fieldwork in the summer of 1996, it had not yet occurred to me to focus on that tour and the impact of the tourist industry on the Cherokee.

Since people live in small pools of culture, every human's daily lived experience is always, everywhere local, whether that locale is a mountain Indian reservation, an urban ethnic community, a multinational corporation, or a small American town. While a few want to leave and explore the world, the vast majority of the people on this planet are stationary. In the United States, and any other place that fully exploits this technological age, we explore the world from La-Z-Boys in front of the box of shadows we call television. Anything from the latest movie to the Olympics is within the grasp of everyone with access to a TV and a cable or satellite system. Local culture is acted on, augmented, enhanced, and changed by that access. MTV, CNN, Kosovo, Israel/Palestine, Columbine High School, *Star Wars, Austin Powers,* "The 700 Club"; the list continues ad infinitum (or ad nauseam) and is familiar to a vast majority of ethnic Americans.

This book is about a phenomenon that is now concomitant with life for the residents of a small corner of western North Carolina. It has a historical basis and is also a current cultural system that is always already on the verge of the next step, the next change, within an American Indian society of the southeastern United States. The phenomenon is tourism. The people are the Eastern Band of the Cherokee Nation (EBCN), formerly the Eastern Band of Cherokee Indians (EBCI). They reside on what is called the Boundary, not "the rez." EBCN land is federally held; however, unlike most other reservations in the United States, the Boundary is a land grant to the Cherokee. Even though I am a long-standing traveler of this part of the country, I began this ethnographic study in 1996 while working toward a Ph.D. in anthropology. A decade later, I returned to the site of my field experience to observe the changes that had taken place during that time.

This volume presents a history of the tourist phenomenon in Cherokee as well as two distinct ethnographic presents, 1996 and 2006, together. My intention is to illuminate the ways in which tourism, as the fastest-growing economic industry worldwide, has both its ups and its downs for the Eastern Cherokee. In many ways, the changes I will document, a great many of which are positive for the Eastern Cherokee people, only happened due to the tourist industry. In other words, the impetus for change is and was a result of the now-historic interplay between the Eastern Cherokee people and the many streams of the tourist industry throughout the twentieth century. Further, I will present the data I have collected so that others might learn from the Eastern Cherokee's contact with and use of the tourist industry, and hence capitalize on their triumphs and perhaps avoid some pitfalls.

The "tour" that was initially thrust on the Eastern Cherokee people in the late nineteenth and early twentieth centuries by federal, state, and local non-Cherokee initiatives reinscribed a specific Euro-American cultural system based on consumerism and capitalism. Although some Cherokees were involved in the process, the initial impetus for a tourism-based economy came from the Bureau of Indian Affairs (BIA), the U.S. government, the state of North Carolina, and local Jackson County and Swain County officials and landowners. This was accomplished in three major stages: chronologically, these are the building of railroads and then surface roads in the area, both before and after the time of the lumber industry; the creation of the Great Smoky Mountains National Park and the Blue Ridge Parkway; and the establishment of businesses by non-Cherokees who wanted to boost their economic base by "playing up the Indian presence" in western North Carolina (Finger 1991, 1995; French and Hornbuckle 1981; Frome 1980; Gulick 1960; S. H. Hill 1997; Pierce 2000).

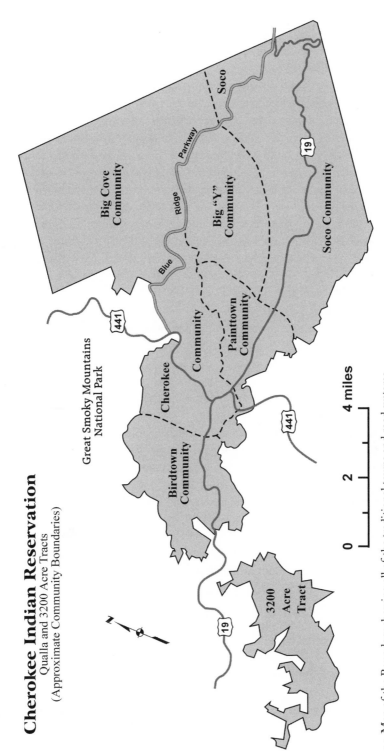

Cherokee Indian Reservation
Qualla and 3200 Acre Tracts
(Approximate Community Boundaries)

Great Smoky Mountains
National Park

Big Cove
Community

Soco

Parkway

Ridge

Big "Y"
Community

Blue

Cherokee
Community

Painttown
Community

Soco Community

Birdtown
Community

3200
Acre
Tract

0   2   4 miles

1.1. Map of the Boundary showing all of the traditional towns and road systems

Millions of tourists come to and through the EBCN Boundary every year (*Cherokee One Feather* 1997c, 1997d). Eastern Cherokee people constantly traverse the blurry line between being thought of as "real" Cherokee or being perceived and characterized as "not real" by their relationships with enrolled members of the Eastern Band, the local white population that surrounds them, and tourists (Finger 1991; Witthoft 1979). This paradoxical reality is lived by autochthonous peoples all over the world who also depend on the tourist dollar in order to live, however marginally, within the cash economy systems that were brought to and imposed on them. This is true whether that imposition began 50 or 500 years ago (Babcock 1994; Berman 2003; Besculides et al. 2002; MacCannell 1984; Medicine 2001a; O'Rourke 1987; Smith, ed. 1989). For the Cherokee, the distinction between "real" and "not real" is doubly confusing, since the stereotype of "Indian"—which is neither "real" nor Cherokee in the Eastern Cherokee schema—is reinforced daily by perceptions and expectations of the "other," the tourist.

As I will show through my data, these centuries of colonization and Euro-Americans' concomitant perceptions of a stereotypical Indian have taken their toll. For the elders, the youth, and all those in between, the tightrope is high and there is no safety net to fall into. Over the centuries of contact and acculturation, factionalism, and removal, the People have had the considerable burden of the simultaneous identification as *first* Americans, maintaining cultural continuity or being "real" Cherokee, and *Americans* first, acting "just like everyone else" or "being American" (Babcock 1994; Finger 1991, 1995; S. H. Hill 1997; Medicine 2001b; Perdue 1998). In the tourist venues this is seen repeatedly from the tour guides' speeches at Oconaluftee Indian Village, to history displayed in the Museum of the Cherokee Indians (MOCI), to the newest coffee-table book about the Cherokee on sale at Harrah's Cherokee Casino. The empirical evidence concurs with findings over more than a quarter century of research on other Indian lands in the United States where mass tourism is also the defining economic base and tourists bring their expectations, as well as much-needed money, along with them (Bowden 1994; Chambers 2000; MacCannell 1994; Rojek and Urry 1997; Rossel 1988; Seiler-Baldinger 1988; P. West 1998).

In an interview I conducted in 1998 at the now-defunct TeePee Restaurant in Cherokee, three Cherokee women, all enrolled members, suggested that tourism and tourists "kept the Cherokees being Cherokees. Because they [the tourists] were willing to pay and look for 'authentic Indian stuff,' Cherokees maintained or revived some traditional parts of our culture, arts and crafts, to take advantage of the opportunity." All three agreed that "if not for tourism, we don't know what would have become of Cherokee and the Eastern Cherokees." These statements, which other Cherokee artisans echo, exemplify the varied ways that tourism affects Eastern Cherokee life. Ten years after my initial sojourn to the Boundary, many things had changed, but the tourist industry and its continuing interplay with all things Cherokee remained.

Despite the many difficulties tourism brings, most Eastern Cherokee people think of it as a necessity of life. Freeman Owle, a stone carver, storyteller, and narrator for some of the Qualla Arts and Crafts Mutual, Inc.'s videos on Cherokee artisanship, speaks eloquently about tourism and about being Eastern Cherokee. In our initial interview in 1998, he said:

> Fortunately, there is beginning to be more education of children outside the Boundary that enables them to realize the humanity of the American Indian in general. It is a long time coming, however. This casino will create some problems that we haven't seen on the Boundary before. Even though it created some jobs, I fear that family-oriented travelers won't come because Harrah's changes the atmosphere. There are not enough cultural events and tourist opportunities. There should be more demonstrations of arts and crafts throughout the year, and not only at the Qualla Arts and Crafts Mutual but also at other craft shops. Tourists in general are not impressed with the Cherokee strip [the long section through the center of the Boundary]. If we work hard at it, I think we could have the junk market closed down in ten years. Some tourists are genuinely looking for the authentic. Those are the people we need to cater to.
>
> I am Eastern Cherokee because I was born of Cherokee parents, I have eight brothers and sisters, I live on the Boundary and have the lifelong experience of Cherokee-ness. I have some conversational use of our language and I am a stone carver. I teach stone carving to children from third [grade] to high school. We [Eastern Cherokees] want to live without hassle and interference by outside governments. The tribal government is becoming more supportive of craftspeople and Cherokee-ness is beginning to be primary. We have been able to obtain land [on] which sacred sites are located and I believe that we are gaining control of our destiny. (Owle 1998a)

A decade later, I realize that Owle certainly called some things correctly. As I present and discuss the facts and factors that went into the making of the tourist industry in Cherokee, it is my hope that these observations will be of use both to the Eastern Cherokee people, as a piece of the ethnographic present as well as the past, and to indigenous peoples in general. Even as I write, one of the Indian tribes of Long Island, New York, the Shinnecock, are seeking approval for a casino in Southampton Township to rival the Mashantucket Pequot complex in Connecticut. Currently, one can go online to websites that offer Sepik

River, Papua New Guinea, or Australian aboriginal arts and crafts or music created especially for the tourist consumer. As mass tourism continues its prodigious growth worldwide, cultural change is occurring at an ever-increasing rate for the fourth world, the indigenous world. For indigenous populations, traditional meaning, language, and practice are rapidly being lost in the onslaught of living within the control of nation-states where forced change to a worldwide cash economy is the norm. However, if Eastern Cherokee lifeways are indicators of the results of long-term indigenous contact with mass tourism, there remains a distinctly private space to be a "real" person.

METHODOLOGY

While I was in the field between 1996 and 1998, whether cooking at Tsali Manor, looking at old photographs with elders, or doing one-on-one interviews, numerous women told me to do original work. Women, especially, were interested in taking an active role in the work. They wanted to be interviewed; they wanted to tell me about the ways in which the Boundary, whether as a whole or in its individual communities, has been shaped through the years by the tourist presence. Many also want to be identified in print with both their knowledge and their opinions. My data from this period include both formal and informal interviews with several dozen people, mostly women but many men as well, who live and work in Cherokee. They are from every community on the Boundary and from ages ranging from 15 to more than 90. They are from all socioeconomic levels. There are people who are primarily Cherokee speakers who have English as a second language, and there are people who speak only English. I have met no one over all of these years who spoke only Cherokee. They are every conceivable "blood quantum," skin color (tawny copper to milky white), and hair color (coal black to platinum blond). Most are enrolled members, but some are married to enrolled members and are a generation or two outside of personal enrollment. A few who are not members of the EBCN are longtime residents of the area who worked with the Cherokee Historical Association or own and operate craft shops, restaurants, or hotels and are considered integral people in the community.

Further, the data include participating in local events and working on a day-to-day basis with the elder population at Tsali Manor, a plethora of photographs (both my own and other people's), videotape, maps, official EBCN and Great Smoky Mountain National Park economic statistics, and newspapers from all over western North Carolina.

One local event which indicates that a "private Cherokee" presence was still alive and well on the Boundary in 1998 was Ramp Day. Every year, there are several food-based events specifically for Cherokee people. The most popular one when I did my initial fieldwork was Ramp Day. On April 4, 1998, as I entered the Cherokee ceremonial grounds (where all collective Cherokee events are held), I noted that the ramps (pungent, local spring onions), chicken, potatoes, and trout fresh from the Cherokee Trout Farm were all cooked outdoors in at least four large electric frying pans.[1] Presumably, this outdoor kitchen was to keep the smell down, as the ramps and fish put out an odor that would drive away most tourists. It was gray, wet, and dreary all day long. The Cherokee Chapter of the Native American Indian Women's Association (NAIWA) served as everyone went through the buffet-style line. The NAIWA members cooked the rest of the food at their homes and brought it in. The menu reflected what it means to eat like a Cherokee in North Carolina. It was as follows:

Fried trout	Fried chicken	Fried potatoes	Fried sidemeat
Hominy/beans	Bean bread	Plain beans	Watercress salad
Ramps w/eggs	Plain ramps	Sochan	Desserts
Boiled cabbage	Boiled collard greens w/fatback		

The cooks were mostly younger men and women. The ceremonial grounds management put on Ramp Day each year to raise money for events throughout the year, especially the Cherokee Indian Fair in October. Principal Chief Joyce Dugan came with her family along with hundreds of Cherokees for their share of the festivities. There was no tourist presence at all.

Lots of other folks were there as well, from the tiniest babies to several elders in their nineties. Long tables were set out so you could eat wherever you wanted, or you could take your meal home in a carry-out. I sat with newly made friends and chatted about the food and what the money would be used for throughout the year. The event lasted throughout the afternoon, as there wasn't a specific time set to close down. One of the most interesting things about the event was who was *not* in attendance: none of the people who are considered white locals were there. Nor could I gain much of an explanation for their absence when I later inquired. "I don't like ramps" or "It was raining" were given as reasons, but for the most part the answers were vague. Even folks who have spent their entire lives on the Boundary—shopkeepers, Cherokee Historical Association employees, and others who are respected and thought of as "belonging" to the community—were absent.

Ramp Day is typical of the events put on by Cherokees for Cherokees that I witnessed and attended. These events are very informal, with many of the same people in attendance over and over again. As with many small towns or communities, there is a core of active members with a large peripheral group that may or may not participate (Redfield 1989 [1956]). The members of the local NAIWA chapter are particularly active in these community-wide events. For

three dollars you receive a heaping plate of food—too much for me to finish—
a drink, and the dessert of your choice. Despite the rain, ramps were cooked
and eaten with delight, though most of the elder women thought they were
not cooked well. Cooking well is, as it has always been, a matter of great pride
for Cherokee women. It can also be a source of individual and family prestige
within both the community and throughout the entire Boundary. Chiltoskey
and Beck's *Cherokee Cooklore* includes this traditional recipe:

> RAMPS-Wa-S-Di-\sd
> Gather young ramps soon after they come up. Parboil them, wash and
> fry in a little grease.[2] Meal may be added if you wish. They may be
> cooked without being parboiled or even eaten raw if the eater is not so-
> cial minded. . . . [Collected from] Mrs. Clifford Hornbuckle, who had
> the training of her mother and grandmother to help her become what is
> often spoken of by many of the Cherokees as being the best cook who
> can cook both Indian and "white man's" food. (1951:54)

The Ramp Day event is specifically for Cherokees, and it revolves around a
major cultural marker for women and women's work: traditional food.

During 2005 and 2006, I returned to Cherokee to follow up with new interviews, photography, and video in order to bring my work up to date. From these
data I analyzed and interpreted the sometimes contradictory positions of the
Eastern Cherokee and some of the conflicts generated by being both "public
Indians" and "private Cherokees." While my field experience is an American
one—that is, it occurs within the borders of the U.S. nation-state, with access
to everything I am used to in my own daily life—that does not mean I could
blithely walk in and just begin my project. I had to "learn the language" of the
people of Cherokee. I am not speaking of the Cherokee language per se, as a
majority of residents speak only a few words of the language themselves, but I
had to understand the much more subtle interpretation of American English
as adapted over centuries of contact and the interwoven, interstitial meanings
of Cherokee behind that interpretation (Silverstein 1996). The accent of the
people is unlike everywhere else in the South. It has a direct relationship with
the Cherokee language. The tonal quality of American English spoken by a
majority of people on the Boundary, unless they have been out in the world and
in constant contact with other regions, is much like that of the Cherokee language itself.[3] Likewise, the way in which Cherokees use American English is
quite different from an outsider's use of the same. For example, the Cherokee
meanings of *maybe* can signify skepticism, dismissiveness, or downright dis-
agreement. An illusion of acculturation has been adopted to get along with
and in American society (Sturm 2002; P. West 1981, 1998). Once I got to know

people over several months of almost daily contact, they started to tease me mercilessly about various things. As a side note, upon returning in 2006 to conduct updated work, the people who knew me in the 1990s are still teasing me. Being the object of teasing means, in Cherokee, that one is well liked and trusted. Being the object of eternal politeness is a sure way of knowing that you're always a real outsider (Thomas 1958). When I began the whole process, I had no idea that that would be the case.

In June 1996, I made the first important breakthrough that would get me started in the field. I made contact with an elder woman who was the private nurse of an even more elder couple. I will refer to the first woman as "Jackie." I needed to plan to make an initial trip to Cherokee to get permission from the EBCI Tribal Council in July. After several weeks, Jackie called me to tell me that I had picked a "mighty poor time to come to Cherokee." It would be the height of tourist season, which meant extremely crowded conditions. Worse still, the Summer Olympic Games, held in Atlanta in 1996, would be only three hours away, so motel space would definitely be at a premium. At first she indicated that she couldn't find anything for me, and I resigned myself to staying in the dorm room that I had secured in case of this circumstance in Asheville, about an hour's drive from Cherokee. Instead, she informed me that she had arranged for me to stay with her daughter in the Big Cove community. I will refer to Jackie's daughter as "Lisa." Jackie mentioned that she had no idea why she felt she should help me or why she should throw a complete stranger in with her daughter "up in the Cove." She said it was "just supposed to be that way."

I was thrilled at the prospect of staying in a Cherokee home in Big Cove, Gulick and company's stronghold in the "traditional heart" (anthropologically speaking) of the "conservative" (culturally speaking) Cherokee people on the Boundary (Finger 1991; Fogelson 1962; Gulick 1960; Kupferer 1968). However, that designation was debatable in 2006, as Big Cove had succumbed to campgrounds and tourists seeking a "wilderness" experience. Simultaneously, conservatism is spread throughout all Cherokee townships, especially Snowbird to the south (Neely 1991).

FIRST CONTACT

Driving over the mountain from Tennessee to North Carolina has always elicited an emotional response in me. I grew from an adolescent into a teenager in that area, and I have an overwhelming feeling that this region of the country is my home. With no fear of driving on tightly curving mountain roads, I am usually enveloped in the peace of the mountains. However, a certain degree of apprehension is inherent in the prospect of meeting and staying with strangers for the first time. I was also very aware of going for a new reason: to engage in fieldwork.

I drove into Cherokee from the national park and noticed something I had never observed before, at least not in the enormity of its presence. The sheer number of tourists, presumably searching for some experience of the Indians who were the "last of their kind" in the mountains, was completely staggering. I knew within a few days that this phenomenon would be central in any study of Cherokee women that I would undertake. As I followed Lisa's directions of Newfound Gap Road onto Big Cove Road and into the community, I found myself in Cherokee backcountry. Even in July, the mountain air was cool and calming. The countryside is beautiful. The winding road follows the course of Ravensford Creek, one of the myriad small streams that tumble off the mountains to the Oconaluftee River, which snakes its way through the center of the Boundary. I drove past a number of privately owned campgrounds, designed for tourists searching for their own piece of the mountain, as well as past the trout ponds at the local Kampground of America (KOA) before I found Lisa's house.

Her house is typical of the homes that the tribal housing division built for enrolled members in the 1980s. The weeds, trees, and brush on the road, coupled with a field of corn, were so tall in front of the house that from the road it was impossible to see anything. I soon learned that Lisa rented out the front acre or so to another family so they could have a decent-sized garden; she received vegetables for her use. Two bedraggled hound dogs greeted me as I got out of my car. Lisa is a phenotypically Cherokee woman with copper skin and long black hair. Her BIA card identifies her as 33/64 (a hair over half Cherokee), but the "white" "half" is barely noticeable. Lisa was extremely nice and talkative. She invited me to accompany her family the next evening, July 4, 1996, to watch the tribal fireworks from their Baptist Church at Yellowhill. The first night I stayed with Lisa, I barely slept because of excitement, expectation, and anxiety. Outside my bedroom window, the frogs chirped loudly. Their sound ebbed and flowed with the dull roar of the camping tourists who nearly surrounded Lisa's house and property.

My son, Matthew, came to stay with me for the last three weeks of that summer trip because he was going to join me in the field the following year. Lisa and her family extended their hospitality to us, and we went with them to the outdoor drama *Unto These Hills* and to the Oconaluftee Indian Village.

During my initial fieldwork in Cherokee, I was acutely aware that, although I felt at home in the South, I was an outsider on the Boundary. But, I am a southern woman with both of my parents' families firmly ensconced in all that being southern means, culturally and genetically. Specifically, there is an assumption, at least during my lifetime, that every southern family has an Indian connection. Nine times out of ten, that connection also translates to "Chero-kee." This is an unfortunate predicament when one wants to be taken seriously as a researcher. Because of this, during that first six-week period I was run through a mental gauntlet by every Cherokee woman that I met. Why had I picked Cherokee, North Carolina, for my project? Did I think I *was* Cherokee? Was one of my grandmothers a "Cherokee princess"? What did I want from them? My reply, over and over again, was that I did indeed have an untraceable Cherokee ancestor, probably female, from the 1830s era. However, I was fully aware that there was no such thing as a "Cherokee princess" and that I was just a southern girl down here to do research that I thought was important. Even-tually, they became convinced—perhaps because I was staying with Lisa in Big Cove, perhaps because her mother appeared to think I was OK, or perhaps be-cause I maintained the same story no matter who asked me. But, that summer tested my mettle insofar as getting me ready to return the following year to live and work with these Cherokee people. By the time I returned home in August, I had a formal letter of permission from the EBCN Tribal Council.

LIVING AND WORKING ON THE BOUNDARY

When I arrived back in Cherokee in August 1997, Lisa again let Matthew and me stay with her and her family until I found a suitable apartment for us. Once I was ensconced in a place in Birdtown on the lower Oconaluftee River, I began the long process of participant observation that would allow me to get to know people well enough to carry out interviews on the Boundary. To accomplish this, I adopted three major tacks: first, I volunteered at the Tsali Manor Senior Center; second, I taught and audited courses on the Boundary through the lo-cal university, Western Carolina University (WCU), as well as the local com-munity college, Southwestern Community College (SCC); and third, I made a point of becoming a regular at the TeePee Restaurant, the local grocery stores, the launderette, and a few of the well-established craft shops. An equally im-portant component came from an unexpected source. Matthew started sixth grade at Cherokee Elementary School, and I became a school mom. This out-let provided me with insights into how Cherokees are socialized to be simul-taneously Cherokee and American adults. Being a Cherokee American is very important to almost every person I met on the Boundary, and the school sys-tem stresses that in a number of ways.

Tsali Manor and the Elders

In late September 1997, I started to think about how to make contact with my target population. I decided to ask to be a volunteer worker for the elders, and

1.2. Tsali Manor, Cherokee, North Carolina, 2006 (Author's photo)

the best place to do that is at the Tsali Manor Senior Center. Tsali Manor provides transportation, hot lunches, and a variety of activities and trips to elders (55 and older) who live on the Boundary.

When I went to Tsali Manor to introduce myself and my project, permission letter from the Tribal Council in hand, I met the center's director, Deb West. When I first presented myself to volunteer, she was a bit reticent, as I expected she would be. Cherokees who are in managerial or care-taking positions that deal with preschool children, elementary through high school students, and elders are extremely protective of their people. Too many "unauthorized" researchers have barged in to ask questions, take unauthorized photos, and generally upset the most vulnerable people on the Boundary. I presented my permission letter from the council, gave her the names of the people I had already spoken with about my project, and explained why I was there. I wanted to show my sincere interest in the elder women and their personal histories; in other words, in the *people,* not just the *study.* She easily received approval from her supervisor, Kathi Littlejohn; they decided my interest was fortuitous, as they needed immediate help with the arts and crafts area—activities that were nearly always peopled by the women (the men had little interest in the arts and crafts except to hang around and tease the "hens" doing their "stitchery").

I began work at Tsali Manor on October 1. I was prepared to help with crafts, but I didn't quite know exactly how to proceed, so when other requests for my help came in, I responded. To get me started and introduce me to the staff as well as all of the elders, Deb suggested that I begin with kitchen duty. I prepared, cooked, and served the elders at the daily lunch buffet, cleaned, swept, and set up tables and chairs. The elders were very interested in what I was doing there, and many people asked me to sit at their tables and answer innumerable questions about myself. After a few weeks of working in the kitchen, I began to develop and set up workshops for the elders and the staff. One of these, a family tree workshop, helped me get a feel for the kinship networks that are still in operation on the Boundary and about the people with whom I would actually be working.

Through my work at Tsali Manor I got to know the elder women in a way I would not have been able to otherwise. Once they got to know me, they offered to introduce me to their daughters, granddaughters, sisters, nieces, and aunts. Throughout this book, I continually return to my experience at Tsali Manor and its relevance to my understanding of the palimpsest of being Cherokee while living with the tourism industry. I also include some individual stories of women and men who have been involved with the industry as well as those who have taken other avenues, such as nursing.

Teaching and Taking Courses on the Boundary

Beyond Tsali Manor, one of the first places I went to introduce myself and my project was WCU. Before I arrived, I made some inquiries to the chair of the Anthropology Department, Anne Rogers, about both teaching and meeting with her to discuss my project and talk about some ways to begin in the field. As a result, she hired me as an adjunct for the department, and through her connections I was also able to teach for the local community college, SCC. While the WCU course was on campus, the SCC course turned out to be a telecourse at the Cherokee campus. There I was fortunate to meet the two enrolled members who ran the campus on a day-to-day basis, Jan Smith and Vida Nations. Both had lived on the Boundary their entire lives, and both were of the opinion that every high school student should plan for at least an associate's degree from SCC. They felt that "education can only improve conditions and circumstances on the Boundary" (Nations 1998; Smith 1998), although many people at the time disagreed. Some felt that a college education pulled kids away from the Boundary. The Eastern Band was losing residents, and cultural traditions were becoming more and more diluted with the strong current of mainstream American culture.

Teaching courses gave me a wonderful opportunity to reach an entirely dif-

1.3. The author (in white shirt and black sandals) chatting with elder women at Tsali Manor, 1998 (Author's photo)

ferent set of Cherokees, college students, and I interviewed several students who enrolled in my classes. I found that most students were dedicated to getting an education and then staying at home to improve conditions on the Boundary. I also found that not one of them had aspirations toward the tourist industry for either themselves or their children. Some, however, were interested in continuing in Cherokee arts and crafts as a way to carry on the cultural traditions of their forebears.

While in the field I also had the opportunity to audit a course in the Cherokee language. Auditing that course also gave me the chance to meet other students—Cherokee, other Indian, and white—who were interested in keeping the language alive by learning it and passing it on.

BECOMING A "REGULAR"

One of the primary events that the Eastern Band has sponsored every year since the early 1900s is the Fall Fair. While I was living in Cherokee during the 1990s, it became clear to me that this event was probably the most anticipated one of the year. Much work and skill went into preparations for this week-long event, and I was fortunate to be involved in two fairs while I was there.

Because of my associations with the elders and staff at Tsali Manor and my friendship with its director, Deb West invited me to come back to Cherokee in October 1998 for the Fall Fair. I was to be a judge for the Junior Miss Cherokee Pageant. This turned out to be an interesting position to be in, both as Deb's friend and as an anthropologist. When I had attended the 1997 fair during my first year's stay, I was so new to the residents that I remained primarily an observer, not a "regular." This time, since all of the Tsali Manor elders knew me and knew that I would be writing about my experiences and interviews, they told everyone they knew that I would be a pageant judge. When the daughter of a Tsali Manor employee won the competition, some residents accused Deb—and by extension me—of "rigging the competition." That wasn't true, as I had never met the young woman in context with her mother, and I had no idea that she was connected with Tsali Manor at all. The objectivity that I strived to maintain as an anthropologist was put to the test.

Since my son was a student at Cherokee Elementary School, I also attended some fair events that directly involved the school's children. When I was invited back for the 1998 fair, I was welcomed by my friends and acquaintances. I was also expected, as both the volunteer and the anthropologist, to help out where I was needed. This allowed me to videotape some special events and to have on-camera interviews with people who had been shy and reticent before I had left the previous summer.

My experiences of both the 1997 and 1998 fairs and other events that are by, for, and about the Cherokee population and their kin underlie my conclusions about identity, the Cherokee, and tourism. People come from all over the United States to share in their community, if only for a week or so each year, to remember and strengthen the very vital ties to history and tradition. These experiences, which I discuss in this volume in detail, have brought me a greater understanding of the nature of the Eastern Cherokee community and of how its distinctiveness is maintained. In fact, this experience is what revealed the title of this book—*Public Indians, Private Cherokees*—to me. As I progress, I offer personal stories, historical facts, and ethnographic data about how the tourist industry has produced, both by outsiders and by natives, the phenomenon of "Indians in the street" and Cherokee culture and traditions at "home."

Cherokee women have remained my central focus of research and interest, but I realized just how pervasive was tourism's reach. Although some jobs and careers on the Boundary do not revolve directly around tourism, approximately 80 percent of the economic opportunities do. Most of the other 20 percent— from the tribal government offices and all of the programs that fall under that purview to all the vital services of the Boys' Club to the Cherokee school system—is funded by the tribe's profits from the tourism industry. This is especially the case since the casino was built in 1997. So, as I tried to meet women who were interested in talking about their lives, families, work, and communities, I also began to investigate the tourist industry, in microcosm on the Boundary and as a metaindustry in the social science literature.

The juxtaposition of the fieldwork with Cherokee women and the academic study of tourism is a fascinating blend of political-economic analysis and the investigation of oral history with some really great storytellers. I have collected and heard numerous stories from women all over the Boundary. They are about tourists, family and relationships, working in the tourist industry, working in the Cherokee Historical Association attractions, *Unto These Hills* and the Oconaluftee Indian Village, making crafts and not making crafts, old times and new times, and many others. I've also come up with a few stories of my own. One of my favorites involves ladybugs. Everyone has his or her own ladybug story in the mountains, and here's mine.

When I came to do my extended fieldwork in August 1997, I promised Lisa that I would have a new place by October 1. I just needed to stay with her and her family until I could find a rental property. Well, there just wasn't much available. Qualla Housing has a waiting list several pages long, and they give preference—and rightfully so—to enrolled members. Since it was still summer, motels, trailers, and cabins were all at their tourist-season prices. I finally found something, but I had to move a few hundred feet off the Boundary for it.

The apartment turned out to be a nice, little fully furnished number on Highway 19 at Whittier just outside Birdtown. Old and quaint, but with new paint and carpet inside, it backs up to the Oconaluftee River. My son and I moved in during the first week of October. By the end of that month we had a huge surprise that we had to deal with until we gave up the apartment the following May. The weekend before Halloween, the temperature outside plummeted. When we returned home from a day of driving in the cool mountains, we encountered an invasion of literally thousands of ladybugs. On the walls, on the ceilings, they were crawling, flying. I'd never seen so many ladybugs in one place. Naturally, I asked people I knew for advice. It wasn't as if I hadn't known about them, either. Lisa's house in Big Cove occasionally gave up hidden ladybug carcasses no matter how many times it was swept. But, the experience of the immensity, intensity of the bug bodies, flying past my head, landing on my legs in the shower, inviting themselves to dinner, was, at times, overwhelming.

Then, a friend on the Boundary put the whole ladybug affair into perspective for me. She said, "Well, Chris, ladybugs are just a part of being here. You know, they're just like the *unegs*.[4] *They* just keep coming and coming and *you* just have to learn to live with them."

You just have to learn to live with them. Tourists come by the millions, even in depressed years, to and through Cherokee. As with the ladybugs, the immensity, intensity of tourism can be overwhelming. The industry has yet to be subjected to a critical analysis of the positive and negative influences and all the combinations in between. That, however, will have to wait for another moment in academic time. My work focuses on the Cherokee themselves, and as a result I did not interact with tourists except in the company of Cherokee people; that is, I did not interview tourists. However, based on listening to tourists in the various craft shops and restaurants and from teaching in the counties outside the Boundary, I would say that most of the tourists who come to and through the Boundary do not consider themselves to be racist or to be looking for something "exotic." The Cherokee react to this ignorance in various ways. Throughout the course of this work, numerous stories, photographs, and personal histories underscore the importance of "being Cherokee" to the "Principal People."

2
The Trail of Tourism

Tourism—the state of being a tourist and/or the state of being toured—assumes travel and moving in order to see or gaze at a place, person, or thing that is other than one's everyday geographic location (Babcock 1994; Clifford 1997; MacCannell 1973, 1994; Smith 1989; Urry 1990). According to Valene L. Smith, "tourism as a form of mobility suggests that culturally sanctioned reasons exist for leaving home" (Smith 1989:1).[1] In 1980, when the anthropological study of the phenomenon of tourism was less than a decade old, Nelson Graburn stated that "the study of the nature of tourist motivations and behavior reveals much about the underlying value systems of the modern world . . . we [anthropologists] cannot neglect tourism, which is one of the major forces shaping (and changing) meaning in the lives of the people of today's world" (1980:64). Much of the literature since the mid-1980s has added to the depth and breadth of the knowledge about the tourist and about mechanisms of tourism, as an industry, that have been employed to produce the multibillion-dollar business it is in the twenty-first century (Chambers 2000; Divisekera 2003; Teo and Li 2003).

One of the major ways the economics of tourism works is by encouraging "socioeconomically 'divergent' groups to adopt life-styles embedded in and geared to world system commoditization" (Smith 1997:200). This chapter will introduce a brief history of the tourism industry of the late twentieth and early twenty-first centuries in Cherokee, North Carolina. This chronology is important to the subsequent ethnographic detail and research that form the core of this work. It is vital to understand how the Eastern Cherokee fit into, were "commoditized" by, and ultimately learned to use the tourism industry for their own economic sovereignty and heritage to retain their "place" in western North Carolina and in the annals of the American Indian experience and heritage/cultural tourism (Chhabra et al. 2003; Medina 2003).

The advent of tourism on the Qualla Boundary in western North Carolina was neither planned nor directed by the Cherokee, as was the case with most indigenous peoples throughout the world in the nineteenth century (Babcock 1994; Chambers 2000; Sears 1989; Smith 1989). Since tourism is a Euro-American construct, it is necessary to analyze both the process of tourism and the results of its power as a marker of the expansion of capitalism. This discussion is also vital because it clearly describes how "tradition" is inscribed onto the Eastern Cherokee psyche through the vehicle of tourism from the nineteenth century, throughout the twentieth century, and into the twenty-first century.[2] Through archival research and the rich narratives of women and men intimately involved in the industry since childhood, I show the influences of the mass tourist industry on the daily lived experience of the Eastern Cherokee—and by extension, other diverse indigenous populations.

The southern Appalachian region has been the home of the A-ni-Yu-n-wi-ya for at least a thousand years (McLoughlin 1986; Mooney 1982 [1891]; Riggs 1997; Ruehl 1998). The name "Cherokee" was adopted by European tradesmen and the military as a result of asking tribes other than the Tsa-la-gi who they were.[3] Tsa-la-gi (cha-la-gee) meant "cave-dwellers" in the Muskogean language to the south and west. After going through many permutations (e.g., Chirrakee, Charakey), tsa-la-gi was ultimately transliterated into "Cherokee" (Adair 1775; Bartram 1955 [1791]; Mooney 1982 [1891]; Timberlake 1765).[4]

ROADS AND RAILS

Until the eighteenth century, when European traders brought the trappings of "civilization" in earnest for the pure fur of this place, there was little travel via either animal or land vehicle. Among the autochthonous peoples of North America, everything from hunting to trade to migration was on foot or by water. Horse culture did not appear in the plains until after the Spanish invasions of the sixteenth and seventeenth centuries. That hunter-gatherer cultural adaptation never made its way into the mainstream cultural system of the Cherokee. However, wherever Euro-American settlement was started, horses as working animals certainly made an impact on the already-changing lifeways of Cherokees, especially in the Lower towns. By 1806 in the Holston River area of what is now Tennessee and Alabama, white settlers negotiated with Cherokees to move onto traditional land and build a trade road through Cherokee lands (Mooney 1982 [1891]). Hatley recounts that "sweet potatoes and domesticated animals, probably pigs, were introduced and accepted by Cherokee women farmers in 18th century. . . . Horses were also introduced in the 18th century, but Cherokee tended to reject cattle until the 19th century in preference for pigs" (1991:41, 44).

However, in the high country of the Appalachian Mountains, the country-side did not begin to open up until the railroads came into the region (Frome 1980). As modes of transportation and the economic boom of the lumber industry began to change the face of the mountains around 1900, the tourist industry also began its precipitous growth from the first Indian Fair in 1914 to the multimillion-dollar industry of the present (Chiltoskey 1995; Duggan and Riggs 1991; Finger 1991, 1995; Gulick 1960; Leftwich 1970:2; Redman 1998). For example, the entire United States was feeling the importance of changes in transportation to the advent and burgeoning of incipient mass tourism. As Albers and James note regarding Wisconsin, "Prior to 1915, much of [the Wisconsin Dells] region was remote and visited by small numbers of travelers who reached the area by train. Many of the travelers came for extended summer vacations and stayed at lake-side resorts which catered to the region's recreational pleasures. As roads were still primitive and not suited to automobile touring, the sightseeing traveler (the prototype of the modern tourist) was a minor figure" (1983:133–134).

By the time the Cherokee Nation ratified its constitution in 1827, modes of travel had radically changed in the Lower towns that were located on the river valleys of northern Georgia and western North and South Carolina (Frome 1980; S. H. Hill 1997; Kephart 1983 [1936]; Kupferer 1968; Perdue 1998). There, also, the way of life of the majority of the Cherokee Nation had become a mixture of Euro-American and Cherokee cultural traits. Already, the meaning of being Cherokee was in the midst of radical change (Duggan 1998, 2002b; Finger 1995; Perdue 1998). Among the wealthiest Cherokee families, Euro-American education and religion were both sought and privileged. By the 1820s there was an official, written Cherokee language, and literacy was a reality for an impressive 90 percent of the Nation. Even so, English was the chosen language for official Nation business and was the preferred language for a majority of the people who lived in these most populous areas. However, the new constitution and the Christian Bible were translated into Cherokee from English so that the wider population could read them (Finger 1991, 1995; McLoughlin 1986; Perdue 1998; Taylor 1997).

In the mountains, though, the rhythm of life, trade, and travel went on pretty much as usual. The Overhill and Middle Towns of the Cherokee remained more isolated (Burt and Ferguson 1973; Finger 1991, 1995; Smith 1979). These people had always carved out spaces from the mountain valleys and hollows of what is now northern Georgia, western North Carolina, and eastern Tennessee for clan gardens of traditional corn, beans, and squash; fished the abundant streams; gathered wild berries, nuts, mushrooms, greens, and ramps from the hillsides; and hunted game in the vast wilderness. The people of these regions were among the few who escaped the degradation of the 1838 death march to the "Indian Territory" that was ordered by President Andrew Jackson, against the edict of the Supreme Court, and executed by the U.S. military of the day (Finger 1991, 1995, 2001; Smith 1979; The Unknown Author 1932:56–123; Wallace 1999). According to Duane King:

> The sequence of events at the time of removal is best understood in light of the predicament of the Eastern Cherokees prior to this period. In 1819, the Cherokees ceded to the United States a large tract of land which included the present Qualla Boundary. Although most of the Cherokees residing in the ceded territory in North Carolina moved into the remaining tribal land, some did not [among these], Yonaguska encouraged them to resist inducements for removal west. He asserted that the Cherokees were safer among their barren rocks and mountains than on land that the white man might find profitable. He believed that the Cherokees could be happy only in the country apportioned to them by nature. He advised them to remain in North Carolina, considering that state better and more friendly disposed to the Indians than any other. If they went west, he feared that they would soon again be surrounded by white settlements and eventually "be included in a state disposed to oppress them." (1979b:166–167)

Yonaguska's fears, of course, became reality less than 100 years later with the passing of the Dawes Severalty Act of 1887 and the breakup of the Cherokee Nation in Indian Territory (contemporary Oklahoma) before the turn of the twentieth century (Debo 1966:23). The primary reason why the Eastern Band of Cherokee was unaffected by the Dawes Act was that William Holland Thomas had acquired ownership of the land for them in the mid-nineteenth century. This bold move in effect created the land base which is very much the same as today's Boundary configuration (Finger 1991, 1995).

Because of the remoteness of their homeland and the diligence of the Oconaluftee Citizen Indians, who, according to historical record, "had worked hard to project an image of model citizenship," a small group remained in the last vestige of their ancestral home. There were no military orders to remove these 60–70 families, and they "were not affected by the Treaty of New Echota and were never expected to remove" (Finger 1991, 1995; King 1979b:177–178). According to *The Cherokee Perspective,* a collection of stories, narratives, newspaper reprints, and selected population data, "about a third of the North Carolina Cherokees elected to remain east, and of those, only a small proportion legally complied with the conditions set forth in the 1835 Treaty [for the removal

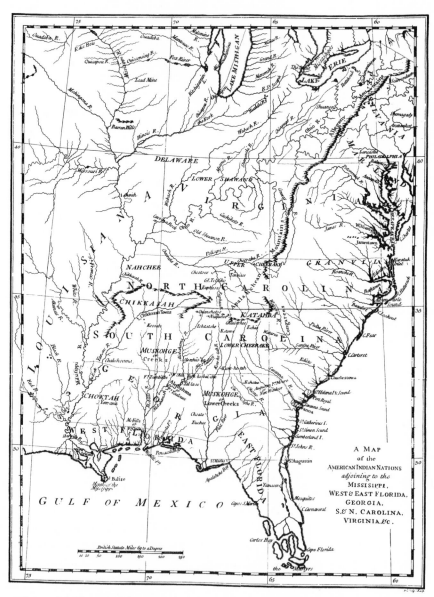

2.1. James Adair's map of American Indian nations, ca. 1770 (From James Adair, *The History of the American Indians* [London: Edward and Charles Dilly, 1775], i)

of the majority of the Cherokees and rules for those who stayed behind], that of registering individual land tracts (deeds) and filing for state citizenship. Apparently, these Cherokee only wanted to retain their old lifestyle and had little interest in adopting the legal and social structure of North Carolina" (French and Hornbuckle 1981:25). The lifeways of the Oconaluftee Citizen Indians changed irrevocably as more and more Americans (both homesteaders and business entrepreneurs) encroached on the land base set up for them in the mid-1800s (Finger 1991, 1995; King 1979b; McLoughlin 1986).

It was not until the late nineteenth to early twentieth century that a few small wagon roads began to be carved out of the rugged country of the Eastern Cherokee Boundary. In a relatively short time, these roads became the railroads of the timber industry. The green deciduous floor of the lower Appalachian chain began to fall, and so did the isolation of the EBCN. Railroads and skid roads made their way into the wilderness of the Cherokee territory. Today in Big Cove, beyond the winding paved road into the Cove, one can still walk—or drive in an all-terrain vehicle—the paths, roads, and rail beds used to bring old-growth timber from the mountain early in this century. It is also obvious which parts of the forest are still rebounding from more than fifty years of felling.

Until the latter half of the twentieth century, travel remained difficult. Gulick and his associates reported in 1960 that "walking is [still] a very important means of locomotion, and most people take for granted the necessity of long walks (for example, the twelve mile[s] from Upper Big Cove to Cherokee Village), and frequent visiting by no means occurs only between people who live closest to each other. In Big Cove, and doubtless elsewhere, the network of trails over the ridges makes [for] frequent communication between households which seem quite far apart in terms of mechanized transportation" (1960: 112). His description of the late-1950s transit system goes on to mention that "the automobile and the truck have begun to take an important place in the communication patterns of the reservation. In Painttown, in 1957, 54 percent of the households owned one or more automobiles and/or trucks. . . . It is of interest that in Big Cove, where the possession of expensive equipment is generally so much less than that in Painttown, 47% of the households had automobiles in the summer of 1956" (1960:112). At the time of Gulick's study (1955 to 1959) there were several taxi services from the Big Cove community into the Cherokee Village (Yellowhill), and at least one car owner refused payment for services rendered. The population of Big Cove, where Gulick's study was primarily concentrated, felt the need for a regular bus service that would include the entire Boundary (Gulick 1960). In the 1990s there were some public conveyances to take tourists from one site to another, but these were few and far between and were specifically for the tour, not for the Cherokee people's convenience.

THE GREAT SMOKY MOUNTAINS NATIONAL PARK AND THE IDEA AND IMPETUS OF "THE TOUR"

When the Great Smoky Mountains National Park was demarcated in 1930, the land was chosen in part because of the proximity to the EBCN Boundary (Frome 1980). In 1899 the Eastern Band had sold 33,000 acres (the Love Speculation) to the Department of the Interior for the purpose of developing and establishing an Appalachian national park (French and Hornbuckle 1981:26). The Boundary of the Eastern Cherokees is approximately 54,000 acres situated within the state of North Carolina. It straddles the North Carolina counties of Jackson and Swain. French and Hornbuckle state that

> in 1933, North Carolina and Tennessee both transferred Southern Appalachian acreage to the federal government to be used for the park. It was during this time that Cherokee laborers began building the main access road (US Route 441) through Cherokee territory to the proposed park site. And in order to ensure national regulation of both the proposed park and its main drawing card, the Cherokee Indians, the federal government assigned official reservation status to the Eastern Band in 1934 under the Wheeler-Howard Reorganization Bill. These plans were contingent upon the development of the Tennessee Valley Authority, the Blue Ridge Parkway, The Great Smoky Mountains National Park, the Cherokee reservation, Gatlinburg, Tennessee and other towns as tourist attractions to the park. The Great Smoky Mountains National Park opened in 1938, transforming the Eastern Band from an isolated, obscure Indian group into the most visited Native American group in the United States. (1981:26–27)

As a result of the Roosevelt administration's Civilian Conservation Corps and Works Progress Administration road-building projects and the "Indian New Deal" developed by John Collier of the Department of the Interior and the Bureau of Indian Affairs (BIA), during the Depression years this mountainous region, which had only been open to limited rail traffic from the lumber industry, became accessible by automobile to vacationing middle-class families (Sutter 2002).

According to Sarah H. Hill, "In the summer of 1932, the 'Across the Smokies Highway' was completed from Gatlinburg, Tennessee, across Newfound Gap to Smokemont, approximately five miles north of the reservation [Boundary]. When more than a thousand cars crossed the gap in a single day, it appeared that boosters had correctly estimated interest in a park" (1997:278–279). Meanwhile, Superintendent Harold Foght of the Cherokee Indian Agency watched this new boon with anticipation, stating that "the Across the Smokies Highway will bring a very large number of tourists through here . . . and will afford a ready market for a great deal of [Cherokee] products" (Martini 1989:14). However, the park service and boosters had their own ideas about how to "use" the Cherokees. The park service hoped to persuade Cherokees to come to Smokemont to dance and weave baskets, as American Indians already did in Glacier National Park and Yosemite National Park (S. H. Hill 1997:282; Sutter 2002). The Seminole, another southeastern Indian nation, had been residing in tourist villages in Miami for more than a decade by this time (West 1981:202). However, Foght had other plans for the Cherokee. "Ours are a different type of Indian," he related, "who would not wish to lend themselves—at least most would not—to exploitation of this kind. . . . [Performing at Smokemont] would be setting up competition of what we are planning to do throughout the summer with pageantry, Indian games, dances, etc., here on the Qualla Boundary" (Foght 1935:3). This attitude appears to have been the general BIA stance on Indians and tourism during this time (West 1981). Two years later, Foght's goal of bringing the tourists to the Cherokee appears to have succeeded. The 1937 tourism brochure, *The Eastern Cherokee: Their History and How They Live Today* (J. L. Caton 1937), was published in Knoxville and sold on the Qualla Boundary at the few new tourist shops for 25 cents per copy. Foght had no need to be concerned about the exploitation of the Cherokee for tourism so long as the BIA and *not* the Great Smoky Mountains National Park was the instigator and perpetrator.

Even though some paved highways were making their way into the area in the 1930s, most of the roads on the Boundary were unpaved (Sutter 2002). Albers and James state that the same was true for the Wisconsin area: "the more mobile, sightseeing tourist was also on the rise but did not become a major component until the 1930s" (1983:134). Myrtle Youngbird, Maryjane Taylor, and Charlotte Taylor (sisters née Welch) related some of their childhood memories from the 1930s about the condition of the Boundary roads and the beginnings of the tourist industry: "When we were little, all the roads were just dirt—mud, really. There was one old taxicab, I guess it was an old T-model that you could jump on. That one taxi driver was Wiley Wilkes. He could go anywhere you wanted to for 50 cents. Once a month we got to go to town in a car. That was Whittier. Back then, it was the best and closest town around. There was a train station, a service station, a mill, and a grocery store. Reynolds had a big store with feed and all that" (C. Taylor 1998; M. Taylor 1998; Youngbird 1998).[5] In the 1930s and 1940s, tour guides brought the few people who came through in small groups to private homes. In the case of the Welches, this was Wright's Creek, a secluded area of Painttown.

> The first tourist place we had was in town. It was just that I can recollect right now. Lloyd's Gift Shop, right across from where the Pizza Inn is now, up in Cherokee. They did take people out to buy stuff from people on the reservation. They were brought by a guide by the name of George Owle and he knew my parents. So he knew that my mother made pottery and he brought people up to watch her make pottery. Us, being children and curious, so we'd always come out and see who was there. They [the tourists] always talked to us too, and took pictures. We all helped with the pottery 'cause that's the way we bought our groceries. We shined the pottery. Mother molded them, Daddy carved them, and we washed them off with a cloth to make them smooth and then used a rock to shine them. They were sort of special rocks, but they came from the rivers. Sam Beck used to bring people up there too. (C. Taylor 1998; M. Taylor 1998; Youngbird 1998)

I asked the sisters whether they thought having tourists buy directly from the family was a positive experience for them. "It was OK," they said, but they also indicated that the tourists wanted to pay as little as possible for their family's efforts. Pottery sales were not the family's only source of income. Their father worked for the BIA, but he worked seven days a week and more than eight hours a day.

By the time World War II ended and life in the United States began to return to "normal," tourism was being recognized as *the* leading avenue to economic growth and economic stability for the western North Carolina region. Although this remote region remained difficult for everyday tourists to reach, the Cherokee suddenly found themselves in the perfect geographical and culturally exotic position for a group of primarily white entrepreneurs to initiate the first major expansion of that tourist trade (Finger 1991, 1995; French and Hornbuckle 1981).

In 1945 this group of businesspeople decided to take advantage of the expected tourism created by the Great Smoky Mountains National Park. The Newfound Road (Highway 441) had recently been completed over the park's rugged terrain, and for the first time there was "easy" access from Gatlinburg to the Qualla Boundary in North Carolina. Gatlinburg and its neighbor to the north, Pigeon Forge, just sleepy hamlets, would prove in time to be real competition for the tourist dollar. Gulick describes the situation in the late 1950s:

2.2. Maryjane Taylor (*left*), the author (*center*), and Myrtle Youngbird (*right*) at Tsali Manor, 1998 (Author's photo)

Although souvenir shops began to appear early in the 20th century when the road which is now the section of Highway 19 between Cherokee Village and Birdtown was improved for modern traffic, the tourist business did not begin to take on serious proportions until automobile traffic suddenly increased after World War II. It was only then that Highway 19 was completed eastward through Soco Valley. Despite earlier precursors, the present tourist business has essentially been a recent and sudden development. In little more than two decades, highways have made the Cherokee Reservation, previously an isolated mountain area, into a major thoroughfare. But people's attitudes and values do not transform so easily. (1960:24)

However, the main draw in the 1940s in the mountains was scenery and Indians. Many businesspeople in the towns surrounding the Qualla Boundary quickly became aware of this public fascination and began to focus on how best to capitalize on it in Cherokee. Thus, the Western North Carolina Associated

Communities (WNCAC) and ultimately the Cherokee Historical Association (CHA) were brought into being in the late 1940s (Connor 1982).

Margie Douthit was involved with the CHA since its first days in 1946. Although she claims no Cherokee ancestry, she lives in an outlying town near the Qualla Boundary and has spent more than half a century working on the Boundary. Margie has liaisons with many Cherokee people through professional connections and through friendship. I asked her whether the advent of the four-lane roads helped tourism in Cherokee, and she replied: "I think so. In the fifties we had tremendous visitation of *Unto These Hills,* but you have to keep in mind that we were new and we were one of the major, well, *the* major attraction in a 50- to 75-mile radius of Cherokee. But, now, there are many attractions in that radius and our attendance is not as much as it was in the fifties and sixties because we have much more competition for the tourist dollar" (Douthit 1998). I noted that these are the only attractions that are really *about* the Cherokee, and she replied:

> Yes, it [*Unto These Hills*] and the Indian Village. There was a little museum here before and the collection was already here that they have across the street, but it was in a small building and it was not advertised. They were open for those who just dropped in to see it. They did have quite a few visitors in the summer because they were the only museum in the area, but the enlarged museum across the street, Oconaluftee Village, and *Unto These Hills* were the historical parts of the "Cherokee experience," so to speak. Most of the other things . . . well, I've always been of the opinion that what is provided is what the public wants. Otherwise, it's like somebody said, they went into one of the shops here in the fifties or sixties and they were just astounded that there was not more Cherokee craftwork. But they couldn't sell it, so they didn't put it in because it was higher than people would pay so they put into the shop what people bought. It's supply and demand. (Douthit 1998)

Here, Douthit is talking about the imported "Indian" souvenirs, made mostly in Asia, as opposed to the "authentic," Cherokee-made crafts (which will be discussed in chapter 4). Handmade Cherokee crafts are more expensive, priced as art for art's sake, and have been since the 1950s and the advent of the Qualla Co-op.[6]

A history of the Cherokee Historical Association was commissioned by the group's executive council in the late 1970s. Written by Dr. William P. Connor Jr., *History of Cherokee Historical Association, 1946–1982* contains detailed accounts, almost day by day, of the CHA through about 1980. This slim volume is sold at bookstores and craft shops and is sold to the tourist consumer at the CHA venues *Unto These Hills* and Oconaluftee Indian Village. The history goes into minute detail about the CHA's beginnings:

> Shortly after the Second World War drew to its explosive conclusion, communities across the United States sought ways to protect and to expand the sense of prosperity and pride that arrived with the war's end. In the forefront of this effort at community self-development stood the "land-locked peninsula" of the eleven western counties of North Carolina. . . . The barriers to development were not, however, insurmountable, and by the summer of 1946 a group of civic leaders had emerged to point the way to a new beginning for the region. At the invitation of Felix Picklesimer of Sylva a group of eighteen individuals representing the communities of Asheville, Brevard, Bryson City, Cullowhee, Sylva, Waynesville, the Cherokee Indian Reservation and Western North Carolina Teacher's College convened at Dillsboro in Jackson County on June 27, 1946 . . . they [laid] the foundation for what, in two weeks, would become the Western North Carolina Associated Communities. (Connor 1982:7)

In addition to stressing "industrial expansion, tourist business, game and fish, and roads," the WNCAC discussed the possibility of producing a "western North Carolina drama, similar to THE LOST COLONY of Roanoke Island" (on the outer banks of North Carolina) (Connor 1982:7–8). According to Connor, this suggestion was not the first of its kind. "In 1941 Ross Caldwell, a trader residing in Cherokee, discussed with several friends the idea of producing a pageant concerning the history of the Cherokee in North Carolina. . . . After the war Caldwell discussed his idea with Joe Jennings, the Superintendent of the Cherokee Indian Reservation, but the scope of the project discouraged them from pursuing it further without professional advice and help" (1982:9).

The CHA, as a "satellite" of the WNCAC, was fully incorporated on February 23, 1948 (Connor 1982:14; Umberger 1970). From the start, the CHA's goal was to create a venue, the outdoor drama, as a draw for the newly booming middle-class car tourist that was coming into the Great Smoky Mountains National Park. According to Charles A. Collier (John Collier's brother), "the development of tourism . . . offered the one great opportunity for economic vitality [to the Qualla Boundary]" (quoted in S. H. Hill 1997:304). BIA supervisor Joe Jennings went along with this estimation and joined the WNCAC at its first meeting. When the CHA was incorporated, there were twenty-seven incorporators and subscribers (Umberger 1970), of whom eight were members of the EBCN and one was Western Cherokee. In addition, six of the thirteen members of the CHA Board of Trustees were members of the EBCN, and one was Western Cherokee. The trustees thought this was adequate Cherokee representation on the CHA board. Every account of the proceedings of the board meeting reported they leaned toward the positive eventual impact of the CHA on the Cherokee people.

By the summer of 1948, a site had been chosen for the outdoor drama, and a playwright, Kermit Hunter, had been hired for the production. According to Connor:

> [There were] plans for seating five thousand people (in two sections) in the amphitheater. However, the $65,000 budget included only enough to pay for the first section. A projection proposed that twenty performances would net $45,600 (at $1.50 a ticket). The brochure plan called for a quarter of the needed $65,000 to come from expenditures and other assistance donated by the United States Indian Service Administration at Cherokee. This important contribution to the establishment of "Unto These Hills" was to be largely the work of Superintendent Joe Jennings. He offered to provide parking, improve the access road, contribute the site (thought to be on the Agency's land) and supply materials and labor. (1982:14)

"THE PLAY'S THE THING"

A pamphlet produced for the WNCAC by George L. Simpson and Harriet L. Herring points to the play that was eventually written and accepted by the CHA: "A historical drama is perhaps the best way to characterize and make known the peculiar appeal of a region to hoped-for travelers and vacationers. It advertises and attracts; it becomes the prime reason for visiting the region" (1956:24). Samuel Selden, a professor at the University of North Carolina–Charlotte, came to Cherokee in 1947 to find out if a drama about the Cherokee could be written that would be as compelling as *The Lost Colony.* At the same time, Mary Ulmer (Chiltoskey) had written a paper for the WNCAC regarding the history of the Cherokee. It is likely that the paper she wrote was researched entirely from the Mooney (1982 [1891]), Royce (1887), and Kephart (1983 [1936]) versions of Cherokee removal history.[7] This history was also reproduced for the above-mentioned tourism brochure (J. L. Caton 1937:22, 25). According to historian John Finger, although some "facts" can be gleaned from primary source material, these versions leave much to be desired in interpretation (1983, 1991). Ulmer's paper convinced all parties that "a worthy drama would result from their efforts" (Connor 1982:13). When Hunter began to look into the history of the Cherokee for a theme for the play, he turned to this paper and the several popular versions of Cherokee history mentioned above for a suitable story. He selected for a central theme the most popular historical legend of the Eastern Cherokee, that of Tsali (Charley) and his family (Connor 1982). According to Duane King, "This story is not only ingrained in the oral tradition [of the Eastern Cherokees], but it is also reinforced by the reservation's only outdoor drama, which has re-created the tragedy six nights a week throughout the summer months since 1950. Unfortunately, however, the account cherished by the majority of the Eastern Band and accepted by the several million tourists who have witnessed the play is at best a romanticized version of an important period of Cherokee history" (1979b:166).

Primary sources—including military records of Major General Winfield Scott and Colonel William S. Foster, the letters of William H. Thomas, and North Carolina State Records—contradict the now ingrained and accepted "traditional" story that all of the Eastern Band were "escapees" from the 1838 removal (Burt and Ferguson 1973:213; Finger 1991, 1995; Hobsbawm and Ranger 1983; King 1979b:176–178). In fact, the primary material shows that this belief is "a distortion and oversimplification of a very complex episode in Cherokee history" (King 1979b:176).[8] Tsali has been credited with martyring himself and two of his sons so that the Eastern Cherokee could remain on ancestral land. While the story has basis in fact, Tsali and his immediate family were to be among those removed to Indian Territory. There was brutality against the defenseless Cherokee by the federal troops that acted to remove them. The entire act of removal violated an edict from the U.S. Supreme Court stating that the Cherokee Nation next to the state of Georgia was a separate entity and could not be dislocated from its land and possessions (King 1979b). Tsali and his kinfolk did, in fact, escape from the troops and in the process accidentally killed a soldier. However, the story as told in *Unto These Hills* is of the legend, not the fact, of Tsali. As Finger points out, the "poorly written 'Unto These Hills' version of how the Eastern Band came to exist is a 'Creation myth'" (1995:30). For this rendition, I turn to scene descriptions from the drama's 1996 program.

> *Scene 9:* a Cherokee Village, 1838. Back in the Smokies life went on. A party was gathering for the wedding of *Nundayeli,* daughter of *Tsali.* As the wedding party gathered, Major Davis of the US Army appeared and read the orders which proclaim that before another moon the Cherokee must be transferred to Indian territory west of the Mississippi, in the vicinity of *Tahlequah, Oklahoma territory.*
>
> *Scene 10:* The Village, 1838. The Cherokee were herded into stockades in North Carolina, Tennessee, Georgia, and Alabama. When the soldiers came to take *Tsali,* his wife *Wilani,* and their sons, they set off down the trail. *Tsali's* wife stumbled and a drunken soldier clubbed her to death.
>
> *Scene 11:* Tsali's Cave in the Mountains. Major Davis sent Will Thomas

and Drowning Bear to find Tsali's cave, and to tell him that if he will come in and surrender all of the others hiding in the mountains will go free.

Scene 12: Village, Next Morning. At daybreak it was evident that Tsali has been to the village. As the villagers gathered, Tsali came in bringing with him his three sons. Tsali and two sons were placed before a firing squad. The life of his youngest son was spared. Because of his sacrifice a remnant of his race was permitted to remain in the Great Smokies. His people were sent streaming into exile, and only those who had hid out were allowed to remain. (*Unto These Hills* 1996:7)

In the play, William Thomas, the only "white" chief of the Eastern Cherokee, who had been adopted as a young man by Yonaguska, told of the incident that actually provoked Tsali's family. It was actually told by Wasitani, Tsali's youngest son, whose life was spared: "A soldier struck his mother with a horsewhip for stopping to care for her infant. To make better time, Smith ordered two of his men to dismount and give their horses to the women and children. Tsali's wife and infant were placed on a white horse. Wasitani asserted that as the horse started, his mother fell, catching her foot in the stirrup and releasing the infant. The infant apparently sustained a fractured skull and died" (King 1979b:172). Tsali and his family retaliated, killing two soldiers and wounding another, and fled on the soldiers' horses into the mountains. It is also important to note that the troops in the area, led by Major General Scott and Colonel Foster, did not submit Tsali and his sons to a firing squad. In fact, only one group of Cherokee fugitives was affected by the capture of Tsali and his family. Foster insisted that this group of Cherokees, who were also in flight from removal—Euchella and his people from the Nantahala area about 50 miles south and west of Qualla—find and kill Tsali (Finger 1991, 1995; King 1979b). Tsali's was not a voluntary sacrifice but a chance for Euchella's people to disassociate themselves from the murders of the troops and "demonstrate their loyalty (*or submission*) to the federal government [emphasis mine]" (King 1979b: 177; see also Burt and Ferguson 1973; Finger 1991, 1995).

The story perpetuated by *Unto These Hills* may be true for some of Tsali's kin and for Euchella, who finally tracked, captured, and killed Tsali. In reality, however, the Oconaluftee Citizen Indians are the forebears of what became, by 1850, the Eastern Band of Cherokee Indians (Burt and Ferguson 1973:213–215; King 1979b; Ruehl 1998). Tsali's remaining family and Euchella's kinfolk were allowed to go to live with the Oconaluftee Citizen Cherokees, and their descendants are still on the Qualla Boundary today (Burt and Ferguson 1973:215; Finger 1991, 1995; Ruehl 1998).

Perhaps all of this was unimportant in 1949, especially since the sole purpose of the Drama (as *Unto These Hills* is known) was to give the passing tourist a glimpse of a Cherokee story. Artistic license is, after all, an accepted excuse for taking liberties with historical "fact." Connor observes that "the task was further complicated by the average American's highly romantic mythology concerning Indians. Show business Indians were expected to wear full-fringed leather outfits with splendid eagle-feather headdresses, not the breechcloths, scalplocks, and turbans of the historic Cherokees. Hunter wrote to Selden that authentically portrayed Cherokees would appear 'decidedly plain in contrast to what the average theatre-goer conceives of being American Indian'" (Connor 1982:18). Controversy has swirled around the play since its first reading. Connor relates that "when the script draft was read to people in Cherokee, it faced 'harsh criticism' because of the numerous historical inaccuracies." One aspect of the play that came under fire was Hunter's use of the Eagle Dance as an important ritual dance of the Cherokee. This choice is unfortunate in two ways. First, the Eagle Dance was intended for hunting and giving thanks; it would not have been included the participation of the entire population and therefore would not be *the* important event of the Cherokee cyclical year. Second, when casting the dance, Cherokees themselves have never been part of it. Instead, dance students from the University of North Carolina filled the ranks of the "eagle dancers." In this, Selden argued for "the 'spirit' of the truth over literal factuality" (Connor 1982:18).

Despite all the difficulties encountered in getting the Drama into production, the first summer of *Unto These Hills* was a "spectacular success" (Connor 1982:26).[9] The Drama delighted large audiences every time it played, and the huge debt was paid off in an unprecedented one month. Summing up the first season, the *Asheville Citizen-Times* commented that the play's success "probably exceeded the fondest expectations of its most enthusiastic booster. It gives western North Carolina keen pride and satisfaction in its latest tourist attraction. . . . It would be difficult to over-emphasize the contribution this colorful drama will make to the entertainment and inspiration of this region's visitors in the years to come" (1950:14). According to a fact sheet produced by the CHA in 1997, from 1950 to 1990 more than 3 million people attended the Drama, an average of 2,133 per performance.

THE OCONALUFTEE INDIAN VILLAGE

The other major venue produced and maintained by the CHA that is still in operation is the Oconaluftee Indian Village.[10] The Village, like the Drama, was intended to offer tourists a glimpse into the past of the Eastern Cherokee. When I stayed with Lisa, she used her enrolled status to take me through the Village the first time as a guest.[11] Because I had taken the tour previously as a tourist, I could see immediately that, except for the fact that the forest which had been cleared to make way for the Village had grown back into a lush canopy, most of the tour was exactly the same. This was affirmed by Lisa, Amanda Swimmer, Shana Bushyhead, Deb West, and numerous other former or current employees. The tour of the Village has changed little since the 1960s. First, I will discuss the conception and layout of the Village.

Shana Bushyhead worked at the Village as a tour guide for the duration of my fieldwork. An enrolled member who returned yearly to stay with family, Bushyhead is not native to the Boundary. She is the granddaughter of one of the more famous lifetime resident elders, Robert Bushyhead, and was quite eloquent during her interview.

> The script is exactly the same. Everything is the same. It would be cool if they could do anything to update. I heard they went through the speeches and checked them, but I think they could still use some work. They try to get the guides to read a history. Sometimes they do, sometimes they don't. But it's a summer job, and the kids that work there aren't going to put as much time and effort into it as, say, I would, as a college student trying to find something out about my culture. I've been reading and reading and reading and reading, so I know weird [factual] answers to questions that no one else really knows. It feels like Cherokee trivia. More seriousness [on the part of the employees] would be a big help as far as the training for the tour. (Bushyhead 1998)

As I go through the stations, it is possible to imagine fifty years' worth of tourists, well over a million, seeing the same basic representations that were original to the exhibition. The Village tour includes two basic types of stations: artisanship demonstrations and cultural/historical areas. The two are interwoven so that the tourist is led into the village and has the opportunity to alternate between them.

Tour Guides

Each group of about twelve tourists has a single tour guide who will stay with them throughout the tour. The female guides wear calico tear dresses, and the male guides wear jeans and ribbon shirts, both of which are considered traditional Cherokee wear. In this case, the traditional women's costuming is from the early nineteenth century, well after deer hides had been replaced by the Euro-American trade item, calico cloth (Hatley 1991; Perdue 1998). The term "tear dresses" has a distinct meaning for the Eastern Cherokee. I was told that women tore calico into strips and sewed them together to create the dresses (probably originally skirts). This was a good thing, as few women had scissors to cut fabric and the knives used to cut buckskin were too rough for the more delicate calico. The men's costuming has evolved through the Village's fifty years from buckskin with no shirt to the now "traditional" garb of the powwow circuit (Hobsbawm and Ranger 1983).

The tour guide's primary goal is to keep the group moving at a pace that allows each member of the group to see each station while keeping a suitable distance between the preceding and succeeding groups. It is important for tourists to have one-on-one encounters with the Cherokees working at each station. The tour guides are chosen for their phenotype and for their affability with the public. The artisans at each station are also encouraged to answer questions, but many focus primarily on their work and say little to the tourists.

The Stations

The thirteen demonstration stations provide seasonal income to artisans from all over the Boundary. Examples of baskets, pottery, beadwork, carving, and finger weaving are all executed at the station sites. To illustrate the egalitarian nature of the Eastern Cherokee schema, I note whether women or men tend to be involved at each station.

Beadwork (Women)

While beadwork is considered one of the defining crafts of pan-Indianism, there is little evidence in the historic record that the Cherokee actually produced much of what is now considered "Indian" in the pre-contact through pre-removal periods. Fired clay beads may have been used with animal claws, teeth, quills, and beaks along with shell beads—either produced from local mussels or traded with coastal tribes—for jewelry. Some archaeological pieces remain in the collections of the western North Carolina/eastern Tennessee region (R. M. Abram 1998; Chapman 1985). According to Perdue, trade beads from Europe were introduced to the Cherokee at least by the eighteenth century: "[In] the process of enlisting their aid in an expedition against St. Augustine in January 1717, the South Carolina House of Commons appropriated funds to purchase gifts for three visiting Cherokee headmen. Each received 'One Gun, on [sic] Cutlash and Belt, a Cagg Run, a Bagg Sugar, a stript Duffield Blanket, a Peece Calicoe and some Strings Beads'" (1998:102). There is no mention, however, of how the beads were used. Since this was a European "gift," it can be assumed that the beads were glass from the Continent. How-

2.3. Beading stop, Oconaluftee Indian Village, 2006 (Author's photo)

ever, Perdue also cites an incident between the Cherokee of the Southeast and the Iroquois of the Northeast: "[The Cherokee] had come [to the Northeast] to recruit Iroquois warriors for an attack on the French in the Ohio Valley, and they were impatient to get on with the business. A little over a decade later, the war chief Oconostota conducted a Cherokee delegation to a council in New York. No Cherokee women were present, and so he presented a wampum belt they [the Cherokee women] had sent to Iroquois women and he delivered their message urging peace" (1998:93). While this may seem like a small point, it shows that Cherokee women were doing beadwork in the eighteenth century. However, the term "wampum belt" is a Northeastern Algonquian one and has no equivalent in the Cherokee language. The above description comes from the papers and records of Sir William Johnson, 1757 and 1763, who was familiar with and in contact with the Six Nations in the New York area (Johnson 1757, 1768). Wampum is a specifically indigenous New England invention for use and trade. There were sacred beaded belts, however, as the following passages describe:

> The Keetoowah's bible is not written on paper. The words are woven into seven wampum belts which are shown only in rare occasions. The belts are very old, and are made of pearls and shell beads, woven with seaweed fibers from the Gulf of Mexico. *The wampum belts are shown only on very sacred occasions.* The history behind the belt is that many years ago, the tribe was preparing to go on to war with another tribe, when the medicine men foresaw which would survive, and cut the original wampum belt into seven pieces, giving one to each warrior. After the war, the belts were scattered, some being hidden and disappearing, the last one was recovered by Redbird Smith around 80 years ago. (Hickman 1992; emphasis added)

The Algonquian word *wampum* is used in the present day to describe Cherokee beadwork, or a-de-la di-ya-tso-di (Chiltoskey 1972). Perhaps this is because of the loss of a great deal of language or because *wampum* is such a recognizable word in English. These might have been descriptions of beaded bandoliers, that is, cloth or leather strips embroidered with beadwork. According to Paula Giese, an educator and activist on American Indian issues,

> Though bandolier bags are mainly associated with Anishinaabe people, and especially with Midewiwin dances, a few early ones were found among the southeast Woodland tribes. Peabody Museum identifies . . . one—which is made of trade wool broadcloth and glass beads—only as made by a southeastern tribe, prior to the time of Removal—the 1820–1840 period. They call it a doctor's bag. Cherokee women made bandolier bags, which women wore (men usually wore Ojibwa bandoliers). One was made sometime prior to the Trail of Tears death marches removals (May 1838–March 1839) of Cherokees from the southeast to Oklahoma. It may have been looted during the removals. It is presently in the National Museum of the American Indian. (Giese 1996)

In contemporary times, most women engage in some form of beadwork. At the Village, beadworkers create many types of jewelry, including rings, earrings, bracelets, and necklaces. They also do the more intricate forms of beading to produce elaborate designs on buckskin moccasins, medallions, and clothing. While the beadwork done at the Village is intricate and exquisite, it is a distinctly twentieth-century "invention of tradition" for the tourist industry (Hobsbawm and Ranger 1983).

2.4. Pottery-making stop, Oconaluftee Indian Village, 2006 (Author's photo)

Pottery (Women)

With at least two potters working at all times, the pottery station is always humming. Two methods of pottery making, pinch pots and coiled pots, are demonstrated. Each method is equally intricate and requires skill, knowledge, and patience to achieve the desired results. Pots of all types and at all stages of construction are on display. Lumps of fresh clay may be in the process of being kneaded, coils may be in production, and tennis-ball-sized blobs of clay may await their transformation into delicate pots. Many of the pots are based on the archaeological shards unearthed and identified with Cherokee pottery from the fifteenth century through the eighteenth. Wooden paddles with various designs are used and on display, and stones and shells for decoration and to produce sheen are there as well. A fire for "burning" the pots was nearby in the 1990s, and tourists could occasionally see the end result emerge from the flames. Pottery is important in Cherokee traditions, both of craftwork and of cultural continuity. I will discuss how the loss and recovery of pottery making became a turning point in Cherokee lifeways in chapter 4.

Blowguns (Men)

The Cherokee undoubtedly used the bow and arrow for hunting throughout their pre-removal history, as there are stories of such contained within the mythology of the people (Mooney 1982 [1891]). However, for the Village tour the art of the blowgun has been central to the tourist's understanding of Cherokee hunting. The tour guide describes in detail the process of making the blowgun: "The cane is gathered and stored to dry . . . when dry the cane is crooked. It is straightened by holding it over an open fire and then [being] bent over [the] knee [of the artisan]. After it is straightened it is cut into the length of the blowgun needed. . . . Before the introduction of metal . . . a long wooden shaft with a piece of flint attached to the end . . . was used to knock out the joints inside the cane. By placing sand in the cane and using the end of the shaft with an in and out motion, the joints could be smoothed out."[12]

The dart used with the blowgun is usually six to eight inches long and is traditionally made from yellow locust and bull thistle down. It is not known what materials were originally used for the tail down.[13] The down is rolled onto the dart shaft with twine, and the ability to make the dart tail even is still an art form. The blowgun was said never to have been used in warfare but only for hunting small game. While men currently are the primary manufacturers of the blowguns and darts, both women and men acquire skill in their use and engage in contests at the annual fair. Blowguns and darts are manufactured in the Village and can be purchased in local craft shops.

Basketry (Women)

The primary examples of basketry completed at the Village in 1996 were white oak and honeysuckle, which can be worked fairly quickly. This offers the tourist a chance to see the baskets move toward a finished product while on the tour. Several women are generally at work on the baskets. An apprentice might finish off handles and closures while more experienced weavers make the forms and begin weaving the intricate patterns that are distinctive to Cherokee basketry. This is a rather large station with basket-making materials on display for the tourist and for use by the artisans in various stages of the basket-making process. Bundles of honeysuckle vines, white oak splints, vats of natural dyes of various shades with the different woods and vines soaking in the rich colors available in the mountains, and white oak and red maple handles carved by the men in the woodcarver's station are all available for the tourist group to examine.[14] Basketry is probably the most notable of all Cherokee craftwork. Books are dedicated to it, and photographs of women weaving rivercane with over 100 different splits sticking out in every direction exist from the time of James Mooney's excursions onto the Boundary more than a century ago (S. H. Hill 1997). A large section of chapter 4 is devoted to basketry and to the women who keep the basket-making tradition alive and thriving.

Arrowheads and Traps (Men)

While flint knapping and hunting traps are described in separate but adjacent segments of the tour, their descriptions are generally brief.[15] There are examples of arrowheads and traps, but these stations lacked actual production of the goods in 1996. There are presumably still men who have the knapping skill, but I did not meet or hear of any at the time of my initial stay.

The traps area of this station is generally not staffed with a trap maker. The

2.5. Basket-weaving stop, Oconaluftee Indian Village, 2006
(Author's photo)

three basic types of hunting traps are the dead-fall or bear trap, the fish trap, and the figure four or bird trap. All use materials available in the environment and are said to be very effective.

1750s Log Cabin Reproduction

In a clearing of the trees and a widening of the path just beyond these several stations, the tourist comes to reproductions of dwellings that the Cherokee built during the eighteenth century and then the early nineteenth century just after the American Revolution. Replete with hides, drying gourds, and reproduction furnishings, these cabins are open for tourists to enter, examine, and ask questions. Corn pounding is a part of women's work that is documented from the eighteenth through the twentieth century. During his initial ethnological fieldwork with the Eastern Cherokee in the late 1800s, Mooney noted that every family in Big Cove used a mortar and pestle made from logs. Some-

2.6. Reproduction of 1750s house, Oconaluftee Indian Village, 2006 (Author's photo)

times, two women worked together in a rhythm not unlike driving railroad stakes to produce cornmeal and hominy (Mooney 1982 [1891]; Perdue 1998). However, the tour guide's speech for this area refers to the use of stone and metal tools for this work. This is the kind of historical inaccuracy that caused dissent among the Eastern Cherokee when the CHA first began these projects in the 1950s. In the present, however, the Eastern Cherokee accept whatever the tour guide scripts say as tradition and fact (Finger 1991, 1995; Berkhofer 1978).

Sweathouse

The presence of a sweathouse in the Village and its explanation on the tour are completely out of context for the Cherokee. In the 1990s I spoke with more than one elder who was quite upset with this part of the exhibit, saying that "if they put a sweathouse, they oughta go ahead and put in a teepee in here!" G. B. Chiltoskey, a renowned Cherokee woodcarver, was adamant that "Cherokees didn't sweat!" (Chiltoskey 1996). Here, "Indians" are confused with Cherokees. Laurence French, in *The Qualla Cherokee: Surviving in Two Worlds,* calls this exhibit an "aboriginal medicine lodge" (1998:48). However, the tour guide's scripts clearly refer to this area as a sweathouse.

Finger Weaving (Women)

The ancient art of flat braiding, a method that predates the loom, is not as prominent as the pottery and basketry stations on the Village tour. Cherokee women make beautiful woven sashes and belts in the same manner that peoples of the Eastern Woodlands employed for thousands of years (Leftwich 1970). "Finger weaving is a technique which evolved in many parts of the world, cultivated into a fine art by Native Americans. Native Americans of the eastern forests are well known for their finger woven yarn belts and sashes. Archaeological remains of pottery in the Northeast show where woven textiles were pressed into the clay some 3000 years ago. The constant wet environment of peat bogs in Florida have produced a piece of finger weaving 6,000 to 8,000 years old" (NativeTech 2002a).

Often, new employees or artisans at the Village begin in the finger-weaving station. However, this fine art is extremely complex. Even though today's weavers use contemporary threads, cords, and yarns—mostly of cotton or wool—the traditional dexterity it demands is difficult to master. Shana Bushyhead started her employment at the Village as a guide, but she became interested in becoming an artisan in the finger-weaving station. "I am learning how to finger weave. I think it is actually the closest that any of [my family] has come to doing craftwork. . . . I don't know if that just comes from being here, because I feel like I should [learn a craft]. . . . That's the impression you get when you work at the village, that you should be able to do at least one craft. I chose finger weaving and I love it. It's so frustrating and so hard but now that I'm getting it, it's getting to be a lot better. I hope to keep it up. I'm learning it from Tasha Maney, she's teaching it, she's 16 or 17, and she learned in high school" (Bushyhead 1998).[16] It can take many years to gain competency in this craft. The competent weaver manipulates up to 60 threads at a time to produce the myriad designs that become sashes and belts for sale.

1540s House Reproduction

This station is small and can be considered an homage to Cherokee archaeology and pre-contact Cherokee society. The description is short: "The house was constructed by first placing large poles in the ground. These were covered with smaller saplings, the saplings with mats, and the mats with red clay. . . . The roof is made of thatch and is raised in the center to allow the smoke to escape. This is because our people always built their fires in the center of the room. The furs on the beds are buffalo hides. At one time the small bison roamed in our territory." This description is probably more accurate for Tugaloo, the site in northern Georgia upon which the Oconaluftee Village project was based. However, since the Cherokee were not confederated in any sense

2.7. Finger-weaving stop, Oconaluftee Indian Village, 2006 (Author's photo)

in the pre-contact period, their building style (as well as language) was varied and distinct, with at least four areas and three dialects: "The Lower (*Elati*) dialect was spoken in the settlements along the Keowee, the Tugaloo, and the headwaters of the Savannah River in what is now northwestern South Carolina and northeastern Georgia. The Middle (*Kituhwa*) dialect was spoken in the settlements on the Oconaluftee, Tuckaseegee, Nantahala, and Little Tennessee rivers in western North Carolina. The Western (*Olati*) dialect was spo-

2.8. Reproduction of 1540s house, Oconaluftee Indian Village, 2006 (Author's photo)

ken in all the towns of East Tennessee and in the towns along the Hiwassee and Cheowa rivers in North Carolina" (King 1979a:ix). Thus, the early architecture of the Cherokee area of North Carolina can better be described as being in the Pisgah phase.

Canoe Making (Men)

This is one of the more popular stations on the tour. Because the work is ongoing and time consuming, tourists never know what phase of canoe making they will encounter. The method shown, burning the center out of a large felled yellow poplar, can take months to complete in the Village setting. This kind of canoe would have been impractical in the deep mountains of the pre-contact Overhill Cherokee, since canoes could not have traversed the rocky rapids of the western North Carolina mountains. Like the 1540s house, the canoe-making exhibit is an homage to other areas of Cherokee habitation that were on the large rivers of what is now southeastern Tennessee, northern Georgia, and northwestern South Carolina.

Woodcarving (Men)

The importance of wood and stone carving to the Cherokee cannot be overstated. They appear throughout the archaeological and oral records of the

2.9. Woodcarving stop, Oconaluftee Indian Village, 2006 (Author's photo)

Cherokee in the same ways that basketry and pottery do. Some pieces—especially stone and wood pipes—are definitive of the pre-contact Cherokee (Blankenship 1987). This station is the last craft area that the tourist encounters on the tour. Dozens of examples of masks, dough bowls, eating utensils, rattles, farming implements, and weapons (e.g., bows and arrows and spears) are on display for perusal. Artisans are always on hand and produce utilitarian pieces. Contemporary items are produced specifically for the collector and the tourist trade as "art for art's sake."

Stone carving is also featured here. The primary items created and displayed are pipes originally used to smoke ceremonial tobacco. According to the tour script, "Pipes are carved from pipestone which is a soft stone that can be easily carved with a knife. The seven-sided pipe represents the seven clans of the Cherokee people. . . . The pipe with the four holes represents the four directions of the earth." Beautiful pieces of stone sculpture of the same type as the wood pieces are also carved and displayed for the collector.

Council House

Once the tourist group has passed through all of the artisan stations and smaller ethnohistorical exhibits, the guide leads them into the reproduction of the Cherokee council house and leaves them in the hands of the council house speaker (the guide then returns to pick up the next group and start the process over again).

As they are ushered into the council house, tourists enter a building that is built partially into the earth. The council house is the first place on the tour where one can sit, rest, and listen to the explanations of the ways of life of the pre-contact Cherokee. Photographs from the original construction reveal that the house was built first and that the earth was filled in around it later (Connor 1982:31). The resulting feeling, however, is that the council house was dug into the earth. It is dark and cool inside. The council house is seven-sided— one section for each of the clans—and the center has a large hearth that is always lit. Artifacts representing different historical periods of the Cherokee are placed along the walls and in the center area from which the guide speaks. The explanations of the clan system of the pre-contact Cherokee are explained in some detail here.

The council house speaker is always eloquent and has a flair for theatrics. She or he draws the tourist into the "mystery" surrounding the events that took place within the councils. The speaker also briefly explains the pre-removal village system. "Every Cherokee village had a council house, a squareground, seven clans, and two chiefs—a war chief and a peace chief. Over the entire Cherokee Nation was a third chief who was known as a principal chief. Where his home was located was considered the capital of the Cherokee Nation. The last established capitol was in New Echota, Georgia, in 1838 at the time of the Removal. The principal chief at that time was John Ross who was one-eighth Cherokee. The principal chief was known for his wisdom and ability as a leader." It is relevant to note that there was no principal chief until the European conquest and subsequent colonization of Cherokee lands. Each village was autonomous, and they all came together only in times of war (Finger 1991, 1995; Goodwin 1977; King 1979b; Perdue 1979, 1998). Persico states that "beyond the level of the town, the Cherokees of the early eighteenth century recognized no higher authority. The Cherokee tribe consisted of a number of politically independent towns held together by a common culture, language, and history. No formal political mechanism existed on the tribal level" (1979:95). Upon completion of the speech and after questions and answers from the tourists, the group is led to the final area of the Village tour, the square ground.

Square Ground (Ceremonial Dance Ground)

Upon arriving at the square ground, tourists are seated in a clan area. The guide for this portion—who also stays at this position and doesn't lead individual groups—explains that the pre-contact Cherokee had at least seven clans. "Seats were built around the square for those who did not take part in the ceremonies. These were constructed in the manner [seen] here [in the Village] with coverings to protect the people from the sun. The seats were divided into seven sections with each clan having their own section to sit in." The seven clans are Blue (Panther), Long Hair, Bird, Paint, Deer, Wild Potato, and Wolf. According to a tourist-oriented booklet written by Marcelina Reed, an enrolled member of the Eastern Cherokee, "A dramatic decline in clan affiliation occurred during the middle of the twentieth century (1940–1969). Today on the Qualla Boundary of western North Carolina there are still a few Cherokees who can identify their clan through the generation. If the clan affiliation is not known, it is very rare that it will be identified. The task is made very difficult because there was no record of clan membership kept on file" (1993:26).

At least one private stomp ground is active on the Boundary. While I don't have any firsthand information about it, I do know some who have long practiced the stomp and tell the old stories. Terrapin rattles on the legs of Cherokee women and songs sung in Cherokee after ritual scratching and "going to water" are keeping the old ways alive into the twenty-first century (Woodhead 1994).

The objective of re-creating the pre-removal village is to introduce the tourist to the individuated experience of the social and cultural system unique to the Cherokee. Has it succeeded after half a century? When I compare the number of tourists who come through Cherokee with the number of tourists who come through the Oconaluftee Indian Village, I must answer both yes and no. Yes, because those who do go through the Village may come out with some knowledge of the Eastern Cherokee themselves. They may learn that the Southeastern Complex of American Indians is not the same as the Plains Complex, which is the American tourist stereotype. And no, because only a small percentage of the millions of travelers passing through each year take the time to come to the venue. These tourists want the quick shot of another ethnicity, of the "exotic other," that they can write home about on postcards and take photographs to prove their actual presence with "them" (Albers and James 1983; Markwick 2001). Despite the fact that the Village and the Drama are well advertised, they still draw less than 1 percent of the tourists who snake their way through the Boundary each year (*Cherokee One Feather* 1997c, 1997d).

BILLBOARDS POINT THE WAY

Signage is particularly important to the Cherokee, North Carolina, tourist enterprise and questions of Cherokee identity. Certain venues have always been the subject of roadside advertising, including Oconaluftee Indian Village, *Unto These Hills*, bear zoos, craft shops, Santa's Land, and food establishments.[17] Most important to my analysis are the signs for the Oconaluftee Indian Village and *Unto These Hills*. Billboards for the Village have been in place since 1956, while billboards for the Drama have come and gone. None have been intact and maintained for as long as those advertising the Village, some of which are probably from the 1960s. However, between 1996 and 1998 there was a movement to add Drama billboards back to the scenery. When the historical billboards are compared with those erected between 1996 and 1999, some clear differences emerge.

The "traditional" billboards for the Village on the roads leading into the western North Carolina area are large and contain all the information a tourist needs to visit the Village, including the distance and which exit to take. The models for these billboards are elder women doing their craftwork, most often baskets or pottery. The women are dressed in post-contact tear dresses and head rags and are always deeply engaged in their work. The older billboards are beginning to show age, but none actually *need* to be replaced, though occasional touch-up is required.

The billboards that went up in the late 1990s, in contrast, are about one fourth the size of the originals. They appear less frequently and are less effective in leading the tourist to the Village. But the most glaring change is that the model for the new billboards is a young, stereotypically beautiful, generic Indian woman. She, too, is shown in a post-contact tear dress, but her flowing straight black hair is not discreetly put up in the head rag that is customarily worn to keep one's hair out of one's way when working with clay, basket weaving, or finger weaving. Instead, she is the ideal of the "Indian princess," very much like the Disney version of Pocahontas. In addition, compared with the very real likenesses taken from photographs of the elder women doing craftwork, the new billboard representation appears as a caricature, a cartoon.

From 1996 to 1998 no men appeared on any of the billboards, either new or old, for the Village. I find this fascinating, since numerous postcards available for purchase show men in the Village demonstrating weapons or at craftwork. This is an indication that the tourist public, in the minds of the CHA advertising board, identifies the peaceful Indian woman hard at work with their comfortable notion of what is American Indian. Would the appearance of a man using a traditional blowgun or flint-knapping arrow and spear points on a billboard frighten away tourists? I could find no rationale for this decision in my interviews with the CHA administration or in my literature review. This question was easier to answer in 2006, as there *were* traditional male Cherokees on billboards then. I will discuss this in the epilogue.

In sharp contrast to the existing Village billboards were the new ones for *Unto These Hills.* These new billboards were the same size as the new ones for the Village, but each was filled, nearly border to border, with an eagle dancer from a small section of the Drama. All the eagle dancers are male, and in the Drama they are all non-Indian dancers with heavy, coppery-colored makeup all over their bodies (*Unto These Hills* 1997). Many people consider the lead

2.10. Old and new billboards for Oconaluftee Indian Village, 1998 (Author's photo)

eagle dancer and his entourage the highlight of the Drama. This billboard image also adorns the many tourist pamphlets and tourist newspapers for the western North Carolina region as well as the Drama program. Just as no men are depicted on Village billboards, no women are on billboards for the Drama. The contrast is stark. Do tourists expect something different from a play than from a re-creation site? What message about women and men do these billboards convey? One of the facets I will later discuss in detail is the salient social dichotomy of the domestic and the public. These images also fit into the American schema for the stereotypical Indian. As such, a few pictures fill the need for Americans to think that Indians are "just like us" (Mihesuah 1995). Non-Cherokee, non-Indian people make all of the decisions about advertising for the CHA. The rationale for the new billboards was explained to me by the director of the CHA, Barry Hipps. When attendance at the CHA venues dropped throughout the 1990s, these new billboards were made in an attempt to restore interest (Hipps 1998). Instead, the billboards continually reinscribe the inherent misconceptions and stereotyping that come from this overlay of a Western social schema onto indigenous people.

3

Academic Perspectives on Tourism and the Case of Cherokee, North Carolina

Both traveling and touring take on great significance in the light of two centuries of change resulting from colonialism and imperialism in the southern Appalachian region of the United States. The initial point of reference for the early American imagination was "sacred space" and "frontier," even though the territory was extensively used by human populations for millennia (Finger 2001; Riggs and Rodning 2002; Sears 1989). In their discussion of certain aspects of tourism among the Maasai, Edward Bruner and Barbara Kirshenblatt-Gimblett point out that "tourism gives tribalism and colonialism a second life by bringing them back as representations of themselves and circulating them within an economy of performance. Mass tourism routinely recycles dying industries, dead sites, past colonial relations, and abandoned ethnographic tropes to produce industrial parks, living historical villages and enactments" (1994:435). The Cherokee Historical Association's outdoor drama, *Unto These Hills,* certainly fits Bruner and Kirshenblatt-Gimblett's hypothesis. Many Cherokee people would see the truth of the above statement while simultaneously acknowledging that if not for the tourist enterprise, much of the cultural systems of their ancestors, especially the traditions of artisanship, would have been lost to ensuing generations. Others would retire to the silence of the mountains and go on with a subsistence lifeway that would neither agree nor contend with mass tourism as a catalyst for the maintenance of cultural traits. These Cherokees point out that many people do not participate and have never participated in "the tour" and have managed to remain "conservative" or "traditional," keeping in touch simultaneously with both their small communities and the larger mainstream (S. M. Abram 1998; Finger 1984, 1991, 1995; French and Hornbuckle 1981; Gulick 1960; Neely 1991). Still others state emphatically that colonialism has never been arrested anywhere in the United States and that the tourist industry continues to be a way to exploit that still inverted power and economic relationship (Plane 1996; Povinelli 1991).

Since the 1970s, when explorations into tourism analysis began, this area of inquiry has grown steadily. My work relates most closely to the literature that concentrates on indigenous populations worldwide who have had to learn to cope with and/or capitalize on the phenomenon of modern mass tourism that began in the sixteenth century (Echtner and Prasad 2003; Hollinshead 1991; Kehoe 2005; Maybury-Lewis 2001; Moreno and Littrell 2001; Stronza 2001; Takaki 1993). Geographically close to the Cherokee, the tourist industry of the Florida Seminoles has been chronicled and analyzed for more than two decades by Patsy West (1981, 1998) in particular, and it holds many correlations to both the upside and the downside of the industry. Tourism research also moves well beyond North America and includes the Maasai, traditional Welsh villages in England, the tribal peoples of the Sepik River in Papua New Guinea, the many Australian Aboriginal peoples, the Toraja of Indonesia, the tribal peoples of the Upper Amazon, and the widely varied societies of the South Pacific (Adams 1995; Bruner and Kirshenblatt-Gimblett 1994; Maybury-Lewis 2001; O'Rourke 1987; Rajotte and Crocombe 1980; Seiler-Baldinger 1988). More general work on the interface between tourism, identity, and the "fourth world" has led many scholars to question whether tourism is a viable and sustainable practice.

It is the indigenous reaction to the circumstances of being "the toured," in both public and private settings, that concerns the tourist industry and its effects on those populations which are assumed by large numbers of the "mainstream public" to be "extinct." Questions that concern the importance of geographic place and the intertribal and intratribal politics of land dispersal also come into play in this analysis (Foster 1995; Narayan 1996; Sahlins 1995; Sarris 1993; Swedenburg and Lavie 1996).

Since the publication of Valene Smith's edited volume *Hosts and Guests*, anthropology has been problematizing and theorizing the growing phenomenon of tourism (Smith 1989). The work has followed in the vein of all the subcategories that came before it. In other words, the anthropology of tourism is as varied and complex as anthropology itself (Lett 1987). Theron Nuñez said in *Hosts and Guests* of the turn to an anthropology of tourism that "as a subject of scholarly study, tourism may be new, but it may be treated within traditional methods and theories of anthropological research for the present [1977] and will benefit from the application of more recent, more sophisticated models as data and understanding accumulate. By the time a discipline is beginning to attempt definitions and prepare taxonomies . . . the subject has achieved legitimacy" (1977:274). Within the literature there are multi-vocal, multi-storied works that pointedly attempt to include the voice, face, and perspective of the toured (Besculides et al. 2002; Errington and Gewertz 1991; Grünewald 2002; Medina 2003; O'Rourke 1987; Seiler-Baldinger 1988). This is especially true for anthropological work concerning American Indians of the Southwest and the Seminoles of Florida (Babcock 1994; Bowden 1994; Norris 1994; Rodriguez 1994; P. West 1981, 1998). Two examples correlate well with my work: those of Barbara Babcock and Patsy West.[1] While West's work is more ethnographically relevant, Babcock writes theoretically of the exoticism and racism inherent in touring the Southwest "other":

> I implicated Edward Said's *Orientalism* in my argument, because I think that the Southwest *is* America's Orient. Like the Orient, the Southwest is an idea that has "a history and a tradition of thought, imagery, and vocabulary that have given it reality and presence in and for" the rest of America. And . . . this Anglo-American tradition is explicitly figured in the trope of Orientalism. Repeatedly, "travelers passing the Pueblo villages of the Southwest in the [eighteen] eighties were invited to recall the villages of ancient Egypt and Nubia, Nenevah and Babylon, rather than to study the remains of American aboriginal life." . . . Then and now, Pueblo men mimed the whiteman in clown performances on dusty plazas, and Pueblo women shaped his [the whiteman's] image in clay. Few whitemen who bought these figures, which were described as "eccentric" or "grotesque," realized that they were in fact portraits of themselves. These *monos* were not regarded highly, and because traders [Anglo-American] . . . encouraged the manufacture of these "primitive idols," they were (and still are) frequently dismissed as "tourist junk" and as wholly "commercial" in origin. (1994:187–189)

Many societies have charades of the whiteman as the outsider, the other, that they understand as mimicking (R. M. Abram 1998; Babcock 1990; Fogelson 1983; Fusco 1995; Maybury-Lewis 2001; O'Rourke 1987). I would argue that Said's explanations of Orientalism obtain beyond tribes of the American Southwest to the entire population of Indians on the North and South American continents (Said 2000). Tourists are constantly in search of the exotic other in their own backyard—for example, Little Italy and Chinatown in New York City, the Shinnecock and Poospatuck Reservations on Long Island—and everywhere they visit throughout the world—for example, the Maasai or !Kung in Africa, the Yanomami or Xavente in South America, or the Sepik River peoples of Papua New Guinea. They buy "tourist junk" as souvenirs and compare the artisanship to European art epochs—baroque, for instance—to hang on their walls and show how far they have been, mentally, at least, away from home (Babcock 1994; Bruner and Kirshenblatt-Gimblett 1994; O'Rourke 1987).

The literature on tourism focuses predominantly on aspects of the economics of the tour itself and on tourists who seek out the tour (Albers and James

1983; Bender 1996; Digance 2003; Poria et al. 2003; Pretes 2003; Ryan and Huyton 2002). However, MacCannell points to another reinterpretation of the "traditional" look and reminds us that "clear exploitation occurs when aspects of everyday life of a formerly colonized people (their cuisine, music, or anything else that is important in the cultural life of the community) are taken from the people and turned into industrial products that *displace* the original—that is, when people are forced to buy back a devalued simulacrum of their former lives. This is unethical" (1994:174).

It is not difficult to find this displacement on the Boundary. A major source of this is the Cherokee Crafts and Moccasin Factory, a cottage industry formed in the 1960s by an "enterprising local white man" to make moccasins and children's toys (e.g., tomahawks, "pretend" blowguns and darts, bows and quivers with arrows, drums, dolls, and headdresses, both Plains chief and brave styles) (Sharpe 1998). The factory had been a constant, continuous employer of Cherokee people for decades until 2001 (Chiltoskey 1986:17; Sharpe 1998). Beginning in the late 1990s, however, the dropoff in the tourist trade throughout the region had an impact on the economic strength of the factory. Machinery, some of it 30 years old, for cutting the piecework so that employees could assemble the many items kept in inventory began to break down. With no money to replace or repair the machinery, the factory faced closing in 2002 and was kept running by the determination of about half a dozen women who refused to quit altogether. An enterprising white from "over the mountain" in Tennessee tried to reopen the factory in 2003 (Sharpe 2003). Even though the factory has offered continuous employment to Cherokee people, its products precisely fit MacCannell's description, as inexpensive, mass-produced imitations replaced handmade utilitarian items for Cherokee people and provided tourists with "real" and affordable "Indian" paraphernalia to purchase. Cherokee children are as likely to be seen sporting these products as tourists' children are. There is another difference, however. The Eastern Cherokee people recognize that the products made at the factory are "fake" or "pretend," but they do not shun these items as they do the Asian-produced versions of the same. This is because Cherokees actually make these products—and earn a decent living while doing so.

For the Eastern Cherokee, the trail of tourism is a narrative that is contradictory to the extreme. The Cherokee Crafts and Moccasin Factory is just one of those contradictions. Two primary articles concerning the tourist industry (Duggan 1997; Stucki 1981) combine some of the major historical notes about the advent of tourism, oral stories of days gone by, current views—which always occur at a specific ethnographic moment—of the contemporary scene, and/or indictments against the enterprise. Betty Duggan's meticulously researched "Tourism, Cultural Authenticity, and the Native Crafts Cooperative:

3.1. Author's son sporting headdress with raccoon tails, bear-claw necklace, and tomahawk purchased at the Medicine Man Gift Shop and produced by the Cherokee Indian Crafts Factory, 1989 (Author's photo)

The Eastern Cherokee Experience" includes analysis of numerous interviews and archival research. Duggan concentrates on the Qualla Arts and Crafts Mutual and its much-revered place in the traditional craft-making community. In her narrative she writes:

> The Qualla Arts and Crafts Mutual, Inc. has experienced remarkable financial success in tapping into the mass tourism market that burgeoned in Cherokee, North Carolina, after World War II. The organization's ability to recognize traditional economic and social values that underlie and reinforce continued production of Cherokee crafts has contributed significantly to its emergence as the oldest and most successful Native American crafts cooperative in the United States. In both aspects, the Co-op provides a fine example of the positive economic and social benefits that tourism can engender when it is culturally informed and indigenously controlled. (1997:48–49)

Duggan rightly leaves the reader on an upbeat note, as the Co-op has long been a Cherokee success story. On the other end of the spectrum, Larry R.

Stucki took the "Devil's advocate" approach to Cherokee tourism in "Will the 'Real' Indian Survive?" He states:

> One [would not] be likely to include as evidence of the survival of "real Indianness" at Cherokee the violence, drunkenness, and shabbiness that is all too often visible there as it is on most other reservations in the United States. The "empty" symbols that distinguish many Cherokees (especially those with very European facial features) from their nearby White neighbors are often no more than a few "Indian-style" items of jewelry, clothing, and/or household artifacts together with the coveted tribal enrollments cards and "possessory titles" to particular parcels of tribal land. And even those local residents more blessed or cursed (depending upon one's viewpoint) with darker skins and "Indian-type" facial features—who are often encouraged to retain their "Indian identity" by being packaged as "chiefs" and "princesses" by gift shop owners, hired to be craftsmen, demonstrators, and guides in the Oconaluftee Indian Village, or recruited for crowd scenes in the Drama—have in a sense merely become actors in a Disneyland-type fantasy world created to serve the needs and desires of the local tourist industry. (1981:70)

Although from my time on the Qualla Boundary I can see the validity of both Duggan's and Stucki's statements, I want to push farther than either position and analyze the whys and wherefores of how Cherokee tourism grew to the level and configuration at which it existed in the 1990s and continued to exist a decade later. Rarely is anything completely positive or completely negative, and here I explore the interstitial space between the two poles.

While a great deal of the research has focused on the American Indian populations of the Southwest, less has been done on native peoples of other cultural areas of the United States (Babcock 1994; Bowden 1994; Deitch 1977; Desmond 1999; Gómez 1994; Rodriguez 1994; Schulte-Tenckhoff 1988; Sweet 1989). The experience of the Eastern Cherokee is quite similar to that of American Indian nations in the Southwest and Native Hawaiians who have been the subject of the tourist gaze for a century or more as well. According to Patricia Capone, in the Southwest "the present-day artistic tradition of pottery production for sale outside Pueblo communities has been part of a pottery production revival that has also been called a 'commercial revival.' This revival began in the 1880s with the arrival of the railroads carrying a new audience of consumers to the Southwest from the East. It intensified and blossomed in the 1970s and 1980s through efforts to develop tourism in the Southwest, a place portrayed as an exotic landscape with exotic peoples" (1998:35–36). In a similar vein, Jane Desmond tells of the seductive exoticism that Hawaii presented for tourists from the States from the late nineteenth century to the beginning of the twentieth. In her American studies volume, *Staging Tourism*, she notes that "an increase in future tourism is taken for granted. Hawai'i is presented as a marvel of nature. Unique races and unique geological features combine with nationalism in this narrative of the pleasures and fears involved in being at home, abroad, in the United States and the Pacific. The tourist industry discourse masks these discussions of 'racial mixing' and of present cosmopolitanism to produce the trope of the 'pure' Native" (1999:88). What is so interesting about the differences between mass tourism in the Southwest and Hawaii, according to Desmond, is that "unlike the mainland American West, where the image of the noble savage in the form of the male Indian came to stand for a vanishing way of life and covered over the bloody expansions of Euro-American settlement, in Hawai'i it is the image of the female dancer that stands for a paradisical past, unspoiled by modernity yet willing to be its entertainment" (1999:88). For the Cherokee, women and men within the tourist industry mark both ends of the spectrum simultaneously. The noble male savage is staged and restaged for the public in war bonnet and face paint while the demure stereotypical "Pocahontas" or wise elder woman looks out from many a billboard, newspaper, and advertisement to simultaneously draw the tourist to the beautiful and the rare, the mystical and the vanishing.

A TOURIST WHO BECAME AN ANTHROPOLOGIST

Prior to my arrival in North Carolina to conduct research, I made numerous summer excursions as just one among the millions of tourists who come annually to consume the commodities that are the Great Smoky Mountains National Park and the tourist strip through Cherokee. I first came to the mountains as a child with my parents, who had come as children with their parents. Then, as a parent myself, I brought my young son, eager to introduce him to the mountains. I have many photos in my personal collection that represent the typical tourist view of the Cherokee.[2] I took them long before I became interested in the phenomenology of tourism and its effects on indigenous lifeways. They are representative of the tourist experience in Cherokee, with the Cherokee presentation of being a "public Indian."

I was always an eager participant in the tour. I was socialized toward this enthusiasm because my family wanted to learn about and visit historical sites, as did many other families of the 1950s and 1960s. Wherever we went, our itinerary included historical venues (Clifford 1997; Kaplan 1996; Urry 1995; Wilson 1994); for example: Cherokee and the 1750 re-creation of Oconaluftee Indian Village and the outdoor drama *Unto These Hills;* Kitty Hawk and the Wright brothers museum; Colonial Williamsburg; Old Boston with all of its historical buildings and events; the Liberty Bell and the birthplace of the United States in Philadelphia; San Antonio and "Remember the Alamo"; the first Spanish forts in Florida; and the site of the disappearance of Virginia Dare. This is not to mention the sites close to home, such as Shiloh and many other Civil War sites in western Tennessee, the Hermitage and Belle Meade Mansion in Nashville, and Mammoth Cave in Kentucky. Like most lower-middle-class tourists, we accepted what historical societies nationwide presented as the "facts" of history. Such presentations were vital to both our tourist experience and the experience of the peoples representing that experience. What was not and is still not presented to tourists is perhaps of more interest than what is presented. In the 1950s and the 1960s we didn't hear about the fact that a black man discovered Mammoth Cave, or about the cruelty visited upon the slave population at the Hermitage, or that Andrew Jackson personally saw to it that the Cherokees were forcibly removed from Georgia, Tennessee, and northern Alabama, in defiance of the Supreme Court. While much more interpretive history is now available, this particularizing of historical "truth" holds true whether one is discussing the tour at Monticello, the White House and the D.C. tourist package, colonial Williamsburg, the many historical sites of famous artists nationwide, the pueblos of the Southwest, or American Indian sites nationwide (Babcock 1990; Chambers 1997, 2000; MacCannell 1992; Urry 1990). As historical geographer John Towner writes: "A thorough history of the development of tourism requires paying as much attention to the social and cultural conditions of tourists' ordinary, nontouristic lives (what he calls the 'visitor-generating area') as to their choices of tourism styles and destinations. In other words, it is as important to pay attention to where tourists are coming from as it is to look at where they are going" (quoted in Chambers 2000:8–9).

In his discussion and review of Dennis O'Rourke's acclaimed documentary *Cannibal Tours,* Dean MacCannell recognizes that the tourist is masterfully fooled into thinking that nothing is lost or stolen from the "natives" so long as money changes hands. The tourist is played by what spin doctors call "misinformation." Specifically, the tourist is ignorant of the understanding of "exchange within exchange relations." MacCannell writes:

The fable is as follows: the return on the tour of headhunters and cannibals is to make the tourist a real hero of alterity. It is his coming into contact with and experience of the primitive which gives him his status. But this has not cost the primitives anything. Indeed, they too, may have gained from it. Taking someone's picture doesn't cost them anything, not in any Western commercial sense, yet the picture has value. The picture has no value for the primitive, yet the tourist pays for the right to take pictures. The "primitive" receives something for nothing, and benefits beyond this. Doesn't the fame of certain primitives, and even respect for them, actually increase when the tourist carries their pictures back to the West? It seems to be the most perfect realization so far of the capitalist economists' dream of everyone getting richer together. (1990:16)

The taking of photographs to "capture" the "other" is a specifically touristic activity that takes place at tourist sites all over the world, all of the time. My own photographs are a testament to this.

To illustrate the similarities between the rise of tourism in the indigenous societies of the United States and around the world, I employ R. W. Butler's tourism cycle. This graph shows one idea of the progression of tourism evolution at cultural or ecotourist sites. The vertical axis represents the number of tourists coming to a given area, while the horizontal axis represents the passage of time (Butler 1980). In the late 1990s, the tourism cycle at Cherokee and the Great Smoky Mountains National Park adjacent to the EBCI Boundary lay between stagnation and either decline or rejuvenation. The massive building projects of Harrah's Cherokee Casino, the reworking of the Museum of the Cherokee Indian, and the addition of several new motels and restaurants between 1995 and 1997 were aimed at rejuvenating the tourist market. During my initial stay in Cherokee to gain permissions and entrée, the 1996 Summer Olympics were taking place in Atlanta. For those few weeks, the tourist flow was burgeoning and not a single room was available from Atlanta to Asheville. But as that excitement passed and autumn came, many people complained that the tourists weren't coming anymore (C. Abram 1998; Sharpe 1998). In an attempt at rejuvenation, Harrah's opened to tumultuous uproar from local white people, the Cherokee—both pro and con—and a multitude of press. Every newspaper within 200 miles of the Boundary announced its opening. The media blitz was aimed at gambling tourists who had never had a place so close to home to indulge their pleasures (Abram 1997; Davis and Wall 1997; Martin 1998d; Cherokee Tribal Travel and Promotion 1997).

In the following section I will further discuss the Oconaluftee Indian Village, one of the primary areas in which "othering" is most obvious. The previous chapter gave the Village's layout and described what takes place in each area. After I read through CHA material that explains and justifies the creation of an Indian village, participated in the actual tour with Lisa and a group of tourists, and interviewed several women who either worked or had retired from working at the Village, the fact of "othering" became crystalline. It is also quite clear that the researchers of the 1950s, as well as the Cherokees who were involved in the creation of the Village, were unaware of the implications, even while research from more than a century was available to draw on to elucidate

Time

3.2. Variation on Butler's graph (1980)

and avoid this exoticizing of the Cherokee people. Exoticizing American Indians is a form of racism.

RACISM: THE PROBLEM THAT PERSISTS

It is evident that racism has been and remains a problem on the Boundary and for tribes of the Southeast in general, and that its effects are felt simultaneously in various ways (P. West 1998; Greenbaum 1991; Lossiah 1998). The following excerpt is from a letter to the editor, "Racism Hurts Tourism," from the *Cherokee One Feather.* Rosalie Rowell wrote in May 1997:

> It seems racism is rearing its ugly head in Cherokee recently. The really hard-to-believe part is that is it coming from our own ethnic minority who have historically been the recipients of racism in its worst form. Cherokees from the youngest to the very oldest are made aware of the

"Trail of Tears." Many of us, including me, have personally experienced racism because of our Indian heritage and should therefore be even more sensitive to others in an ethnic group that's vulnerable to verbal, physical, or psychological attacks. Examples of racism that have come to my attention include a family of Indians getting up and moving from booths in a local eatery because a black family sat behind them. . . . A second example of ugliness includes a young woman recently doing her hob answering a phone and was called the "N" word . . . by faceless, nameless cowards. . . . How about an Indian citizen provoking a fight with a car load of another minority group . . . or another non-Indian woman having rocks thrown through her windows just because she is a member of another minority group. . . . In Cherokee, we are dependent on the tourist dollar. If we don't make our tourists and temporary citizens feel welcome and comfortable in our community, they won't come back. If bigoted individuals insist on driving away the people who are feeding our lifeline, they don't need to be whining and crying about not being able to feed themselves and their families and expecting handouts. (1997:2)

Clearly, racism is harmful. The fact that tourism exoticizes the Eastern Cherokee to such a degree that there is a swift and sometimes destructive backlash is seen in this letter.

Tourism—especially mass tourism—*is* institutional racism and discrimination at its worst as people go away in search of a different experience from their "normal" lives (MacCannell 1973, 1976, 1994; Nash 1977; O'Rourke 1987; Macionis 2002). Most tourists are unaware of the institutional racism that drives their fascination with the "exotic other" (Dominguez 1986; Fusco 1995). They are just as unaware of the distinct history and mythology of each individual nation, band, or tribe of American Indians. This inevitably allows them to ask a multitude of degrading and disturbing questions of the Eastern Cherokee who make their income in the tourist industry. I've heard some of these questions when out with Cherokee friends and at CHA venues: "When do Cherokee boys begin to grow their feathers?" "Where are all the teepees that your people live in?" Inevitably, someone asks, "Did you know that *my* great-grandmother was a Cherokee princess?" This is usually followed by, "Can I be a real Cherokee?" The most disturbing question, and the one that creates the most anger among the people I worked with, was, "Where are all the Indians?" In my experience, the Cherokee people just look at each other and shake their heads.

After being put in the position of the "exotic other" for more than a century, Cherokees have little patience with such ignorance. Yet, very few of them would dream of insulting tourists face-to-face. It is not part of the harmony ethic that persists from pre-removal times (Thomas 1958). Hence there is a pervasive sense of calm and acceptance that eases the tourist. This allows the tourist to be unaware of the problems she or he is reinforcing. Little does the uninformed tourist imagine that her or his ignorance is the subject of equal portions of hilarity and anger beyond their hearing. The tour guides at the Village are a perfect example. According to Shana Bushyhead,

> The biggest complaint is that people don't know anything. OK, when anybody complains about a group, that's the biggest thing. No, we don't live in teepees, no, we don't all live here in the Village. But what I do find impressive is that when somebody [a tourist] asks a question that we don't know, we'll try to find out. How were the houses constructed without permanency in mind? What were the roofs made out of? That's cool. It's frustrating, especially for people who have worked there for years and years and years to get the same questions over and over. From what I hear, it hasn't gotten any better over the years. You get a few people who know a bit about Native culture, but for the most part it's families looking for fun. And with those people, they really don't know *anything* about your culture and they believe you're all [all Indian peoples] just one big group. Like all tribes are one. . . . Do you want to know the biggest complaint at the village? The thing we hear night and day from every person is, "My grandmother was full-blood Cherokee," or "My grandmother was a Cherokee princess." You hate hearing it, because you know that when the tourists get a bit comfortable they tell you that. We're like, "Ooh, I'm sure she was." So we always say, "Oh, yeah? My great-grandmother was white." It takes them back a little bit when we say that. It's funny. (Bushyhead 1998)

Owing to this lack of education about the differences in American Indian nations as a requirement of American history classes at every level and the inherent racism in the governmental system under which all "domestic dependent nations" must still abide, tourists exhibit a classic example of the "hidden curriculum" of the public school system, namely, that each particular ethnic group of Americans is viewed as exactly the same, from sea to shining sea, no matter what actual differences exist (Macionis 2002:70).[3] All male American Indians wear war bonnets, all female American Indians are subjugated "squaws," all Italians have Mafia connections, all Irish drink, all WASPs are middle class, all African Americans belong to gangs, all Hispanics are lazy, all Asians excel at math, and so on (Frankenburg 1993; Takaki 1993:2).

THE SPATIAL CREATION OF THE OCONALUFTEE VILLAGE

Cherokees as a group often dislike and distrust white people (Bushyhead 1998; Stucki 1981). Parts of the beginnings of the tourist explosion in which the CHA was such a part include the idea of actually having Cherokee families live in the Village to depict the "time gone by." To accomplish this idea of literal "living representations" on the CHA's agenda for Cherokee tourism, it was decided to build a replica of a pre-removal Cherokee village (White 2001:15). As with the Drama, the Village was begun with what appears to be only the best intentions by the Cherokee Indian Agency, the CHA, and the scholarly community that joined in the process. These intentions—namely, to offer the tourist public an "authentic" perspective of the Eastern Cherokee in their mountainous home and to provide a stable economic base for the Cherokee—have been and are still proclaimed in the tourist literature (J. L. Caton 1937; Cherokee Tribal Travel and Promotion 1991–1994, 1996–1997; Connor 1982; *Unto These Hills* 1997). However, the politics of the late twentieth century combined with the continued growth and enhanced educational opportunities for the Eastern Cherokee population at large have sometimes pushed the original intentions to their limits (Abram 1997; Bender 1996; S. H. Hill 1997; Neely 1991). The Village was the first place where those limits were explored.

When the site for the Village was first plotted in 1951, the area was mostly meadow due to the logging of the earlier century and clearing land for the boarding school and its farming enterprises. That meant that the first visitors to the Village were in very little shade, and the newness of the buildings did not lend itself to the feeling of a 1750s village. It was also the site of an ancient village. According to Connor's history of the CHA, "Carol White, Harry Buchanan, T. M. N. Lewis, John Parris, Madeline Kneberg, and Joe Jennings met to discuss the project. They talked about the sort of buildings and materials used by the 18th century Cherokees, and they spoke at length about the possibility of a Ford Foundation grant, perhaps for the [Old Tugaloo Town (Tugaloo, Georgia)] excavation. . . [All] agreed that support from the Indians [EBCI] would greatly assist [the] effort" (1982:29–30). As a result, an offshoot of the CHA was born, the Tsali Institute of Cherokee Research. The institute's official purpose was described in the Certificate of Incorporation: "To engage in scientific research into early Cherokee Indian History, customs, and modes of living. To study, collect data, public information and in every way practicable to sponsor projects of investigation and education, including the excavation of archaeological sites of supposed Cherokee occupation, and anything calculated to inculcate a wider public understanding and appreciation of the early Cherokee Indian customs and traditions" (Tsali Institute of Cherokee Research, Inc. 1951). The Oconaluftee Indian Village, first called the

Pioneer Indian Village, opened in August 1952 as a "monument to the Cherokee's ancient culture . . . a living museum" (Lewis and Kneberg 1954:2; Hipps 1998). I find the name "Pioneer Indian Village" ironic, since the Cherokee were never "pioneers" in the Euro-American sense, which includes being "the first person[s] to explore territory" and "go[ing] into unexplored territory" (Soukhanov 1999:1371). This could have been true of the Cherokee in the Mississippian cultural era (ca. 1300–1500 CE), but certainly not in the 1750s, since the Cherokee had been established in the area for at least four centuries.

The goal of the Tsali Institute was to achieve an extraordinary degree of authenticity. According to a report from the institute,

> The village must come alive if it is to serve the purpose of giving the public a knowledge of Cherokee life as it existed shortly after the Cherokees had established permanent contact with the white people, and give the Cherokees of the present an insight into their own past way of life, of which they have now only a vague knowledge. . . . In order to provide an atmosphere of reality, Indian families are expected to live in the village. Their household utensils will be like those of long ago, and they will wear clothing such as is described by the travelers who visited the Cherokee towns of that period. They will work at the same tasks and use the same tools as their ancestors. (Connor 1982:32)

That the thought of having Indian families live in the Village even occurred to the Tsali Institute's board is disturbing enough. That similar activities took place throughout the nineteenth and twentieth centuries is noteworthy in that the practice was nothing new. However, this shows a blatant racist "othering" that was critiqued by no less than W. E. B. DuBois from the fin de siècle. The discussion continues through numerous critiques of indigenous cultural tourism in general (Bruner and Kirshenblatt-Gimblett 1994; Desmond 1999; French 1998; S. H. Hill 1997; MacCannell 1984; O'Rourke 1987; Urry 1990).

In 1935, Franz Kafka wrote a story that was "presented as the testimony of a man from the Gold Coast of Africa who had lived for several years on display in Germany as a primate" (Kafka 1983:250). Kafka's point was that indigenous people all over the world must somehow prove their humanity. In *English Is Broken Here*, Coco Fusco compiles a "short list" of thirty real-life "aboriginal samples" that spans five centuries of European and Euro-American curiosity (1995:41–43). She writes:

> Since the early days of European "conquest," "aboriginal samples" of people from Africa, Asia, and the Americas were brought to Europe for aesthetic contemplation, scientific analysis, and entertainment. Those

people from other parts of the world were forced first to take the place that Europeans had already created for the savages of their own Medieval mythology; later with the emergence of scientific rationalism, the "aborigines" on display served as proof of the natural superiority of European civilization, of its ability to exert control over and extract knowledge from the "primitive" world, and ultimately, of the genetic inferiority of non-European races. Over the last 500 years, Australian Aborigines, Tahitians, Aztecs, Iroquois, Cherokee, Ojibways, Iowas, Mohawks, Botocudos, Guianese, Hottentots, Kaffirs, Nubians, Somalians, Singhalese, Patagonians, Tierra del Fuegans, Kahucks, Anapondans, Zulus, Bushmen, Japanese, East Indians, and Laplanders have been exhibited in the taverns, theaters, gardens, museums, zoos, circuses, and world's fairs of Europe, and the freak shows of the United States. (1995:41)

Unfortunately, Fusco leaves out the Florida Seminoles.

Tourism among the Seminoles shares many characteristics with tourism in the Southwest and in Cherokee, and throughout the world. Some of the ideas for the Oconaluftee Indian Village reflect knowledge of the Seminole tourist attractions in the Miami area just east of the Everglades. Because the whites were draining the swamps, and "with adverse environmental conditions in the Everglades, many Seminoles took advantage of employment in Miami's tourist attractions. . . . In 1917, Henry Coppinger, Jr., of Coppinger's Tropical Garden, N. W. Avenue and the Miami River, hired two Mikasuki Seminole families to set up a village in his tourist attraction. . . . This new source of employment was appealing to the Indians, who received salary, food, and yard goods as an incentive to live seasonally at this location for the enjoyment of tourists" (West 1981:202). There are some differences between the Seminole village and the Cherokee village, however. West's work constantly reminds us of two important points about how the Seminole people were living at the tourist villages. First, it was seasonal, lasting from January to April. In fact, one of the reasons for the villages' popularity was that at the beginning of the first year, "the Indians came to Coppinger's to get warm during the 1917 cold spell and remained as part of the attraction" (West 1981:203). Coppinger's hammock was located on the site of a Mikasuki Seminole camp, so it was a natural place to which the Indians might retreat. Another such camp with similar conditions, called Musa Isle Village, began in 1919 and continued operations for nearly 50 years (West 1981).

Second, the Seminoles were living in the villages just as they were living in their own camps in the Everglades. "The Mikasuki Seminoles' lifestyle in the tourist attraction followed much the same effortless schedule as it did in the Indians' Everglades environment. The men at both Coppinger's and Musa Isle involved themselves periodically in hewing canoes. Craftwork and clothing were produced by the women. Men also produced crafts. Additional chores were undertaken on a periodic basis: hunting, coontie gathering, and fishing. . . . In fact, there is little difference between the daily activities in a Tamiami Trail camp and those in the tourist attraction camps of Miami" (West 1981:205). The primary difference between the Seminole situation, which was welcomed by the Indians, and the Cherokee situation, which never drew the support of full-time residential Indians, was the methods of the owners/founders. As I quoted earlier, the Cherokees would have been "expected to live in the village. Their household utensils will be like those of long ago, and they will wear clothing such as is described by the travelers who visited the Cherokee towns of that period. They will work at the same tasks and use the same tools as their ancestors." That was asking a lot of Eastern Cherokee peoples of the post–World War II era, who had given up lands, children, lifeways, and language to "be like white people." Granted, there were and are numerous "living history" programs throughout the United States to re-create and represent past lifeways. However, from colonial Williamsburg to the Living History Farms in Iowa, none of these Euro-American exhibits have asked modern Americans, caucasians, or African Americans to live full-time under the conditions described above (Colonial Williamsburg 1997; Living History Farms 2007). Creating living history is one thing; exoticizing the "other" is quite another.

Based on my research into CHA documents and interviews with a range of people—from director Barry Hipps to new and longtime Village employees—no Indian families were ever permanently put on "zoological display" for the tour (Desmond 1999; O'Rourke 1987). However, even though the employees of the Village were paid for their efforts and were "allowed" to sell the items they produced, there is still an overtone of racial othering to the tour guide's speeches. This is especially noticeable in who is and is not hired to represent the "1750s Cherokee" (Bushyhead 1998; Hipps 1998; Swimmer 1998).

A 50-year history of the Village, beyond the initial arguments among various scholars from the University of North Carolina, the University of Georgia, and the University of Tennessee about periods, land use, and demonstrations, is told in picture postcards, highway billboards, and the oral history of the women and men who have worked there, some for more than 40 years.[4] Amanda Swimmer, one of the most photographed potters at the Village (she appears on many postcards and billboards in the region), told this story about how she acquired her skill:

I was employed 35 years, almost 36. Well, when I first went to work I just had to go and learn, you know, some things I've had to learn. When I'd worked with them, sat with them for about a year, then I tried to make

3.3. Amanda Swimmer crafting at Tsali Manor, 1998 (Author's photo)

something. The first thing when I went to work was pounding corn, demonstrate corn pounding. And then I stayed there all summer long and then the next thing I had to do, well, they moved me over to the finger weaving. I learned how to finger weave and I sat there one year at the finger weave, and then the year after that they decided they'd move me up to the top to relieve the workers for lunch. I was just a relief worker for baskets and a little bit of everything. Then, with the women at the pottery, I'd just sit there and help them with the pottery and I'd make some and finally caught on more. Well, I used to make 'em before, but I caught on more by working with these women that was good at pottery, the Bigmeats, and I think I worked with them all summer long as a relief worker. They really moved me on the pottery from there. They kept me on the pottery because it's what I enjoyed the most and I did it pretty good after I learned to catch on to what I can do. I still had a lot to learn about making pottery even after they came and took all of those pictures for the side of the road and postcards. I was learning more and more every year. (Swimmer 1998)

According to some scholars, tourists are interested in the disappearing or extinct Indian in order to replace or enhance a sense of loss of their own cultural continuity and meaning (Baudrillard 1988; Desmond 1999:144–145). The ever-present question of who is a "real" Cherokee or a "real" Indian, or even of "what" is an Indian, is put to the test by the institutional racism and exoticism that tourists bring to the Boundary. Swimmer went on to say that it would be a lot more pleasant if the tourists were nice, which many are not.

A lot of people are not very nice when they go through the Village, see. You can tell them something and they say, "Oh, that's not what Indians do." The tourists don't even listen to what we tell them. Lots of people don't talk at all. Sometimes they ask if it's good for Cherokee people to be in the Village working. I said that we're in here to show you what we make. I said we demonstrate things to you so you can see how it is on the Boundary and that's our work. That's all I tell them. Some people show us that they hate Indians. If they start being smart [condescending or sarcastic] we just tell them to go on their way. I guess the dumbest question someone ever asked me while I was making pottery was, "What is clay made out of?" [She gave a hearty laugh.] What do you say to something like that? They want to know "Where's your teepees?" We didn't ever live in teepees. It's on and on, the same thing every day. (Swimmer 1998)

Shana Bushyhead described an incident that happened while she was guiding a tour at the Village that exemplifies the difficulties which the Cherokee, and all American Indians, have with a mass tourist population. First, though, I have to mention that at 21 in 1998, Shana was a lovely young woman and the epitome of the stereotypical, phenotypical "ideal" Indian woman for mainstream U.S. society. Tall and athletic, she had copper skin with a sleek nose and high cheekbones, long, straight coal black hair, and dark brown eyes. This is her story:

I was on a break from my tours when one of the other guides came rushing up to me. On one of the tours that was winding its way through the Village, a three- to four-year-old blond-haired, blue-eyed tourist girl child was throwing a tantrum in the middle of the tour to see Pocahontas. The Disney animated movie had just come out a few months before on home video. This child was sure that she was going to the home of Pocahontas. They were at an Indian village, after all. Differences between the Cherokee or Powhatan peoples did not exist for her. In order to appease the girl, the guide with that group began searching frantically for me. There had been a discussion amongst the guides prior to this incident about how much I looked like the Disney stereotype of an Indian maiden, Pocahontas. Their tour guide *begged* me to pretend to be Pocahontas so they could go on with the tour without having to ask the family to leave. So I did. At the next craft station that the tour was approaching,

I went and sat down on one of the benches along the trail that are designed for people to rest or sit on to watch the craft demonstrations. This way, the child would not be able to miss seeing me. As the tour group rounded the corner, the child was still crying wildly until she spotted me sitting on the bench. The tour guide who had initially come to find me pointed to me and said to the child, "Look, there's Pocahontas now!" The child absolutely shrieked with delight and ran to throw her arms around "Pocahontas's" neck. The child told me how much she loved me. After that, the only thing the little girl really wanted to know was why I was wearing shoes. After all, Pocahontas didn't wear any shoes in the movie and she could run and jump and dance through the woods without them just fine. I told her that the Cherokees gave me the shoes to wear while I was with them. That apparently satisfied the girl and [she] skipped happily away with her parents to the next craft station waving and shouting, "Bye, I love you, Pocahontas." (Bushyhead 1998)

On the surface this might seem like a sweet gesture by the Village staff that has little relevance beyond appeasing a distraught child. But, after Shana told the story she was very upset because of the implications about her worst fears for the mainstream American public and their lack of knowledge of the specific histories of American Indians. This story reveals merely the tip of the iceberg of misunderstanding and miseducation of non-Indian America concerning the myriad lifeways among American Indian peoples.

In order to understand the tourist industry from the Cherokee perspective, I turn in the next chapter to those tourist venues that the Eastern Cherokee took at least partial control over by 1950. This includes tourist attractions and shops that were and are under the direct supervision of the Eastern Band of the Cherokee Nation as well as those that are entrepreneurial in spirit. In some ways, Shana Bushyhead's concerns are shown to be quite well founded. However, the primary way in which "Indianness" is presented for the tourist gaze, "chiefing," exemplifies the general practice of the mass tourism industry both in Cherokee and for indigenous populations worldwide.

4

Eastern Cherokee Ingenuity

In this chapter I discuss the long-standing Cherokee ability to adapt to whatever the Euro-American majority of the United States throws at them. Far from being defeated by events that have continually shaken up their social world since the earliest European contact, the Eastern Cherokee continue to adapt what is dropped into their laps, or thrown in their faces, to their own societal understandings (Adair 1775; Bartram 1955 [1791]; Burt and Ferguson 1973; Duggan 2002b; Finger 1984; Raymond D. Fogelson, personal communication, 2003; Goodwin 1977; Kehoe 2002; Kephart 1983 [1936]; King 1979b; Kupferer 1961). I discuss the wave of modern tourism that crashed upon them in the mid-twentieth century and show how the ever-resourceful Eastern Cherokee have turned at least part of the tourist industry into their own culturally specific undertaking.

In the 1940s, as travel by automobile and the accompanying tourist culture boomed (Sutter 2002), the fledgling Cherokee Historical Association began its push to exploit "Indianness" and "being Cherokee" for the incipient tourist trade. Once again, the Cherokee came upon a way to make the tourist industry their own. The EBCI had owned and operated several major enterprises since the 1950s, while others had come and gone. The primary venture that has been successfully maintained by the EBCI for more than half a century is the Qualla Arts and Crafts Mutual, Inc. This chapter will also discuss what has come to be called "chiefing," though this particular enterprise is only recently regulated by the Eastern Band. It is also important to discuss another important annual event, the Cherokee Indian Fair. The Eastern Cherokee transformed this event from one created as a public Indian spectacle to a private Cherokee celebration of tradition and heritage.

THE FIRST TOURIST ITEMS

Baskets for Barter

From the time that long-term contact began around the mid-seventeenth century, a sort of "tourist trade" began between Europeans and the Cherokee in the form of the fine baskets and pottery that the women made. In Cherokee country, basket making is an ancient practice.[1] For most of the tribe's history, women made baskets for their own use in farming, carrying everything from babies to firewood, nuts, berries, ramps, corn, squash, and beans from the well-tended communal matrilineal clan fields (Adair 1775; Duggan 2005; Duggan and Riggs 1991; Hatley 1991; S. H. Hill 1997; Mooney 1982 [1891]; Perdue 1998). There is evidence that baskets were used in the long-distance barter between tribal peoples of the continent long before Europeans made landfall in the sixteenth century. However, the utilitarian aspects of basket use and basket making were ensconced in the traditions of the people. Since the beginning of the twentieth century, however, basket making has been primarily an "art for art's sake" form.

At the time James Mooney came to the Qualla Boundary of the Eastern Cherokee in 1887, basketry was undergoing a change to please Euro-American tastes. Natural dyes from indigenous plants were being replaced with modern aniline dyes in a range of bright primary colors. Mooney, after purchasing baskets in 1887 and again in 1900, stated that Wadi-yahi, who died in a grippe epidemic in 1897, was "the last old woman who preserved the art of making double-walled baskets" (quoted in S. H. Hill 1997:176; see also Dykeman and Dykeman 1978; Frome 1980:140; Pierce 2000). This was hardly accurate, as double-walled rivercane baskets are still being produced and are among the most highly sought after artisanship items in the Cherokee repertoire (Duggan 2005; Duggan and Riggs 1991). Mooney's assumption may have stemmed from his relative confinement to the Big Cove area, which was until recently assumed to be the stronghold of "conservativism" on the Boundary (Frome 1980:140; Gulick 1960).

Throughout my fieldwork I was regaled with stories about mothers, grandmothers, sisters, and aunts making arduous walks over Rattlesnake Mountain or Balsam Mountain and down to Andrews, Sylva, and Bryson City to sell baskets so that they could buy shoes and cloth for clothes. Betty J. Duggan reminds us:

Traditionally women were the culturally sanctioned basket-weavers among the Southeastern Indian tribes. Generation after generation, they have handed down prized baskets and passed knowledge of particular basketweaving traditions to their daughters and granddaughters (and other female kin), primarily through example in daily life and sometimes through joint social activity. Several historic accounts of the Southeast report that at times Native children and elderly men also made or assisted women with making baskets. Many contemporary basketweavers describe learning the rudiments of their craft as small children, picking up scraps of river cane, then imitating their mothers and other matrilineal kin who sat working together. Only a handful of Southeastern Indian men in the 20th century have made and marketed baskets under their own names. Many, however, routinely help female relatives and spouses with gathering raw material and performing specialized tasks, such as handle making. (2005:32)

One of the women I interviewed was Arnessa Maney. In 1998, at the age of 91, she was lively and talkative and related many stories about her lifelong residency on the Qualla Boundary. Her sister, Roweena Bradley, was among the most celebrated basket makers on the Boundary, and her daughter-in-law, Louise Bigmeat Maney, is equally celebrated for her pottery. All three of these Cherokee elders are now deceased. In 1998, Arnessa told me about the experience of her mother, Nancy Bradley.

Arnessa Bradley Maney was born on Wright's Creek above Painttown in 1907. She went to boarding school at an early age and had vivid memories of the transition from speaking Cherokee to speaking English. She also had vivid memories of her mother's basket-making process. Like most folks on the Boundary, the Bradleys did not have much money to buy necessities such as shoes for the winter, cooking pots, or sugar, although there was always plenty to eat, a roof over their heads, and clothes to wear, Arnessa related. During the cold winter months, her mother would weave the basket materials that she and the rest of the family had collected during the summer into salable merchandise. It seems that long before the advent of the "tourist" per se, Cherokee baskets were sought after by the surrounding white communities (Duggan 2005; Duggan and Riggs 1991; S. H. Hill 1997). Arnessa recalled the times, probably in the 1910s, when her mother would load up her baskets and walk to the next town—at least 10 miles over rugged mountain terrain—to sell them either to shop owners or door to door to the Euro-American women of the towns. In *Weaving New Worlds*, Sarah Hill writes that Arnessa's mother "walked from Painttown to Tahquette's store on Soco Creek. . . . Like other weavers, she could only trade as many [baskets] as she could carry and could only bargain for what she was able to walk back home with" (1997:263). It is also a vivid memory for other senior women whose grannies and mothers, aunts, and sisters helped provide for their families in this way. According to my own sources, which are

4.1. Arnessa Maney (left) and the author at Tsali Manor, 1998 (Author's photo)

corroborated in Hill, many of these baskets sold for as little as 25 cents, and many were bartered for shoes and trade goods.[2] Hill states:

> Nancy George Bradley's basketry winds in and out of her daughter's memories . . . "she did a direct trade. She wouldn't sell them for money." . . . When Aggie George finished a load of baskets, she and her husband would "tie them together, put them on, and take off." They went to trade at Duncan's or Tahquette's in Yellow Hill, and "sometimes they'd take them over to what they call Shoal Creek, over in there" to white communities. (1997:269)

Arnessa did not acquire the skill of basket weaving from her mother or her sister. When I asked her how she felt about tourism on the Boundary, she related what I have come to recognize as the ambivalent relationship with tourists in Cherokee:

> We're used to 'em. They don't bother me. They don't bother us. They just mind their business and go on and do what they want to do. They

liked to take pictures, though, sometimes of different people. My mother made baskets. I didn't even try to learn to make it. I got a sister who makes them and she makes most of her living at it. Roweena Bradley. Go over to a shop and look at some of her work. I worked one summer [making baskets]. I didn't do it the next summer. Just too many people. I never did take an interest but now I wish I could. My sister Roweena sure did. You know people have taken her baskets and put them in the big museum [Smithsonian] up in Washington. My mother's baskets too. (Maney 1998)

When I asked Arnessa about working in the tourist industry, she told me that she didn't want to do that kind of work, although she did work in a craft store for a little while (probably during the late 1950s or 1960s): "I didn't like foolin' with the tourists because they always asked dumb questions. I worked in a craft shop with Kate Arkansas one time. I didn't like it. Tourists, they get on your nerves sometimes 'cause you have to wait on them. I'm just a Indian and when the tourists came, they wanted to see a Indian. Then some would come and say 'Where are all the Indians?' The white people are all around us. They all wanted to take my picture too. I guess I look like a Indian" (Maney 1998). Arnessa went on to say that she felt tourism was vital to the community so that the "old timey crafts weren't lost."

Sally Allison, an older elder, and Bertha Chiltoskie, a younger elder, agreed with this perspective. I conducted an interview with them set up through their younger kinswoman, Kayce Crowe Wiggins, at the TeePee Restaurant in Cherokee. Kayce was one of my students at Southeastern Community College during my stay. She is the daughter of Rev. Denny Crowe, the leader of the Yellowhill Baptist Church and the principal leader in the 1997 movement to reject all Harrah's Cherokee Casino benefits. Sally stated that "even though everyone [complains] about the horrible traffic and the difficulties with the tourists by the Fourth of July, come November they are all missing the dollars [tourists] bring in." She recalled going to town with her mother to sell crafts in the 1930s. Her mother made Indian dolls and beadwork and "raised six children on that income." All three women from different generations agreed that "the tourists kept the Cherokees being Cherokee." When I asked them to elaborate on that statement, they said, with voices sometimes overlapping, "Because they [tourists] are willing to pay and look for 'authentic Indian stuff,' Cherokees maintained and then revived some traditional parts of the culture to take advantage of the opportunity. If not for tourism, no telling what would have become of Cherokee and the Cherokee people. It goes farther than just crafts, too. Because of the interest in keeping that part of the culture alive, the language revival was started" (Allison 1998; Chiltoskie 1998; K. Wiggins 1998).

This view is equally recognizable in the discussion of the resurgence of pottery making on the Boundary in the 1930s and 1940s.

Pottery Refound

Unlike basket making, the knowledge of pottery making—how to find and gather the best clay and the traditional adornments for the pots, bowls, and urns—gradually came into increasing disuse for eighteenth- and nineteenth-century Cherokee women. The antiquity of pottery making is observable in the archaeological record. Pottery shards have been found that date from 2500 BCE (Ruehl 1996). Also, a definite continuity in ceramic traditions dates from the sixteenth century CE to the eighteenth- and nineteenth-century historic Cherokee. In fact, archaeologists who specialize in traditions of the Southeast believe that "this continuity reaches as far back as 1000 CE" (Riggs quoted in Ruehl 1996). Dickins states that "between about A.D. 1450 and 1650, there were several important changes in the cultures of the Southern Appalachians. Stimuli for some of these changes were indigenous, while others probably resulted from initial contacts with Europeans . . . [I]n the Blue Ridge, Late Pisgah becomes Early Qualla . . . [this] transition . . . [in] ceramics is clearly documented at several sites in western North Carolina" (1976:22).[3]

In 1767, Englishman Thomas Griffiths documented the high quality of the raw materials used for Cherokee pottery. Griffiths was commissioned by Josiah Wedgewood to investigate the clay pits of western North Carolina. It had been discovered that the Cherokee were using a fine white clay for their pottery, and Wedgewood wanted to secure some of this clay as he began to develop his blue and white jasper ware. A historical marker was unveiled on August 11, 1959, to identify the location of the pit where "Cherokee Clay" was obtained (Leftwich 1970:75–77).

According to Leftwich, the Irish trader James Adair's prediction that the use of European trade goods (in the form of iron pots) caused a decline in traditional skills had become a reality by the time Mooney arrived in the 1890s. The Cherokee almost lost the skill of pottery making, and only three potters were left on the Boundary by that time. The durability of Euro-American cooking vessels most likely made pottery vessels less appealing to Cherokee women. Adair reported that "the Indians, by reason of our supplying them so cheap with every sort of goods, have forgotten the chief part of their ancient mechanical skill" (quoted in Perdue 1998:75). However, Adair seemed to contradict that point in this description of Cherokee pottery: "They make earthen pots of very different sizes so as to contain from two to ten gallons; large pitchers to carry water; bowls, dishes, platters, basons [sic], and a prodicious [sic] number of other vessels of such antiquated forms as would be tedious to describe and impossible to name. Their method of glazing them, is, they place them over a large fire of smoky pitch pine, which makes them smooth, black, and firm. Their lands abound with proper clay, for that use; and even with porcelain, as has been proved by experiment" (1775:458).

How can we resolve these contradictions? Did the art of pottery making disappear completely among the Cherokee? Was it "lost" between Adair's time in the mid-eighteenth century and Mooney's field research in the late nineteenth? According to R. Michael Abram, a longtime resident of the Cherokee environs and independent scholar of Cherokee culture, this skill found its way back into Cherokee country through displaced Catawbas from the eastern Carolinas: "In the 1840s . . . about a hundred Catawbas came north and took up residence near the Cherokee in western North Carolina. This interaction with the Catawbas brought to the Cherokee a renewed interest in pottery as a source of trade outside the Boundary. The Cherokee had something the Catawbas didn't, that was a landbase. The Catawbas had something the Cherokees didn't, that was a marketing technique for the pottery. Those two things meshed together so that pottery was kept alive here. . . . [I]t went from just a mere spark into a burning flame" (R. M. Abram 1998). However, this was only one way that the Cherokee revitalized pottery making. Archaeologists from area universities and the BIA have studied ancient examples of Cherokee vessels for style, shape, material, decoration, and construction (Leftwich 1970:78; Ruehl 1996). Amanda Swimmer related to me her discouragement over the lack of indigenous clays left on the Boundary. One of her favorite spots for the beautiful blue indigenous clay had been covered over in the 1980s by one of the roads of the Blue Ridge Parkway (Swimmer 1998). However, some spots are known only to certain people, and indigenous clays are still being gathered, tempered, and formed into vessels. While other types of craft work have always been important for the Cherokee's utilitarian needs and have now made the transition to art for art's sake (e.g., wood and stone carving, blowgun and dart manufacturing, finger weaving and beadwork), basket and pottery making continue to be a mainstay of artisanship for a majority of Cherokee women artisans. Examples of all of these arts have been on display and for sale since 1946 at the Co-op.

QUALLA ARTS AND CRAFTS MUTUAL, INC.

The Qualla Arts and Crafts Mutual, Inc., a tribal concern established in the 1940s, was first called the Cherokee Indian Craft Cooperative, and Boundary residents still commonly referred to it as "the Co-op." It was begun under the advisement of the U.S. government's Indian Arts and Crafts Board, which was formed as a result of the Indian Reorganization Act of 1934. The Co-op was one of the earliest groups to use the board's services (Richmond 1987). Since its inception, its raison d'être has been the promotion and sale of the work of Cherokee artisans (Duggan 1997; S. H. Hill 1997).

In the early years of tourism as an economic base, the only time when there were buyers in Cherokee was during the six months when the newly built roads into the Boundary and over the mountains of the Great Smoky Mountain National Park were passable (Pierce 2000; Sutter 2002). This left artisans literally without an income for the other six months, from late October through late March (Duggan 1997; S. H. Hill 1997). Mollie Blankenship notes in her history of the Co-op that "some of the problems the craftworkers faced were: low prices paid by the shop owners for their work, no market during winter months, a decline in the quality of their work due to a lack of incentives to improve, and no organization to promote the craftsmen as the artists they could be" (1987:viii). To counter some of these problems, artist/teachers were hired by the EBCI to teach basket weaving, beadwork, pottery, jewelry, and weaving in the Cherokee Indian School, then a BIA school.

The Co-op changed locations as it grew from the mid-1940s to the late 1960s when a shop/gallery was built on the main strip through Yellowhill—Cherokee (where it still is today)—to accommodate the ever-increasing number of artisan members (Blankenship 1987; Duggan 1997; S. H. Hill 1997). Each year, until the early 2000s, the Co-op published numerous placards and brochures to promote individual artisans. These placards and brochures are available for tourists and collectors, as well as locals, to pick up to remember a particular artisan. Deb West, director of Tsali Manor during my stay in the field, worked at the Co-op while in her twenties. She explained:

We did brochures. We would have shows in the gallery and highlight one artist. So we designed, we went out and took pictures [of the artisan at work], we did all the writing for the brochure and had them printed. They usually include a short biography and photographs of the artisan and the artisan's work. These announce a special showing or demonstration in the gallery section of the Co-op by an artisan or group of artisans. Since the Co-op has always been one of the classiest places in town, we had to keep everything really clean every single day. Clean every piece of artwork, vacuum, wash all the windows—every week, sweep the parking lot, pick up trash from the yard. Then we could relax a bit. One of the main differences in working at the Co-op was the sales approach. Since the pieces are high priced, the manager didn't want any of us to crowd

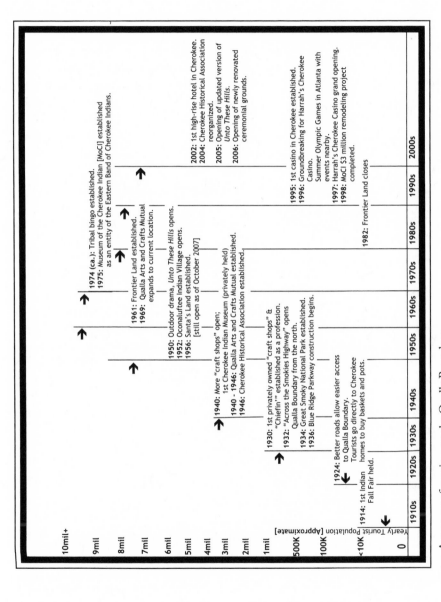

4.2. A century of tourism on the Qualla Boundary

the tourists. We had to wait for them to ask us. The manager considered approaching them to be rude and that it would drive them off. It's a collectors shop. People who just want Taiwan stuff come in and cruise for a couple of minutes, then they're out of there. The collectors come in and want Amanda Swimmer's pottery or Eva Wolfe's doubleweave reed baskets. (D. West 1998)

Over the years, the rules and standards for being a Co-op member have been steadily elevated. As elders pass on the knowledge of artisanship to the youth, some of the ideas of what is women's work and what is men's work is also passing to another phase. Amanda Swimmer, a potter and a member of the board that decides who may join the Co-op, told me about the process of decision making and of some of the difficulties she has experienced:

One of my boys [to whom she teaches pottery, traditionally women's arena] in the Co-op, he's good. . . . He makes them shine so pretty, he uses his fingers. When he shines them, he just uses his fingers. . . . He took [some pieces] down to the Co-op and one lady told him that they wouldn't take them. So, I'm on the committee at the Co-op. Now we've got pottery right here on the table, I said, that's not even fixed right. I said my boy brought some pottery down here and it wasn't accepted and it's better than these we've got right here. These [the pieces already accepted in the Co-op] were made just like a little kid made them, and whoever made them, you took them. But my boy took his that are much better than these and I don't understand why you didn't take his pieces. So they said to tell him to come on in and they'd take them. So I told him to go take five pieces down there and they would take them and he'd be a member. We've got to see how good the new pieces sell, because I can't keep the pottery stocked. I take about two or three dozen down there and they're gone the next week. (Swimmer 1998)

There are pieces in stock that don't sell because they don't have the sheen, the expertise, or the professional look that Amanda's pieces have. Her frustration was over the fact that her pottery students, both boys and girls, are as exacting with their finishing as she is, yet their pieces were being rejected at the Co-op. Amanda went on to say that

there was one man that brought in big pots. If you felt around on the inside, they had been patched up. We turned him down. If one piece of mine has a crack, I take it back. But they take some that you can tell is patched. One man painted the inside where there was a crack with some kind of polish to keep everyone from seeing the crack. I said it's rough in there. There are about eight of us [representing all different types of artisanship] on the Co-op board to accept the crafts people bring in. If we think they aren't worth taking, we turn them down. I told the board that it wasn't right to take this man's pottery that was patched up and rough inside. I told them to put a hand in there and feel how rough it is. The board decided that we'd have to tell him to do better and to come to the Co-op and make his bowl right in front of us. But I don't know if they ever did it. I told them I wouldn't accept it unless he comes and shows us that he actually made the bowl and that he could do it smooth and take all of the roughness off of it. They ended up not taking him. The committee meets every year to decide if the committee will stay the same or if another member will be voted on. We've been retained for another year. If we want to fire the boss, we can do it. The Co-op manager is under us, the board, and she has to go along with whatever we decide. It's like a council. Because we know more about the actual crafts that come in for inspection than she does. (Swimmer 1998)

Stringent rules and standards are—on the surface—a positive step for the Eastern Cherokee. However, the problem that has developed is a high degree of subjectivity in the decision-making process. There are generally around 300 producing members of the Co-op. While this sounds like a large number, it is only 2 or 3 percent of the enrolled population of the EBCI (in 2003 that population stood between 12,000 and 13,000). Many people who are quite good artisans don't qualify to be Co-op members. And some members who "qualify" don't want to be Co-op members, since the Co-op's criteria are so stringent. This means, however, that the shops who carry these artisans' arts and crafts cannot put the label that proves authenticity on them. They can say, however, that they are "handcrafted by Cherokee people" (Abram 2003). There certainly must be guidelines, but other than the qualities that can be measured, such as the roughness and cracks inside a piece of pottery she discussed, the process of judging who meets those guidelines is quite subjective (Abram 2003). As such, it is impossible to identify what would cause an individual not to be accepted as a Co-op member. However, this leaves many would-be Cherokee artisans out of the loop. Many of the craftspeople who sell their goods through the Cherokee Heritage Museum and Gift Shop fall into this category. They have either been rejected after presenting items to the Co-op or they don't wish to associate with the Co-op for factional and political reasons. The reasons why some people stay away from the Co-op come down to whom you discuss it with on the Boundary (Abram 2003).

Nevertheless, the Co-op has had a positive impact on the Boundary. Some

Co-op members have won National Humanities Association awards, including Louise Bigmeat Maney for pottery and Roweena Bradley for basketry. Pieces are displayed in museums nationwide, and collectors are willing to pay what individual items are actually worth (McCoy 2006). The move made from utilitarian handmade objects as a necessity for everyday life in pre-contact times to the "art for art's sake" artisanship of today's handcrafted items has taken individual indigenous cultures to a place entirely embedded in capitalism and ongoing colonialism (Babcock 1994; Deloria 1997; S. H. Hill 1997; Owle 1998a; O'Rourke 1987; Perdue 1998; Swimmer 1998; P. West 1998). The Eastern Cherokee are understandably proud of their Co-op and of the many talented artisans who have been and are currently members. The Co-op is one of the few shops in Cherokee where there are no foreign "imitations" of American Indian artisanship to purchase. This sets the Co-op apart and makes it, as Deb West and Donna Toineeta put it, "the classiest place in Cherokee."

"CHIEFING": A CENTURY OF PRESENTING THE PUBLIC INDIAN

As we saw in chapter 2, the idea for turning the tourist gaze toward the Eastern Cherokee came from the Bureau of Indian Affairs, the Department of the Interior (in particular, the National Park Service, in the form of the Great Smoky Mountains National Park, ca. 1934), and white entrepreneurs from towns and counties surrounding and bisecting the Qualla Boundary. Before usable roads into and through the Boundary were built, making it a "perfect tourist destination" (around 1940), chiefing was unheard of (R. M. Abram 1998; Foght 1935). The Indian Fall Fair gave some intrepid tourists the opportunity to see "real Indians" as early as 1914, but there is no documentation of the Plains Indian ensembles on particular males that so define chiefing.

The phenomenon of chiefing has been cited by social scientists undertaking fieldwork on the Qualla Boundary since the 1950s (Bender 1996; Finger 1984, 1991, 1995; French and Hornbuckle 1981; Fogelson 1960; Gulick 1960; Kupferer 1961). Over the twentieth century it became the most visually prominent and most explicitly gendered tourist feature in Cherokee. Relatively few women take part in the chiefing business, and when they do they are generally referred to as "Indian princesses." This designation in itself reinforces the gender specificity in the work. The women who dress up for tourists and enact the "Indian princess" are, by necessity, young, beautiful, and phenotypically "Indian" (French 1998:137). One certainly does not find an elder woman in this line of work. In fact, most women 25 or older are settled with family and/or job and, perhaps, craftwork and have little time for long hours of chiefing and "fooling around with tourists." On the tourist strip, women are usually behind the

4.3. "Chiefing" postcard with teepee and woman selling baskets, ca. 1920

scenes as service workers and are not on display for tourists. The CHA has the only venue that prominently features women as part of the tourist attraction, the Oconaluftee Indian Village, and women at the Village produce traditional crafts during their time there and have relatively little direct contact with the public.

Laurence French provides the generally accepted history of the chiefing phenomenon: "most sources stated that it began after World War II when tourism began. Two white leaders . . . said they remembered seeing 'chiefs' when they were little boys, over fifty years ago. . . . An older former tribal council member recalled that Mr. Standing Deer was the first 'chief' stating that 'he found out he could make a buck, so he "chiefed."' One shop owner said that his parents started a shop forty-five years ago [ca. 1945, perhaps], allegedly the first in Cherokee, and they supposedly hired the first 'chief,' a man named Tom Jumper" (1998:138). However, there is evidence that chiefing actually began prior to the advent of the Blue Ridge Parkway when the Great Smoky Mountains National Park was just beginning to draw the wealthy from the Asheville area as a result of the Vanderbilts' interest in the park and its viability. Through archival research I located several postcards from the 1930s and early 1940s that feature "chiefs." The 1920s black-and-white postcard is replete with a "chief," a "princess," and a teepee, all of which are reminiscent of the Plains cultural area. However, closer inspection reveals that the "princess" is sitting with—and presumably selling—classic doubleweave rivercane baskets. Unfortunately, there is no description on the back of the postcard and hence no way to identify who these people were or where the photograph was taken.

4.4. Big Cove "chief" and two girls with typical transportation, ca. 1930

Another postcard—which carried a 1941 postmark—is of the above-mentioned Mr. Standing Deer. It is an example of the first color-tinted post-cards that became available in the late 1930s and early 1940s. Standing Deer was undoubtedly one of the first chiefs; there is even a possibility that he is the chief in the postcard from the 1920s. Even though the color-tinted postcard was mailed in 1941, the photograph might have been taken much earlier. During my interview of the Welch sisters (Charlotte, Maryjane, and Myrtle), they told me about the early chiefs. In the 1930s, they said, the first tourist shop was Lloyd's Gift Shop. This was also, according to the Welches and other elders, the first place to hire a chief for the tourists. Over the ensuing years many other chiefs were hired and gained reputations with tourists as the most authentic on the Boundary.

Many personal photographs provide evidence of the importance of chiefing to the tourist industry of Cherokee. The majority of those who came to and through the Boundary were satisfied with a stereotypical representation of the American Indian through the chiefing enterprise, and relatively few stopped to see who the Cherokee actually were. One of the women who participated as an "Indian princess" as a youth told me that chiefing "puts Indians out in the public view. Most tourists don't realize there are different cultures [of Indians]. It was and is a profession. I worked to put food on the table and to be able to tell tourists about actual Cherokee culture. As an industry, tourism is always a

The Cherokee Indians

of the Qualla Reservation   ::   ::   Cherokee, N. C.

How They Live Today   ::   ::   Their Tribal History

4.5. Front cover of tourism brochure, *The Cherokee Indians,* ca. 1930

balance, some painful and some good, and it is a very traditional way of look-ing at life. We became a showcase because of the park and land. Most people bought into this 'showcasing' hook, line, and sinker" (personal communication, 1998). This is the general attitude I encountered on the Boundary concerning the chiefs.

Chiefing is performed nearly exclusively by men age 35 and over for the mil-lions of tourists who pass through Cherokee on the "strip" each year. The tour-ist is, as always, encouraged to stop and have a picture taken with the chief, for a small fee, as a memento of one's trip to one of the few federal trust reservations on the eastern seaboard (Finger 1984, 1991, 1995; French and Hornbuckle 1981:35–37; Tiller 1996). In the early days of tourism, only one older Cherokee man was chiefing, with one woman being the "Indian princess," at the single gas station/craft shop in town. In the late 1990s, however, one could not drive 100 yards through the heavily touristed sections of town without finding an "authentic Indian Chief" (Norman 1995; Chambers 2000). French describes all of these men by what a few Cherokee call them. This story is identical to French's vituperation on chiefing and tourism in his 1980 publication with Jim Hornbuckle (Cherokee), *The Cherokee Perspective.* I never heard any of the people with whom I worked criticize chiefing, either while I was in the field or on subsequent returns to Cherokee. French states:

> These street *Chiefs* best illustrate the *vulgar Cherokee,* token Indian made conspicuously visible for the tourists' sake. The Cherokee themselves refer to these individuals as *postcard chiefs* or *grasshopper chiefs.* The latter reflects the fact that they come out in the spring during the six-months tourist season, and disappear in the winter off-season. Other white-run organizations, such as the Bureau of Indian Affairs and the Cherokee Historical Association, publicly discredit *chiefing* as a humiliating profession and, while this may be true, they fail to mention that both of these organizations, along with all other outside tourist enterprises profit greatly from the *chiefs* and their *Cherokee Princesses,* and the millions of tourists this pseudo-profession attracts to the Qualla Boundary each season. (1998:137)

One spot in particular catches my attention each time I pass through the Cherokee tourist strip, because in addition to a new rough stage with seating for tourists, there are two venerable signs of the "Indian"—a large teepee and "Bill the Buffalo" (stuffed, of course)—that have been on the strip for many years. There is a chief at this location, but there is also a new addition to the classic chiefing staff, the "Indian dancer." Only one woman, if present at all, dresses in buckskin to gather tips from tourists watching authentic "Indian dance" and storytelling. The "Indian dancer" is, again, phenotypically "Indian." Until recently, these men were not necessarily Cherokee and were doing powwow-style dance exhibitions for the tourists. This is a very different variation from chiefing per se and was not consistent from week to week, much less from year to year.

Chiefing, which is now performed exclusively by Cherokees, is their profession, not a pseudo-profession. Chief Henry (Lambert), arguably the most photographed chief ever, had this to say:

4.6. Bill the Buffalo and teepee, Cherokee, North Carolina, 1998 (Author's photo)

I enjoy my work as *chiefing* more than any other job. I worked construction in the wintertime . . . but I'd rather see one happy kid's face than
fourteen happy superintendents' faces. And all kids, regardless of where
they're from, no matter if they're rich, poor, middle-class, they know
what an Indian looks like and if you can make him [*sic*] smile it's worth
a week's pay on construction. . . . Ninety percent of the tourists who
come here look for Indians who live in teepees and run around naked
and hide behind trees and ride horses. Very few people who come to
Cherokee expect to find the Indians as they live today, and the only ones
who know what to expect have been here before. I think there should be
a program set up, not by the Cherokee, probably by the federal government, teaching people . . . of how Indians live today. (quoted in French
1998:143–145)

According to R. Michael Abram, all the men who are currently in this profession view it as street performance. They all realize that Cherokees never
dressed in this way, and they will gladly tell every tourist who takes the time
how things really were and are on the Boundary. However, most tourists aren't
interested. In the 1970s, there was a movement for the chiefs to dress as real
pre-contact Cherokee men and chiefs did. The result was that very few tour-

ists bothered to stop, because they did not recognize the feather cape, turbans, and clothing as "Indian." The bottom dropped out of the chiefing business until they went back to dress of the Plains culture area. Since Cherokee men have been the ones to adjust most to the ongoing transitional time from pre-contact to present, finding a way to fit into the tourist industry schema has enabled them to provide homes, provisions, and educations for their families that might otherwise have been impossible (R. M. Abram 1998). When I returned for follow-up research in 2006 I interviewed the latest group of chiefs. In the epilogue I will show some of the ways this venerable profession has changed and remained the same over seventy years as an attraction on the Boundary.

The Cherokee took an active role in taming the onslaught of early tourism and then, after World War II, mass tourism on a scale that is hard to comprehend if you have not experienced it. But the Cherokee have also made sure that they have a secure place in their own community. The most enduring and prominent of these is the Fall Fair.

THE CHEROKEE INDIAN FAIR:
THE PLACE TO BE CHEROKEE

One of the most fascinating aspects of my time with the Eastern Cherokee was participating in various ways in the fairs. Certain aspects of the fair are American mainstream, but they are *contained* in a specific area, literally cordoned off, and draw mainly the youth of the EBCI, who are especially vulnerable to the constant onslaught of television, radio, movies, clothing fads, and tourists. The Cherokee Indian Fair, which began in 1914, was originally designed as a tourist attraction for the surrounding white communities of the Qualla Boundary and to give Cherokee farmers a place to show their harvest (Chiltoskey 1995). According to a 1976 *Cherokee One Feather* article, "In the summer of 1912, Mr. Cato Sells, Commissioner of Indian Affairs . . . made a special trip from Washington, D.C. to Cherokee. His object in coming to Cherokee was to discuss with James E. Henderson, Superintendent and James Blythe, Farm Agent [both of the Cherokee Agency] the possibility of promoting and sponsoring an Indian Fair. . . . During the year of 1914 the Commissioner of Indian Affairs officially authorized the presentation of the Fair" (quoted in Chiltoskey 1995:5). The fair, which may have originally been remembered by the Cherokee as a vestige of pre-contact seasonal rites and therefore was by and for the people's ritual cycle, changed from the potential tourist haven that the BIA and the Cherokee Agency were looking for into its original purpose for the Eastern Cherokee (Chiltoskey 1995; French and Hornbuckle 1981). It has become a place for homecoming, and Eastern Cherokees from all over the country come *home* for the event. The intended audience is Cherokee,

4.7. Ceremonial grounds with open bleachers, Cherokee, North Carolina, 1996 (Author's photo)

and ownership of the fair and participation in all events is for enrolled people. John Parris wrote in 1977:

> This is the Cherokee's season of Thanksgiving. . . . And they came down from the high hills and out of the coves this week for their annual Fall Festival. . . . Held [almost] annually since 1914, it has grown into a nationally known event. And once again the Cherokee came this week to celebrate and hold up the mirror of their labors. They came from Big Cove and Wolftown, Birdtown and Painttown, Yellow Hill and Snowbird. And once again the age-old trails that wind along the slopes to the valley of the Oconaluftee echoed to the footsteps of young and old. . . . The Fall Festival is a combination of tribal ritual, county fair, and homecoming. . . . It is a time when the Cherokee come home, if they can get home. And usually they do. (quoted in Chiltoskey 1995:57–58)

Indians who are not Cherokee are also present, and these folks are welcomed and treated like honored guests. Some are invited speakers and performers for the nightly rounds of singing, dance exhibitions, comedy acts, and pageants.

Fair Events: Traditional Cherokee and Euro-American Additions

Although no one is turned away from the fair, it is evident upon entering the ceremonial grounds that this is an Eastern Cherokee event. Enrolled members have free access to the fair at all times, while non-enrolled people who live on the Boundary (e.g., spouses and longtime residents who are considered local) receive a discount on the admission fee. Anyone else who buys a ticket—tourists, local people from the counties surrounding the Boundary, researchers, and so forth—pay the full admission fee. Many people buy a week-long ticket that is a bit less expensive and allows open entry for the entire fair. In order to enter contests and win prizes, from pageants to community booths to art and agricultural awards, one must be an enrolled member of the Eastern Band. Invited guests, speakers, judges, exhibition dancers, comedians, and other performers cannot win prizes at the fair.

The first year I went to the fair as part of my anthropological fieldwork was 1997. I had been in the field for just a couple of months and was definitely an outsider. Even though I was living full time with Lisa in Big Cove at the time, I was painfully aware of how much I stood out: I was the "vulnerable observer" in a thousand ways.[4] That year, as I walked around with Matthew, it was he who was the accepted one. Having attended Cherokee Elementary for two months, he had made some friends, verbally fought a couple of racial battles, and proved that he fit in with the Cherokee boys in the sixth grade, no matter what phenotype they were.

Noticeable was the absence of the tourist element that so pervades the Boundary year round, but especially from May through October. If tourists do wander in, they stick out like a sore thumb. There was no one to ask the offending questions, no one to explain to what it was to be an "Indian." One's identity was understood. Similarly, there is no powwow at the fair. In the 1990s, that event was held on the Fourth of July weekend; it included a traditional powwow and was on the official dance tour. Numerous tribal affiliations are represented at the fair, as well as a multitude of vendors offering everything from Indian-made arts and crafts to Taiwanese-made imitations. Many tourists come to the July event to watch the dances, buy "Indian souvenirs," and eat real "Indian tacos." They leave thinking they have had an "authentic Indian experience," bathed in history, unaware that the powwow trail is a twentieth-century answer to a need for pan-Indianism, dance, and contest.

The fair always begins with a parade that starts in Painttown and ends at the ceremonial grounds in Yellowhill (downtown Cherokee). The parade is a steady stream of decorated cars, new and vintage (mostly convertibles), pickup trucks of every kind, floats that represent each of the different communities or clubs, and the Cherokee police force and fire department vehicles cleaned and polished to a shine. The parade route is teeming with people. Both years that I was a participant and observer the weather cooperated beautifully, but I was told that the parade and the fair go on regardless of the weather. Each contestant for all the pageants has a separate vehicle in which to ride. There can be three dozen or more contestants for all of the various pageants, so the parade lasts for quite a long time. Candy is thrown by everyone *in* the parade to everyone *watching* the parade, which makes the spectacle even more exciting as children and teenagers and adults rush to catch the goodies. It reminded me of a small-scale carnival event. Once the parade completely passes into the ceremonial grounds, the fair is officially open and all can enter.

As a stranger with little experience to draw on at my first fair, in 1997, I hung out with new friends and my son, Matthew. The adults participated in the typical fair activities that appeal to youngsters. Here is the very American part of the fair. There is a midway with the average rides, games, and junk food (e.g., burgers, hot dogs, fries, candy apples, cotton candy, Belgian waffles, ice cream) that any county fair in the country would have. The Tilt-a-Whirl (a small roller coaster), the Himalaya (an anti-gravity ride), a Fun House, and a Haunted House ride are all crowded with excited faces from toddlers to adults. For the most part, however, the midway is inhabited by children—elementary, junior high, and high school—ready for a good time. On the second day of the fair, all children in the Cherokee school system get the day off and all the rides on the midway are free for them to enjoy. Since the entire midway is enclosed within the fenced ceremonial grounds and all teachers and staff are present, the children are free to do whatever they want in a safe environment. The numerous games of chance—from water-gun races, to balloon darts, to speed pitching at stacked milk bottles, to shooting basketball, to choosing the perfect plastic duck from its trough in order to win a prize, any prize—were very popular with all the children. The adults and even a number of teenagers come for the social aspects, which bring them together to talk about the exhibits and who has won the ribbons, to eat *real* Cherokee food (but there are Indian tacos, too), and to enjoy the entertainment on the stage of the ceremonial grounds.

The events that take place at the fair are easy enough to describe; it is the psychological and emotional phenomena that are more difficult to put into words. The events that have the most importance, and those which I will go into most detail about, are stickball; blow-dart contests; community exhibits; prizes for horticultural prowess, canning, baking breads and pies, jellies, jams, and artisanship of every kind; dancing and singing exhibitions; and the pageants. I'll begin where the Fall Fair begins, with the intense, dangerous, all-male stickball matches.

Anetso: *Eastern Cherokee Stickball*

Stickball has been played throughout the Americas—especially Mesoamerica, where there are ancient ruins of ritual ball courts, and throughout the eastern seaboard of North America (Burt and Ferguson 1973; French and Hornbuckle 1981; Michael Zogry, personal communication 1998; Zogry 2003). Although the game varied from tribe to tribe, as early as 1586, René Laudonniére described the ball game in the Southeast: "[The Indians] exercise themselves much in shooting. They play at the ball in this manner: They set up a tree in the midst of a place, which is eight or nine fathoms high, in the top whereof there is set a square mat, made of reeds, or bullrushes, which whosoever hittith in playing thereat winneth the game" (quoted in Burt and Ferguson 1973:84). The French christened the game "La Crosse" because the sticks were roughly the shape of a bishop's staff, and they changed the rules until there was little similarity between the original game and the Euro-American version (Burt and Ferguson 1973; Fogelson 1962; Zogry 2003). The field, which is roughly the size of a football field, is set up between the midway area and the grandstand. A small sapling is cut and placed into the ground at each end of the field. There are no markings on the grass, as in American field sports, and the play ranges wildly, as far as players can go. Occasionally, the unfortunate spectator has to run out of the way or is inadvertently "tackled" as the rush of the game proceeds. Points are scored when either team gets the ball past the sapling (Zogry 2003). This means, of course, that sometimes the sapling goes down, too, and must be reinserted before play can resume. Referees make sure that only the goalkeepers touch the ball with their hands and that all the other players use only their sticks (Zogry 2003). In my experience with stickball in the 1990s, all the players were barefoot and shirtless, wearing only shorts. Players on the same team wear the same color shorts to signify that they are teammates. Bartram described "the ball play" among the Cherokee in 1791:

> The ball play is esteemed the most noble and manly exercise. This game
> is exhibited in an extensive level plain, usually contiguous to the town:
> the inhabitants of one town play against another, in consequence of a
> challenge, when the youth of both sexes are often engaged, and some-
> times stake their whole substance. Here they perform amazing feats of
> strength and agility. The fame principally consists in taking and carry-
> ing off the ball from the opposite party, after being hurled into the air,
> midway between two high pillars, which are the goals, and the party who
> bears of the ball their pillar wins the game; each person has a raquet [*sic*]
> or hurl, which is an implement of a very curious construction, somewhat
> resembling a ladle or little hoop-net, with a handle near three feet in

length, the hoop and handle of wood, and the netting of thongs of raw-hide, or tendons of an animal. (1955 [1791]:398)

At the fair, stickball is as emotional and important, at all levels of play, as it was in the sixteenth, seventeenth, and eighteenth centuries. It is also as emotional as any soccer match anywhere in the world. Because the teams practice in seclusion during the year and don't want spectators, as an opponent could be among them watching, the fans are ravenous for the games at fair time. Some elder women told me in no uncertain terms not to bother them during the ball game. They had a favorite team and favorite players, and they brought their lawn chairs as close to the edge of the field as they dared. True to their word, they spoke to no one except each other during the games each day. Rivalries exist from the pre-removal clan times to the present. Men go off the field bleeding and limping, jumping for joy in victory and bent over with despair in defeat (Fogelson 1962). There are always mothers, grannies, aunties, sisters, wives, and girlfriends waiting to celebrate the victories or nurse the wounds, both physical and mental. The games start with the younger boys and then move up incrementally to the adult games. Matt was especially interested in the games for his age as he had learned the basics at school in physical education.

In another type of stickball game, both women and men play. All ages are welcome to play in this game (except very small children), and even some elders were out having a go at it. This game, which usually takes place in the afternoon of the last day, involves knocking an object, usually a wooden fish, off the top of a 20-foot-tall pole. In this permutation, women can touch the ball with their hands, whereas men must use the ballsticks to throw the ball at its intended target. The coed games I watched at the fair both years resulted in women winners. The men were truly handicapped by the use of the ballsticks. This game is an excellent example of an activity from pre-contact times that has remained intact in modern Eastern Cherokee society. According to Michael Zogry, "*Anetso* continues to be a symbol of Cherokee identity and culture both within the Qualla Boundary community and beyond it. For many members of the Eastern Band of Cherokee Indians in North Carolina, it continues to be an important tradition in which they are actively engaged as well" (2003:2). The Eastern Cherokee people were indeed out in great numbers for all of these games, that were played in the ceremonial grounds on a grassy field right in front of the staging area. They came out for other competitions as well.

Blowgun/Dart and Archery Competitions

Hunting for food is not a necessity for a majority of the Eastern Cherokee. Those who do hunt use modern weapons and ammunition, whether bow or gun. However, the ancient art of making blowguns and darts and learning to use them has remained. During the first few days of the fair, large hay-filled targets are set up for archery and blowgun competition. In my experience, most Cherokees found the blowgun competition far more interesting than archery. While skill with the bow was vital in aboriginal Cherokee life, there is a conspicuous absence of making arrows and bows in the cultural displays, such as at Oconaluftee Indian Village. Blowguns and darts are essential to the archetypal Southeastern complex tool kit (Burt and Ferguson 1973).

In the 1990s some women began making their own blowguns and darts from local materials and gaining proficiency in their use. However, men still dominate this competition. It is significant that a few women are taking up the craft of the blowgun and darts and gaining the skill needed to use them accurately. The young women I talked with about this indicated that they wanted to be part of keeping their Cherokee heritage alive. They also indicated that they had no proclivity toward craftwork of any type. This could be extrapolated to be in the tradition of the "war woman" who fought alongside men. In pre-contact/pre-removal times this ability might have been one of the many ways that women of great courage and strength became "Beloved Women." Picking up arms and meeting the enemy or bringing in much-needed meat protein would have required Beloved Women to acquire and perfect these skills just as any man would (Perdue 1998; C. M. Taylor 1998). This indicates that pre-contact ways are being consciously maintained by the Eastern Cherokee. I turn now to the indoor exhibitions that are much like any small county fair in any rural area of the United States.

The Exhibition Hall: An "American Fair" Icon

In 1997, I was not privy to the activities that took place in preparation for the fair. I saw the exhibition hall only *after* the booths were set up, after the ribbons were awarded and hung, and after the official opening of the fair. However, I attended the 1998 fair as an invited guest, a pageant judge, and a videographer for certain events that my acquaintances and friends at Tsali Manor wanted on tape. While the exhibition hall and the concept of a fair itself are classically Euro-American, the Cherokee have taken this idea and made it their own. It was also here, watching the booths go up, that I noticed the harmony ethic at work (identified by Thomas in the 1950s) as well as the practice of triangulation to solve disputes. If the men building the booths made a mistake or a "wrong" decision—that is, one contrary to what they had been told to do—an elder woman watching the process would speak of it to a younger woman, who would in turn gently correct the problem with the builders. During the day I spent watching the booths go up I heard no arguing and nothing that would indicate any problems, yet throughout the day there was an underlying murmur as the elder women checked on progress.

At the 1998 fair, Myrtle Youngbird, an elder Cherokee with whom I had become friends at Tsali Manor, showed me around the indoor exhibits while everyone was still busy putting them up. Some of the exhibits were in the process of being judged, and preparations were being made for the presentations of awards. The most unique aspect of the exhibition hall was the community exhibits. Each township—Yellowhill (Cherokee), Birdtown, Soco, 3200 Acre Tract, Big Y, Big Cove, Painttown, and Snowbird—set up its own elaborate exhibit to compete for a ribbon. Elders and people between 30 and 50 years of age were the ones most involved in putting together the exhibits. The men primarily facilitated the building of the structure of the exhibit itself. The booths were all wood and plywood, painted or covered in cloth, and approximately six feet wide and ten feet tall. The women did everything else, including deciding what would go into the exhibits and how everything would be arranged. The exhibits were all together in a rear portion of the exhibition hall separated from all other types of exhibits. I recognized this solidarity of community effort as another aspect of *gadugi*, the community work and enrichment activities for all community inhabitants (Fogelson and Kutsche 1961; French 1998). The exhibits included produce, jams, jellies, canned vegetables, quilts, all types of artisanship, photos of various contest winners, antiques, flowers—anything to enhance the exhibit and show off the individual community's accomplishments for the past year. Each team of workers and supervisors and watchers got to work the moment they were allowed into the exhibition hall, and they didn't stop until the entire job was complete.

In 1998, Big Y's exhibit won first prize. Everything in the exhibit was handcrafted, from quilts and baskets to pottery, wood and stone carvings, and two-dimensional art in paintings and drawings. There were baskets full of perfect beans, corn, and dried gourds. Accomplishments of the youth, shown in the form of plaques, diplomas, ribbons, and photographs from events throughout the year, graced the entire exhibit. All of the booths were similar in content if unique in design, and each one won a ribbon for their efforts. Pride in community identity in particular and Cherokee identity in general were on display in each booth for all to see and share.

Awards for Growing, Cooking, and Creating

The front left portion of the exhibition hall contained a plethora of agricultural products. Corn and beans of all kinds, squash, and pumpkins all proudly displayed the various colored ribbons and other awards. Many of the agricultural products were produced by school-age children in 4-H Club and Future

Farmers of America. Because there were no animal exhibits, growing the biggest and best vegetables is a definite point of pride for the children.

As at any "American" county fair, there were contests to judge the best-tasting pies, cakes, breads, candies, jellies, and jams. The fragrance of delectable homemade treats filled the exhibition hall on the day of the judging, and all the women turned out to see who would win. There were also contests for canning fruits and vegetables—for judging both the process and the result. Although this is also an import from the Euro-American cultural system, what is particularly Cherokee about this event is the multitude of Cherokee recipes and foodways that are judged. Who makes the best bean bread or the best chestnut bread? Who has the favorite kanuche recipe? Whose cornmeal is homegrown and home-ground? The Ramp Day event in April made use of the early spring harvest of greens of every sort. While no prizes were given, the gusto with which the people ate indicated which cook was considered the best. At the fair in October the ramps were well out of season, but judicious families had kept enough frozen to offer them during the fair as well. The contest spilled over from the judging to the outdoor kitchens that families set up to sell to the public while they watched the games, exhibits, and pageants.

In one corner of the exhibition hall, hundreds of arts and crafts items were on display for competition. Many of these items were made by the elementary through high school students. The Cherokee school system begins teaching all children traditional artisanship at the elementary level, and by the time they get to Cherokee High School many students are accomplished artisans. They are also encouraged to explore more traditionally Western art forms such as pencil drawing, pen and ink, and painting, as well as poetry and prose writing. Every type of art and craft is covered: two-dimensional work, basketry, finger weaving, pottery and clay figures, wood and stone carving, beadwork of every description, doll making, and quilting. There are adult events, too, and as in most county fairs, there are different competitions for amateur and professional artisans. Many artisans leave this competition for amateurs or for new members of the Qualla Co-op. These are mainly elders who have won their awards, gained recognition, and established firm reputations. They take great pleasure in the accomplishments of their children and grandchildren, however, and people are always taking pictures of artists, art, and ribbons. Most of these photographs will wind up in the next fair's community booths.

Walker Calhoun and Traditional Dances

Once the daylight hours are past, the bleachers fill to capacity or more (about 500 people) and the stage comes alive with dancing (both traditional Cherokee dances and powwow-style dances), singing, comedy, bluegrass and gospel music, children's choruses, and the pageants. Thanks to the work of conservative elder Walker Calhoun, traditional Cherokee dances and songs were still being practiced in 2006 to keep them a viable part of the Eastern Cherokee cultural system. Calhoun is the singer, something akin to a square-dance caller, and in the late 1990s he had about a dozen students—women and men in their teens and twenties—who wear traditional Cherokee dress from the early nineteenth century and perform each dance. The dances and songs are centered around hunting formulas that James Mooney recorded around 1900 (Mooney 1982 [1891]). These include the Bearhunter Dance, the Quail Dance, the Beaver Dance, and the Corn Harvest Dance. When these dances were still in full use, the hunting dances were performed only by the hunters, since hunting was men's work, but the Corn Harvest Dance was performed by and for the entire community. The exception may have been the Beaver Dance, as we will see.

The first dance to be performed was the Bearhunter Dance. This dance honors the spirit of the Bear, who, in Cherokee mythology, were once people and a clan of the Cherokee called the Ani-Tsa-Gu-Hi. According to the myth "Origin of the Bear," the Ani-Tsa-Gu-Hi clan made the decision to become bears, *yo-nv*, and live in the forest where there is always plenty to eat. Even though the other clans tried to talk them out of it, they had made their decision, but promised that they would offer up their own flesh to the Cherokee and also taught them the songs and dances that would call bears to hunters (Mooney 1982 [1891]:325–327). Calhoun's troupe performs the Bearhunter Dance in a circle. All dancers take on the posture of a standing bear with claws bared, and at regular intervals they turn and "fight" one-on-one with each other. It is a simple dance, but the song sung by Calhoun is more complex.

Next was the short Quail Dance. This dance honors the spirit of the Quail, *gu-qwe*, which is still coveted as game. Mooney relates many different myths of birds and a Birdhunter Formula, but there is no mention in his text of a specific song to Quail (Mooney 1982 [1891]). Perhaps this song has been handed down from generation to generation to Calhoun, who in turn has handed it down to the people and his students. As Calhoun sings a plaintive song that is reminiscent of the call of the quail, the dancers in two lines go forward and then back, then circle around themselves and back to the straight lines. As the dancers circle back to the straight lines, they face one another and make the call of the quail toward the opposite dancer. This song and dance was very short and simple.

The Beaver Dance, the longest and showiest of the dances performed at the fair, might have involved both women and men in historic times. In several places, Mooney's writings indicate that Beaver, *do yi*, was accessible to all as friend and helper who can also be hunted and eaten and then be reincarnated as its young (Mooney 1982 [1891]:266, 314–315, 465–466, 474). The present-day Beaver Dance is as follows. The beat Calhoun kept and the song he sang are reminiscent of the sound that the beaver's tail makes as the animal builds its dam. The dancers begin in a circle carrying sticks that are held end to end by each dancer. This keeps them connected to one another. One pair, man and woman, break off from the circle and go "in search" of *do yi*. The man searches (some made quite a theatrical show of the search), and the woman follows wherever he decides to go. Once the beaver is "found" (two non-dancers have a rope that has a "beaver" attached to it that they run back and forth between them), the woman of the searching pair must make the first strike before the man can strike. Once this is completed, the next searching pair begins. The dance is completed when all pairs have searched, found their prey, and struck it at least once. This is quite a comical dance, and the audience participated with whoops and laughs of glee during the entire procedure.

The final dance performed by the troupe was the Corn Harvest Dance, or the Green Corn Festival. During the live performance, Calhoun stated that this dance was performed "after the corn was harvested and is in the crib. This was the dance to celebrate the harvest." While the exhibition of this dance was short, it may have been part of one of several major celebrations during the year among the historic Cherokee. In this dance, women and men paired and formed a circle. As Calhoun sang and kept time, the women held out their aprons while the men "gathered" corn and filled the aprons. The dancers also chanted while Calhoun sang. That action in the dance is reminiscent of the story of Selu and Kana'ti, the Origin of Corn and Game (Mooney 1982 [1891]:242–249).

The dance troupe exhibition is one of the most popular and anticipated events of the nightly program. While the dances are the same each night, many people return again and again to watch. This was not the case for some powwow-type dance exhibitions, which were staged earlier in the afternoon (these were not heavily attended at the fairs of 1997 and 1998). Even though the powwow dancers were Cherokee and had won many awards, it was the Cherokee dances that drew crowds from every community on the Boundary.

The Pageants

In 1998, six "serious" pageants were held during the fair. These are, in order of appearance, Teen Miss Cherokee, Little Mister Cherokee, Little Miss Cherokee, Miss Cherokee, Junior Miss Cherokee, and Senior Ms. and Mr. Cherokee. These pageants are taken very seriously by the contestants, their parents, and their extended families. At the closing of each, many tears were shed by both winners and all the losers who had put so much of their time into their appearances. Since I was a judge for Teen Miss Cherokee, I will comment on the procedures for that contest. Miss Cherokee and Teen Miss Cherokee are the two most important events, as the winners represent the EBCI all over the country during their year-long reign at other pageants and throughout the powwow season. The girls go with chaperones to Creek, Seminole, Cherokee Nation of Oklahoma, and southwestern events to represent the EBCI. The requisites to judge the contestants for the pageant are quite clear. Each young woman must meet as many of the criteria as possible—with as much grace as possible—to win the pageant in which she is entered.

The pageants provide an enlightening experience of what are defined on the Boundary as traditional Cherokee lifeways. The construction of the costumes and how well they are worn by the contestants come under serious scrutiny by the entire audience, both during the parade, where most people see the contestants in costume for the first time, and again at the pageants. The older girls come under the sharpest scrutiny. As a spectator, judge, and social scientist, I found the costuming and talents areas to be the most interesting aspects of the pageant events. While each young woman had two clothing presentations, one contemporary and one traditional, the more important one for the audience was the latter. The traditional dress consists of the early-nineteenth-century calico tear dress, a finger-woven sash or belt, beaded jewelry, a handmade basket or shawl, and hair worn in traditional style. Preferably, all of these items were made by the contestants themselves or their families, whether mother, grandmothers, aunts, or sisters. Some fathers also make pieces for the contestants to carry.

Language use and comprehension comes into play in the talent sections of the pageants. Talent should entail some sort of recitation, storytelling, or song (mostly hymns) in Cherokee, playing the flute, or dancing. However, one participant in the Miss Cherokee contest, a college student who was a few years older than the other participants, produced a fashion show that featured dresses of her own design. These were modeled by young Eastern Cherokee women who were not contest participants. Some were very traditional pieces and some were updated interpretations, but all of the clothing had an authentic Cherokee look about it. Most of the clothing was of calico with early-nineteenth-century designs as well as updates of those. This particular talent event was different from those of the other contestants. Each participant also had to be able to say at least a few words in Cherokee and express herself on a topic that would have affected the Boundary in some way. In the 1990s, most of the teenage contestants talked about gangs, drugs, alcohol, and teen depression and suicide on the Boundary. Some talked about their desire to become a doctor or nurse to help with the rampant diabetes and concomitant conditions with which all American Indians are currently dealing (Indian Health Service 2001). All stated in their speeches that they wanted to go to college and return to the Boundary to help with these and other problems.

The male competitions were for 8- to 12-year-old boys and for senior men.

As of 2006, these competitions are not being held. Although in 1998 there were some costuming requirements, such as the ribbon shirt adapted from powwow and southwestern garments, the boys wore jeans. They were not required to complete a rigorous schedule of talent and speaking. Of course, the youngest girls in the Little Miss Cherokee pageant did not have the burden of speaking, either. But these children did have similar requirements of dress and some form of talent competition. That the females were expected to present themselves as cultural icons as a part of the pageant requirements, while males were not, reinforces the fact that women are seen as the purveyors of the traditional in contemporary Cherokee. It is also interesting that the very young girls and boys are not judged harshly. The audience finds all of them adorable, at least in public. That did not hold true for the preteens and the elder women. Within the crowd where I sat with my camera, comments about the inadequacy of this costume or that pronunciation of a reading in the Cherokee language were loud and frequent. People in the crowd also let their thoughts be known about the winner of each pageant.

Miss Pretty Legs

As popular as the pageants are, the pièce de résistance was the final event of the entire fair, the Miss Pretty Legs "pageant." The final night of the fair includes a formal "Recognition of All Princesses" and of the male winners (Cherokee Indian Fair Committee 1998:21). Once these proceedings are over, the grandstand is filled to standing-room only as all await everyone's favorite contest, Miss Pretty Legs. In 1998 I watched this contest with Mike and Sue Abram, who have lived in the area since the early 1970s and have been "adopted" by a very conservative family from the Boundary. I suggested to Mike and Sue that this contest could be considered a contemporary form of the old Booger Dance tradition. Described by Gulick as a "satirical release" from the constraints of the harmony ethic and certain taboos in daily life, the Booger Dance was a "safety valve" to let off frustrations approaching anger at others, especially those outside the Cherokee communities (Gulick 1960:145; see also Fogelson 1983). The Miss Pretty Legs pageant certainly fits the bill. Here is a description of the Booger Dance from *The American Indians: Tribes of the Southern Woodlands:*

> One of the highlights of the winter ceremonial season . . . comes in the form of the boisterous and bawdy ritual known as the Booger Dance. . . . [G]uests come together at the home of a sponsor to perform the sacred and social dances that are associated with the season. Suddenly a gang of four or more rowdies, all of them sporting masks with exaggerated human features, barges into the house. . . . [T]hese so-called

boogers begin chasing the women and pantomiming lewd behavior—to the vast amusement of the assembled audience. When their identity is questioned by the host, the boogers—many of whom boast obscene names—reply that they hail from "far away" or "across the waters." They then demand women and a fight, but agree to settle for a dance.... The boogers then disappear into the night, and the traditional dance cycle resumes. This ribald ritual has been interpreted by some ... as symbolizing the intrusion into the Cherokee world of crude, uninvited outsiders.... The act of parodying them perhaps serves to somehow diminish their threat to the community. (Woodhead 1994:92–93)

Like the Booger Dance, the Miss Pretty Legs contest occurs only once a year, and I can easily account for its popularity. The ambience of the entire "pageant" is lewd and bawdy. Sexual jokes, both outright and in innuendo, are thrown freely at the contestants, emcees, and the audience—especially at the men of the EBCI. From the beginning, the main emcee, a woman named Myrtle Driver, treated the contestants and her co-emcee, Sochani, a man in drag, with contemptuous humor. Strict rules concerning behavior and lasciviousness were laid out, but even before the contest began they were broken by the emcees themselves. For instance, Driver said that Sochani, when given a ride in Driver's car, "began to pick things out from under her dress and throw them out the window." When asked what "she" was doing, Sochani replied that "she" had "recently been sleeping with a Cherokee man and he'd given her bedbugs."

Once the contest began, the contestants were introduced and began to "strut their stuff" around the stage. Each contestant was in drag, and each, while not wearing a mask (as was the case in the Booger tradition), had on lots of facial makeup, a wig with a woman's hairstyle, tight, short dresses or skirts with midriff tops, hose, women's shoes or tennis shoes, and highly exaggerated female body parts—specifically, breasts and bottoms made with balloons. The names of the contestants that year were in keeping with the lascivious nature of the Booger Dance description as well: Madam Liksalot, Patsy Recline, the Rap Stars (three "young ladies" who wanted to win the contest so they could buy the Cherokee Police Department Viagra as they were "tired of the law not being stiff enough"), Groovy Grover and the Job Corp Hoochy Mamas, DooMe Moore, E. Z. Hornytoad, Ineeda Lot, and finally, Monica Screwinsky, with future intern Juicy Lucy from Tuscaloosy.

The entire crowd was uproarious the entire time and enjoyed how the "ladies" made fun of every man on the Boundary. From the principal chief's husband to the vice-chief to the men on the council to the entire Cherokee Police Department to random men they saw in the audience, no one was safe from the satirical eyes of the contestants. The crowd especially enjoyed Ms. Screwinsky and Juicy Lucy as they satirized the 1998 presidential scandal (Isikoff and Thomas 1998). All decorum was dropped, all let out their laughter as well as frustrations with the EBCI government, husbands, boyfriends, and the federal government. Even the contestants were made fun of by women in the audience and onstage. They were whistled at, asked for phone numbers, as well as an array of other lewd suggestions.

The Cherokees have been doing gender-confounding rituals for centuries. "According to the Speck and Broom theory, the ceremony reduces the Cherokee enemy to something psychologically manageable. The offending boogers represented real threats to the Cherokee. Speck and Broom concluded that the masks symbolized Europeans and the diseases they brought. The white man happened to be the most imminent threat of that era, but in earlier times it may have been dangerous animals or enemy tribes. The dance eased threat through the use of humor and mockery" (Orr 2003). This display of role displacement and the continuation of a major Cherokee ritual element into the modern Eastern Cherokee lived experience is further evidence of the continuation of roles and attitudes beyond the acculturated world of mass tourism.

However, the massive mainstream American assimilation machine is never far away. In the following chapter I will discuss one of the earliest ventures, the Museum of the Cherokee Indian, the collection of which was officially bought by the band in the late 1960s, as well as the latest, Harrah's Cherokee Casino, which opened during my fieldwork. I have chosen to deal with these venues in a separate chapter because they have the ability to make an impact on the enrolled in a culturally altering way as no other CHA or EBCI venues have had in the past century.

5

Disneyfication on the Boundary

One day in 2003, as I watched the Travel Channel, a commercial for an up-coming program about the castles of Switzerland came on. As the camera panned over the snowcapped Alps and the lush river valleys where magnificent jewels of architecture from the seventeenth, eighteenth, and nineteenth centuries sparkled in the sun, the program's host, an American "tourist," appeared. Seeming to be completely overwhelmed by these sites, she said, "It's like walking into Disneyland." What? Whoa, wait a minute. Two things stopped me in my tracks. One was the woman's apparent sincerity; the other was that she was describing what had originally inspired Disney to attempt to duplicate the Matterhorn and those castles.

Somehow, a U.S. schema had turned on its head the whole original intent of Disneyland. Theme parks, meant to be mere re-creations of the "real" world, have—for so many—*become* the benchmark against which the reality is judged (Baudrillard 1988; Minnick 2006). The Alps, the castles, the rain forests of South America, the African savannah—these have become mere shadows on Plato's prison wall. As Baudrillard puts it, "The form that dominates the American West, and doubtless all of American culture, is a seismic form: a fractal, interstitial culture, born of a rift with the Old World, a tactile, fragile, mobile, superficial culture—you have to follow its own rules to grasp how it works: seismic shifting, soft technologies" (1988:10). In the late twentieth and early twenty-first century, Americans have allowed these representations of the real to become the reality (Bryman 2004).

Why has it been so easy for this phenomenon, variously called "Disneyfication" or "Disneyization" (Bryman 2004; Kurtz 1995), to occur? The *Oxford English Dictionary* defines *Disneyfication* as "the addition or acquisition of features or elements considered characteristic of Disney films, cartoons, or theme parks; the simplification, sanitization, or romanticization of a place or concept." The Disneyfication of the tourist industry started in the United States.

As the globalization of the Disney worldview continues (Disneylands now exist in Japan, France, and Hong Kong, as well as central Florida and downtown Los Angeles), tourists—especially American tourists—continue to expect more and more glitz, more special effects—more "bling," to use the modern lingo. Disneyfication is for tourism and tourists what McDonaldization is for consumerism in general. The public is directed through the world under as much control as possible (with a few exceptions), and tourism as a global industry is much the same. Humans are being well trained to queue up (Bryman 2004; Cypher and Higgs 1999; Minnick 2006).

For the average American tourist, the "Disney experience" is the reality of travel; it has become the reality that is different from most people's daily lived experience. From the 60-hour white-, pink-, or blue-collar workweek, traffic jams and long commutes from the suburbs, and the constant motion of the "typical middle-class" family all the way through the center and into the opposite American universe of urban blight and unemployment, street gangs, shootings, drug addiction, and family life in the midst of chaos, Americans look to escape from their lives (Bryman 2004; Macionis 2002). Baudrillard writes: "For me there is no truth of America. I ask of the Americans only that they be Americans. I do not ask them to be intelligent, sensible, original. . . . I want to . . . become eccentric, but I want to do so in a place that is the centre of the world. And, in this sense, the latest fast-food outlet, the most banal suburb, the blandest of giant American cars or the most insignificant cartoon-strip majorette is more at the centre of the world than any of the cultural manifestations of old Europe. . . . This is the land of the 'just as it is'" (1988:27–28). I suppose Baudrillard's critique is harsh, but when I hear the voices on my tape recorder of elder women saying "I guess I'm just not a good Indian," I think I have glimpsed the vestiges of a Cherokee lifeway prior to both Europeans and Americans.

CULTURELAND AND REPRESENTATIONS OF CHEROKEES

During the peak of mass tourism on the Boundary, roughly from 1960 to 1980, a theme-park atmosphere encompassed the entire area. As I discussed in earlier chapters, the Cherokee Historical Association's attractions—the outdoor drama *Unto These Hills* and the Oconaluftee Indian Village—were at the forefront of this phenomenon. These venues can be thought of as a CultureLand where tourists interested in Cherokees as Cherokees could find a form of history and *a* Cherokee cultural perspective. As discussed previously, however, even this "history" was more mythic than factual. Two small theme parks were a part of the tourist scene in Cherokee in the 1960s. The first, Frontier Land, was complete with cowboys and Indians, a rodeo, rides of the fair midway type, and typical games such as skeeball. It added to the Boundary's overall theme-park feeling. Owned and operated by white entrepreneurs who leased the land from Cherokees, Frontier Land had nothing to do with Cherokees as Cherokees. It closed in 1982 when tourism began a long, gradual decline in Cherokee and other, similar theme parks opened in other areas of western North Carolina (Butler 1980).

The other theme park, Santa's Land, is still firmly established. Santa's Land has rides and games, but everything revolves around the Christmas and Santa theme. It is disorienting, to say the least, to be on a federally recognized American Indian reservation and come upon Santa's Land. I have wondered at it for some thirty years, and it now seems more out of place than ever. Also owned and operated by white entrepreneurs who lease the land from Cherokees, Santa's Land exists purely for the pleasure of the tourist who perhaps cannot get to Disney World or Six Flags. Cherokees go there for amusement as well. The teenagers I spoke with there complained bitterly that there was nothing for them to do on the Boundary; they were dismayed that they had to go to Santa's Land, "just like we were little kids," for entertainment. It is as if that portion of the Boundary were set apart. The elders don't speak of it, and people of my generation who have young children go only to please them. Santa's Land offers some revenues to the EBCI directly in the form of a tribal levy and a set percentage of the lease. The park property is leased directly from individual Cherokee families who own the land, so it also provides income for those enrolled members. It offers a few seasonal, minimum-wage, non-benefit jobs to individual Cherokees, but a majority of the workers I spoke with there were from surrounding counties. This venue adds undeniably to the theme-park atmosphere of the Boundary. As of this writing, Santa's Land is still going strong and advertises with billboards and television and radio commercials throughout western North Carolina, eastern Tennessee, Virginia, Georgia, and South Carolina.

How do these venues affect the mass tourism that is part of life for the Eastern Cherokee? Do the Eastern Cherokee continue to live their unique cultural system and let tourists remain mostly ignorant of them as private Cherokees? How will the youngest generations of the EBCI be affected as they interact with the next "tourist extravaganza," whatever it proves to be? In the following sections I discuss possible answers to these questions in the Cherokee case by discussing the newly renovated Museum of the Cherokee Indian, truly "CultureLand," and Harrah's Cherokee Casino, the new "GamblingLand," the latter of which opened during my fieldwork in 1997. By textually walking the reader through the remodeled museum and the casino, I will show how the Eastern Cherokee worldview, with all the meanings and histories that lie behind every major cultural system (e.g., the matrilineal clan system) and every small thing (e.g., the perfect ramp patch), is removed from the public tourist gaze and knowledge base. This is especially poignant for future generations of the Eastern Cherokee.

THE MUSEUM OF THE CHEROKEE INDIAN

In the 1970s, the Cherokee Historical Association, together with the Eastern Band of Cherokee Indians, decided to build a permanent, modern museum to showcase the CHA's collection of artifacts. Prior to the opening of the museum in 1976, the collection was small and housed in an old log cabin on the grounds of the old boarding school in Yellowtown. This small facility burned down around midcentury (Raymond D. Fogelson, personal communication, 2004). In the 1960s an extensive collection was donated to the CHA upon the death of a local collector. The decision to build a modern museum and move out of the log cabin had the goal of adding to the attractions for tourists to learn about the inhabitants of the area prior to Cherokee occupation, as well as during Cherokee prehistory, removal, and the contemporary Eastern Cherokee. The collection includes hundreds of archaeological artifacts from the archaic period (8000–6000 BCE) through the pre-removal period (ca. 1800 CE). The collection was displayed in much the same way that any collection of ethnographic/archaeological artifacts are in major museums such as the American Museum of Natural History in New York City. Cases of glass filled to capacity with arrow and spear points, atlatls, spears, ancient bows and arrows, blowguns and darts, pottery shards to full pieces of pottery, baskets, moccasins, buckskin clothing, weaving, and beadwork were all on display. Each item, as is usual for an ethnographic/archaeological collection, was labeled. Each case was also labeled with a paragraph or two about the time period of the items, where they had been exhumed, and sometimes even a map of the archaeological site itself and the location of the site. Center glass cases enclosed eighteenth-century canoes, women's and men's costumes on manikins, and drums used for dances prior to removal. A museum visitor could proceed in a general chronological order or meander through at one's leisure.

Subjects as diverse as the first meeting of the South Carolina town Cherokees with DeSoto to the actual removal of the majority of the Cherokee Nation in 1838 were tackled with aplomb and tact. Historical facts were given with references and copies of parchments of treaties tainted by deceit and land loss. Stories of individual Cherokees, both female and male, who are still considered to be the most outstanding in Cherokee history were prominently displayed as well. The visitor was also treated to two large (3 feet high, 6 to 8 feet in diameter) circular interactive displays at which one could listen to a Cherokee storyteller recount the tribe's major origin myths. The displays were designed by a Cherokee artist in stained glass that depicted the cosmogonic myths of the buzzard and "How the World Was Made," the water spider and "The First Fire," and the animals and plants and "Origin of Disease and Medicine" (Mooney 1982 [1891]:239–251). The visitor circled the displays and listened on a handheld headset to the myth that corresponded with the scenes being lit from beneath to reveal the color of the glass and the abstract shapes of the figures.

In addition to putting together the collection of artifacts, the makers of the 1970s museum created dioramas showing lifeways throughout the known history of the Cherokee in the Southeast. Small, meticulously created scenes showed villages with adjoining gardens tended by women; forests with men hunting deer, boar, and mountain buffalo; a re-creation of the ball game replete with dancers, medicine men, and onlookers; and homes from the 1500s to the early 1800s with life in busy pursuit around them. Set on pedestals so they could be viewed from every imaginable angle, the dioramas were scattered throughout the museum in proximity to filmstrips (later videos) for the museum visitor to watch and listen to narratives about the scenes.

The tour ended with a small gallery of artwork by Cherokee artists from both the Eastern Band and the Cherokee Nation (Oklahoma). The gallery led the visitor into the final area, a theater with 100 to 125 stadium seats. Here a documentary film was shown that depicted current life on the Boundary, noting what had changed over the years as well as what had stayed largely the same. Many enrolled residents were featured in the film, which included major attractions that the visitor might seek out. By the time visitors reached the end of the museum tour, they had the feeling of actually knowing something about Cherokee life from the 1500s through removal and about the current members of the Eastern Band. It was a satisfying experience that I enjoyed on numerous trips to the Boundary from the 1970s to the 1990s.

In 1989 a carving of Sequoyah was commissioned and added to the front of the museum. This appears to have been a wise move on the part of the museum's director, as the imposing carving, which was sculpted from a single giant sequoia redwood from the California coast, makes the museum stand out to the tourist traffic. The carving was produced by a Swede, Peter Wolf Toth, who was traveling in the United States in the late 1980s and was commissioned by the chief of the time and the museum's director, Ken Blankenship. Yet, in spite of Blankenship's good intentions, many of the wood-carving Cherokee artisans felt this was yet another slap in the face. One went so far as to carve three smaller figures of Sequoyah in the same pattern save for the fact that by the third one, Sequoyah had been turned into a grotesque phallic symbol (R. M. Abram 1998). Much like the use of Booger masks and dance in earlier times, this was a way for the sculptor to show his disapproval for the person who was chosen, and well paid, to do such a prominent piece of public art for the EBCI (Speck and Broom 1951).

The 1998 Museum Remodel

By the time I arrived for my full-time fieldwork in August 1997, the plans for remodeling the museum were already completed, and work was due to begin after the tourist season ended in late October. It was obvious that the museum was outdated and in serious need of revitalization, as a number of displays were showing their age and some of the electronic storytelling devices no longer worked. At the beginning of the project, everyone I spoke with was eager to see how the 20-year-old museum would be reincarnated. The museum's doors were closed during the winter of 1997–1998 for a complete overhaul. Except for the gift shop, which remained open during the renovation, the entire building was gutted, and thousands of artifacts, pictures, videos, and paintings were stored for safekeeping (Martin 1998i, 1998j, 1998k). The large lobby, with its limestone floor and plenty of space for artisans to demonstrate their skills, was also kept open.

The directors and other tribal representatives in charge of the museum were excited about the entire remodeling, largely because they had chosen a Disney affiliate to design and film the animated parts of the exhibit. According to Van Romans of Walt Disney Imagineering, "The Museum of the Cherokee Indian is revolutionary in its ability to tell stories and should be a model to other museums that are struggling to engage their audience in their message" (Romans 1999; see also Martin 1998c, 1998e). The total cost for the remodel was approximately $3.5 million (Cherokee Tribal Travel and Promotion 1997:1). There was much speculation in the community at large about what the museum would look like, what it would offer, and how it would present the Eastern Cherokee to tourists.

Disney Arrives

When the museum reopened late in the spring of 1998, a carnival atmosphere was in the air. Admission on the first weekend was restricted to enrolled tribal members of the EBCI, who got in for free upon showing their identification. The designers of the remodel were not on hand, but the people who had been part of the ongoing project on a local level were all there. Once the festivities for enrolled members, CHA board members, and invited locals were complete, the museum was opened to the general public. I went the first week.

The physical arrangement of the museum is the reverse of the original one, starting on the opposite side of the large slate foyer where changing displays and occasional demonstrations are held. One change that is noticeable right away is that the tourist is now directed to view the museum in only one way, whereas the previous layout allowed visitors to wander from one area to another without having to go in any particular order, stay in a line, or be in relatively narrow passages. Now, the "one-way" configuration leads from one section to the next. There are few benches, and no tour guides are available to answer questions. The visitor—whether tourist or resident—merely walks through the maze.

First the visitor is led into the auditorium, which was remodeled to resemble the replica of the council house that has long been on the tour in the Oconaluf-tee Indian Village. The room has seven sides and has heavy, rough-hewn "log" benches on four sides, leaving the other three walls clear. There is never much light in the auditorium; this effect emulates the original design of the council house, which was set into the ground, would not have had windows, and would have had only one door. The smoke from the fire would escape from the hole left in the top of the roof by the seven large beams and bark or thatch cover-ings. In the museum, the simulated sacred fire burns at the would-be "center" in front of the benches, and three screens positioned at the front of the room project a traditional Cherokee storyteller. The storyteller is an old man with long, flowing white hair, beardless, with a bandanna tied around his head. This appearance was presumably chosen because all the "traditional" storytellers begin their tales with "Here is what the old people (grandmother, grandfathers, beloved women and men) told me" (Owle 1998a). The auditorium now holds only 80 people rather than 125. The storyteller narrates a computer-animated film about two of the same cosmogonic myths that were central to the first per-mutation of the museum, the creation and fire myths: "How the World Was Made" (Mooney 1982 [1891]:239–240; K. S. Littlejohn 1998:40–43) and "The First Fire" (Mooney 1982 [1891]:240–242; K. S. Littlejohn 1998:53–55). The visuals presented in this film section of the presentation are very "Disney": brightly colored, well-narrated stories that are easy for all ages to follow and suitable for everyone in the family. The visitor is then invited to continue on a walking tour of the museum, during which, the storyteller promises, the visitor will learn the "authentic history of the Cherokee people." There is no discus-sion of the fissures between the Cherokee people since removal in 1838 (e.g., EBCI, Cherokee Nation [Oklahoma], Keetoowah, Texas groups, Georgia groups, South Carolina groups, California groups, or urban Cherokees all over the United States). They are all the "Principal People"—A-ni-Yu-n-wi-ya.

Walking Tour

There are two large rooms to follow through the various stages from the ap-proximate arrival of modern humans who would populate the continents of North and South America to the Mississippian societies that reached into the early European contact period. "Oak trees" and "birdsong" greet the visitor upon entering the first area of the museum, which holds both artifacts and descriptive plaques. The oak trees are unexpected and quite refreshing.

The Paleoindian Period

This first room presents the Paleoindian period. The generally accepted time frame for this period is from about 11,000 to 6000 BCE (Milner 2004). However, archaeologists disagree about when *Homo sapiens sapiens* came to the Americas. According to Klein and Schiffner, "Based on geological evidence and the discovery of human remains, many assumed that *Homo sapiens sapiens* arrived in America from Asia about 12,000 BP when the Bering Land Bridge was open in one of its periodical dry land phases. This assumption was rooted in the ideas that glaciers blocked these early hunters' land routes to the south from Alaska until the last ice age ended, at about this time. Once the glaciers receded, the founding immigrants were able to people the rest of the Americas in a few hundred years arriving in Patagonia around 11,000 BP" (2003:484). There are no Disneyesque effects or illusions in this area. Appropriately, there is also no direct reference to the Cherokee, as it is generally agreed that that entity did not exist earlier than 1800 BCE, or 3,800 years ago (Thornton 1990:9–10). The displays use the most common archaeological dates for entry into the continent. There are typical museum-written displays and exhibits of artifacts from the earliest periods. It was unclear to me, however, whether the artifacts represent actual material culture from the southeast region of the continent or if they are more general in nature and represent the pan-Paleoindian toolkit (Anderson and Sassaman 1996). This section represents, as is most common in displays of this type throughout the United States, an emphasis on man the hunter. There is no thought toward an egalitarian representation of the Paleoindian period and no exhibit that might suggest women's role in the group. There are a few wall-mounted cases, about 18 squares each, to display a few of the hundreds of projectile points, bone tools, and related objects from the museum's collection.

The Archaic Period

Advancing to the Archaic period on the appointed path, the visitor is greeted with a number of cases of artifacts, again, all presumably Cherokee. The Archaic period can be broken down into three different eras. An extended period of time is represented here, at least 7,000 years, and there are overlaps in timelines and differences of opinion among archaeologists (Milner 2004; Thomas 2000). Milner's brief description of these eras is as follows:

> The Early Archaic is thought to have lasted 2000 or more years and to have ended about 8900 years ago. . . . [There was] a well-established mo-

bile life that characterizes the Early Archaic reasonably well. . . . The next several thousand years spanned a time when people in many places began to live for longer periods in repeatedly occupied camps. . . . [T]he 3000 years following 6000 BCE is referred to as the Middle Archaic . . . it is clear that people began to settle in more or less permanent camps long before they made significant use of any cultivated plants. This period also saw the first purposeful construction of mounds for ceremonial purposes. . . . Some of the most important innovations in the Late Archaic were new kinds of containers for storing and cooking food. (2004:31)

The museum's section for the Archaic period primarily indicates a change in toolkits that adds fishing to hunting. Again, there is no mention of the gathering aspects of daily life, which were primarily women's role, and concentrates instead on an androcentric view of man the hunter (Perdue 1998). Despite the importance of the Archaic period in the development of human cultural systems in North America, this display is a small, transitional area in the museum. The visitor is offered easy and quick large-print reading as well as some maps and panoramic miniature scenes of men's roles in a hunting/fishing culture.

The Mississippian Period

Unfortunately for the educational aspects of the museum, in the next section the designers chose to move directly from the Archaic period to the Mississippian period, skipping the Woodland period. However, it is important to briefly introduce the Woodland period, which is approximately 1000 BCE to 1000 CE, an intervening 2000 years. This time period may well have been when those who would become the Cherokee peoples broke off from their Iroquois-speaking cousins in the Northeast and settled in the Southeast. According to Milner, the Woodland period in the Southeast is rich in archaeological detail.

Societies classified as Early Woodland had appeared by the opening centuries of the first millennium BCE, and they lasted for the next 500 or more years. In the Midwest and Southeast, the next half-millennium or so ending around 400 CE is referred to as Middle Woodland. In the Northeast and along the Eastern Seaboard, Middle Woodland is said to continue longer, as late as 1000 CE. . . . Pottery was acquired where it was previously absent, and it became more common in the Southeast where it dated back to the Late Archaic period. In fact, the appearance of pottery across much of eastern North America is used as a convenient marker for the beginning of the Early Woodland period. (2004:54)

The museum has little to say about the Woodland period. As a visitor with prior knowledge of the history of American Indians, I found the displays confusing at this point. In the same room with scenes that appeared to be part of the Woodland period were displays heralding the final pre-European cultural period, the Mississippian (Kehoe 2002; Milner 2004; Thomas 2000). According to the museum's official website (http://www.cherokeemuseum.org), there is no display for the Woodland period; however, many of the artifacts displayed were from this period. The Woodland and Mississippian periods are so closely intertwined that the visitor has no way to separate one from the other. Depictions of sedentary village life from the Woodland period appear alongside depictions of the massive earthwork mounds that define the Mississippian period.

The story of Kana'ti and Selu is also depicted here (Mooney 1982 [1891]: 242–249). With this story, women appear for the first time in the tour. Here we see the Green Corn Ceremony, and the Eagle Dance is depicted as part of it. According to Mooney, however, the Eagle Dance was never a part of the Green Corn Ceremony, although other dances were (e.g., the Groundhog Head Dance and the Pheasant Dance). Moreover, Speck and Broom state in their lengthy description of the Green Corn Ceremony that the Booger, Bear, and Eagle dances were specifically avoided (1951:52). These dances are still being practiced (Mooney 1982 [1891]; Speck and Broom 1951; Witthoft 1946). I suspect the Eagle Dance is included here because representations of that dance are used in all types of tourist materials, and it was the prominent dance featured in *Unto These Hills* until the updated version opened in 2006. A brief explanation of marriage customs and the sacred fire of the pre-constitution Cherokee is given at this point as well. Sedentary life is stressed, with hunting as the major part of subsistence. A modest display of carved stone pipes appears in this section. It is assumed by the visitor that the pipes on display are actual artifacts. However, a major discrepancy in displays for the next section throws that into question.

At the display for the Mississippian period, the museum turns to an assortment of artifacts, maps, written explanations, and panoramas that blends some generalities about mound-building cultural systems with particulars of the historic Cherokee. The National Park Service's website states that one can divide

Mississippian cultural chronology into Early Mississippian (A.D. 900–A.D. 1200), Middle Mississippian (A.D. 1200–A.D. 1500), and Late Mississippian (A.D. 1500–A.D. 1700). Mississippian sites appeared almost simultaneously throughout the Southeast ca. A.D. 900 and were mainly located within river flood plain environments. . . . The Middle Mississippian area . . . covers the central Mississippi River Valley, the lower Ohio River Valley, and most of the Mid-South area, including western and central Kentucky, western Tennessee, and northern Alabama and Mississippi. This appears to be the core of the classic Mississippian culture area, containing large ceremonial mound and residential complexes, sometimes enclosed within earthen ditches and ramparts or a stockade line. (National Park Service 1997)

This is corroborated by David Thomas in *Exploring Native North America* (2000:152–162, 172–180). According to Vernon James Knight, "By the 1500s, most of the area was abandoned with only a few portions of the site still occupied. Although the first Europeans reached the Southeast in the 1540s, the precise ethnic and linguistic links between Moundville's inhabitants and what became the historic Native American tribes are still not well understood" (Knight 2008). Under the banner of the Mississippian period, the museum places more documentation of the *historic* Cherokee. Among the artifacts displayed in this area are numerous examples of modern basketry and pottery. The "Origin of Disease and Medicine" is related in this section, again with the help of Disney animatronics, holographic images, and the storyteller from the movie the visitor watched in the council house. In this section of the displays, the visitor is told the story of the Nicotani, "The Massacre of the Ani-Ku-Ta-Ni," a priestly clan of ancient Cherokee that was annihilated by the other clans as a result of their abuse of power (Mooney 1982 [1891]:392–393, 501). The story of the "Origin of Disease and Medicine" includes a depiction of a male medicine person wearing skin clothing and using plant medicine as the venerable Cherokee storyteller works holographic magic while telling the story (Mooney 1982 [1891]:250–252). Here also is a brief description of stickball and games of chance such as *chunkey*, as described by eighteenth-century travelers, traders, and military people who spent time in Cherokee country (Burt and Ferguson 1973:92–93; Milner 2004:140; Mooney 1982 [1891]: 434). The exhibit barely mentions mound-building aspects of the cultural systems. A brief nod to the Etowah mounds is offered in the next area.

The Early Cherokee Period

The Mississippian section is the first area in which the few dioramas and paintings portraying Cherokee lifeways include representations of women. There are few artifacts in the next display, which says little about the early Cherokee. Primary source materials have been disseminated by Europeans since the time of DeSoto's journey into the southeastern Lower Towns in 1540, yet little of this is used to enlighten the visitor about the historic Cherokee (Adair 1775; Bartram 1955 [1791]; Brewer and Baillie 1991; Finger 1991, 1995; Haywood 1973 [1823]; King 1977; Mooney 1982 [1891]:23–27).

Also in this section is a single old-school museum-style diorama of a typical

Cherokee homestead. The diorama looks like it came out of the old museum. It is replete with characters, animals, vegetation, and so forth. There is also a brief narrative on a speaker that loops a recording to explain the scene. This alone gives a glimpse into the lives of the indigenous peoples already inhabiting the region. I find this particularly interesting since much of the primary source material has been reprinted—over the last three decades—by the museum's academic publication, the *Journal of Cherokee Studies.* So much primary source information about the lifeways of the first contact to pre-constitutional Cherokee is available that I wonder why no mention is made of it in the premier museum for the Cherokee. The majority of this open space is devoted to the huge mural of a classic mound-building society at its cultural zenith. While the Cherokee and their ancestors or predecessors were known to be mound builders, this mural is more reminiscent of the civilizations of the Natchez or the Cahokia peoples of the Mississippi River valley far to the west of traditional Cherokee lands (Milner 2004).

The fact that disease raged through the nations of North America as often as new Europeans traveled through their lands is given only a single mention (Stannard 1993). Infected by smallpox, measles, and chicken pox, American Indians could not imagine, let alone deal with, these unknown diseases with their own medicines and treatments. Some scholars consider this crisis to be the point of origin for the Booger Dance and masks (R. M. Abram 1998; Fogelson 1983; Speck and Broom 1951; Thornton 1990; Woodhead 1994:92–97). What is ignored is the fact that the Cherokee blamed the diseases on the breaking of sexual taboos by young people and meted out punishment to suit the crime to no avail (Adair 1775).

At this point in the path there is a perfect opportunity to explain to the visitor the Seven Clans and the intricacies of the matrilineal kinship systems, including how the clan mothers' council chose the men who would represent them. This still-important aspect of Cherokee lifeways is left out of the tour (Adair 1775; Brewer and Baillie 1991; Perdue 1998:58, 156–157; Taylor 1997). Instead, the visitor is ushered into a room that looks like a piece out of the "Pirates of the Caribbean" ride at any Disneyland complex. The area is exquisitely finished. Seaports, wharfs and Europeans, ships and cargo are shown in the attempt to explain to the visitor just how the decimation of the Indians began. Several male chiefs of white villages, peace villages, including Moytoy, are also depicted here, presumably as they are about to sail to England in the early seventeenth century to meet with the king. The artwork is excellent. These Cherokee chiefs look like they could walk right off of the wharf. Yet it was difficult for me, even with prior knowledge, to pull this scene together with the previous rooms. There are no explanations, no speakers with descriptions of why there is such an abrupt shift from the mound-building cultures to Europeanesque cultures. It was disturbing, contextually, as the Qualla Boundary is some 300 miles from the nearest seaports on the Carolina Atlantic or Florida Gulf coasts. This portion is very short, and history is again compacted from the late sixteenth century to the early nineteenth century, when the push for the removal of the Five Civilized Tribes began in earnest.

Next, however, there is an excellent piece of cultural education. As visitors turn the corner to the next section of displays, they encounter the historic moment when the Cherokee gained literacy. Here, in prominent display, the famous visage of Sequoyah in a turban with pipe and a copy of the Cherokee syllabary in hand is seen. A printing press (ca. 1880) similar to one the Cherokee Nation used in the production of the *Cherokee Phoenix,* the first tribal newspaper produced by and for Indian peoples in the United States, stands here as well. The syllabary is prominent here in the form of a backlit display and recording that simultaneously flashes the symbol while playing the sound spoken by a female Cherokee speaker. Since there are 87 discrete syllables in the Cherokee language, hearing them all and watching their corresponding symbols flash takes a few minutes.

Here also is a small section that tells of a single famous Cherokee woman, Nancy Ward. A Beloved Woman who lived from the late eighteenth century to the early nineteenth, Ward called for peace with the Euro-Americans and an end to war. Her male counterpart, Dragging Canoe, led an infamous Revolutionary War skirmish against white settlements to try to drive them out of Cherokee lands. Beyond this section, a circular area called the "Chamber of Dissenting Voices" presents short readings from the letters, diaries, and speeches of both the U.S. government and Cherokee peoples concerning the removal of the Cherokee to the West.

Abruptly, then, this section ends with the larger-than-life portraits of those chiefs of each of the Five Civilized Tribes who led the people to Indian Territory: Cherokee, Chickasaw, Creek, Choctaw, and Seminole. These heroes are all male, and as throughout the museum, the faces of women are obscured behind tears and scarves and illness from their part in both surviving the arduous journey and establishing the Cherokee Nation in Indian Territory. The already narrow walkway becomes even more enclosed and the lighting becomes dim. Replicas of 1830s Cherokee houses from the New Echota area of the Cherokee Territory are shown. Dishes are left with food still on the plates, doors are askew, and evidence of people being rousted from their homes transports the visitor to what it must have been like when the removal to Indian Territory began. While this is particularly evocative and effective, it is very dramatic, especially when added to the special effect around the bend. Without warning, one is transported to a concentration camp, a stockade, in which too many Cherokee women, children, and men have been crowded together to await removal. As fall turns to winter in the painted landscapes, the visitor is taken directly onto the "Trail Where They Cried" with hundreds of Cherokee families. A chill wind blows from air-conditioning vents directly onto the visitor, and the life-size dioramas show women, men, and children being marched through the snow at gunpoint. Some have fallen. Some have ragged and tattered clothes, are shoeless, and are clearly sick and dying. The walls are painted in a dramatic panoramic mural of a snowy and bleak landscape. At the first break from the unrelenting scene of the Trail of Tears, another life-size diorama of the Tsali story, once again as told in the original *Unto These Hills* drama, is portrayed (see chapter 2). Tsali, the culture hero, surrenders himself to an armed militia so that the Cherokee remnants may remain in the mountains. This particular history is repeated again and again throughout Cherokee tourist venues. Here, on the museum's pathway, the visitor walks past the scenes with a cold wind blowing down her or his back and more and more desperate faces in the dioramas and on the murals. The terror and sorrow that the Cherokees must have felt on the Trail of Tears are palpable. It is similar to the experience of walking through the Holocaust Museum in Washington, D.C., for the first time. The Museum of the Cherokee Indian was one of the first museums to require visitors to face human tragedy and human suffering. That theme is now repeated in multiple museum sites around the Western world from the Holocaust Museum in Washington, D.C., to the Auschwitz-Birkenau Museum in Poland. While I see the need for this type of museum experience, I wonder whether the average tourist who walks through is moved by what she or he sees. I have walked the pathway several times, and the tourists with whom I walked were only eager to get out of the cold, knowing that they could, around the next bend. The answer to that question will have to wait for future research.

The Civil War and the End of the Pathway

The final section of the museum's permanent collection section is very short. A single display case on the final wall of the tour presents the visitor with a brief history of the EBCI and their involvement in the Civil War. A small display discusses the land purchases made by William Thomas and facsimiles of the maps from the 1840s of the multiple parcels of land that eventually became the Boundary of the Eastern Band of the Cherokee. From there the visitor is ushered into a final corral, where a movie is continuously shown.

The storyteller in the movie is, finally, female. However, the figure changes magically from an elder female—white haired and brown skinned with a time-worn face—to the stereotypical Indian maiden (reminiscent of Shana Bushyhead's "I Love You, Pocahontas" story related in chapter 3). This shape-shifting storyteller is there to say that the EBCI are still alive and well. A good message, except for the fact that the story of the Oconaluftee Citizen Cherokees from the 1830s to the present is not told, shown, or related in any way. Nothing about the current lifeways of the Eastern Band of Cherokees is shared with the visitor. As one leaves, a few placards at the end of the pathway provide a few facts about the Cherokee History Association and the advent of tourism, the current principal chief, and a short piece on the Snowbird community. But the rich history of the Qualla Cherokee Indians and the advent of the EBCI is gone along with all vestiges of who the pre-contact and pre-removal Cherokee people might have been.[1]

From this description of the changes between the original modern museum and the "Disneyfied" museum, one can see how traditional gender relationships are negated and qualitatively changed at the hands of the non-Cherokee designer. By omitting the history of the Seven Clans and the matrilineal, matrilocal, and matrifocal systems that the Cherokees lived with prior to and after removal, the visitor is left with the idea that they are "just like us," a theme that, from the 1950s through the 1990s, was repeated over and over in every Cherokee tourist venue on the Boundary. Even while many of the matrilineal processes and relationships remain, the tourist learns little of culturally Cherokee lifeways, and the view on the strip remains that of male Indians with teepees and Siouan war bonnets. Does this change the fact that in their own homes Cherokees still enact many of those matrilineal values? No. But for the generations of Cherokee youth who will go through this museum year after year, an image of non-Cherokee-ness may indelibly leave the same impression it leaves on the tourist: "We are just like them." Because the Disneyfied museum is so compelling—especially for the young—*this* is the history that will stick with them. In the long run, moves like this, which show the same artistic license being taken with the history of the EBCI as the writing of the outdoor drama did in the 1940s, affect indigenous lifeways irrevocably by changing how the youth of the EBCI come to see themselves in relationship to the world outside the Boundary.

HARRAH'S CHEROKEE CASINO

Harrah's Cherokee Casino opened with a grand flourish during my fieldwork in 1997.[2] The opening ceremonies were more than a decade in coming. Bingo had been generating income for the EBCI since 1974, but the casino goes far beyond the Tribal Bingo Hall and enterprise. Although I do not have space here to give a complete history of Harrah's coming to Cherokee, I will relate the concerns that were expressed to me and what newspaper editorials echoed from 1996 to 1998. According to these sources, there were three primary concerns prior to the building of the casino: political, economic, and moral. These concerns fueled each other and were intertwined.

The people with whom I spoke and those who wrote editorials for the *Cherokee One Feather* were upset by the tribal government's refusal to hold a general referendum to allow the enrolled members to give input on whether to have a large casino on the Boundary. For some it was a moral issue, but for others it had to do with the economic means of bringing Harrah's to Cherokee. Although the EBCI runs the casino, Harrah's initially owned the building and its contents. The tribe acquired the land the casino sits on from specific enrolled families, and it is the same land where the now-defunct Frontier Land once stood. This was done to satisfy the state of North Carolina's agreement for exemptions to permit a casino in the state. The land is a prime spot on the Boundary where one of the major roads leads into the reservation. So, what was the economic problem that led to the political upheaval? The deal with Harrah's required the EBCI to put up the Boundary itself—the entire 57,000 acres—as collateral to Harrah's in case of failure. This meant that if the casino failed—if no one came to gamble, eat at the restaurants, and watch the Vegas-style shows—the whole of the EBCI could lose the land they have owned as a people since the 1840s to banks and the state. The Cherokee would be without a land base, just like all the other federally recognized Cherokee nations or bands. Hence people's primary fear was that they would be forced off their lands, displaced, and once again removed.

The EBCI tribal government was so sure that the casino would be successful that they let Harrah's set up a small casino in a building directly across the street from the Cherokee High School. It boomed and generated traffic problems for the high school, its students, faculty, and staff (Cucumber 1998; Pinnix 1998). Convinced even further of the eminent success of a large casino, the tribal government pushed for a major casino construction project and ignored the people's demands for a referendum. Many people became so frustrated that they refused to participate in the government any longer (Abram 1997; Bone 1997a, 1997b; D. Duncan 1998; Martin 1997a, 1997d, 1998o).

Within the first two years of the opening of Harrah's Cherokee Casino, the risk taken was shown to be an unqualified monetary success. As of 2003 the Boundary was again free and clear because of the profits made in the casino's first few years. The EBCI government uses its profits to improve the quality of life on the Boundary, and each enrolled member also makes a profit in the form of per capita checks. Since 1999, new hotels have been built to accommodate the burgeoning numbers of tourists who come to gamble year-round.

Once Harrah's was open and became quite successful, there continued to be a great deal of vocal opposition on the Boundary to the casino—and even to the Tribal Bingo Hall—because of the gambling it promotes. In the 1990s there were two groups in the opposition camp. One was religious and based in Denny Crowe's fundamentalist Baptist ministry. The other was worried about the type of tourist the gambling businesses would attract to the Boundary over the long run (Abram 1997; Davis and Wall 1997). Since the opening of the Great Smoky Mountains National Park in 1938, Cherokee had been known as a place to take the entire family for vacation. Many feared that the casino and the enlarged bingo hall would change this. People I spoke with feared that professional gamblers and organized crime would take over the reservation and the Cherokee residents. They also worried that the type of tourist interested in gambling for a "vacation in the mountains" would not be interested in buying the arts and crafts that are the livelihood for a great many on the Boundary. Susan Abram, who wrote about attitudes on the Boundary about this issue, relates that "a Cherokee male . . . is against the casino. He has sold his crafts for 30 years, growing up in a family that has sold crafts for their living for 60 years. He is against the casino being in Cherokee for numerous reasons stating that he cannot sell as many crafts to the shops because they have decreased business. Also, he is noticing less public interest in the culture, less family atmosphere, more traffic, and less interest in the young Cherokee to learn culture and tradition" (1997:13). This statement sums up her findings well.

Despite these objections, both the EBCI as a tribal entity and enrolled members of the Eastern Cherokee have benefited financially. Each member receives an annual check from the profits of the casino and the bingo hall. Many who are opposed to gambling on the Boundary refuse to accept these checks, and the monies go back into the EBCI treasury. Refusing to accept the gambling money is a way for the dissenting groups to voice their opinions (Martin 1998l). However, people who are against the casino and bingo told me that they are pleased overall with the state of the EBCI infrastructure. They don't seem to realize that every time an ambulance pulls up in their yard to help someone who is ill, they are benefiting from casino monies. Every time they drive over the newly paved and widened roads on the Boundary, they are accepting casino monies. Every time they turn on their faucet and a stream of clean drinking water comes out, they are accepting casino monies. In 1998, after the casino had been open for about a year, Donna Toineeta Lossiah and Deb West commented on this phenomenon:

Lossiah: The casino sure is helping the education system, that's for sure. It's giving a lot of money to education, which our kids need.

West: It [casino money] goes to all these services out here, like sanitation. And education. We're so absorbed in it. Then we have these people who say, I'm not going there or I'm not going to do this and associate with the casino, but yet, we're so absorbed in the gaming money. For example, if it's paying those guys to run that rescue squad, and they have to go pick up that person that's not going to the casino, but yet they get in there [the ambulance] and go to the hospital. (D. West 1998; Lossiah 1998)

As of this writing, the strain generated by the gambling money and a new prosperity for enrolled members continues. I see an emerging middle class that just didn't exist prior to the casino's success. There are numerous infrastructural improvements on the Boundary as well. I discuss this in the Epilogue.

A Tour of the Casino

As I did with the renovated Museum of the Cherokee Indian, I will textually walk the reader through this megaplex to illustrate the theme-park aura. When one drives up to the casino on Highway 19 and enters the parking lots, the first view is of a huge neon, flashing, changing sign to announce the feature attraction of the week. A boxing match, famous singing groups, and dance exhibitions are just a few of the attractions I saw being advertised (Martin 1998n; McKie 1998a). The sign also invites passersby into the casino for the ever-present chance of winning a fortune. It also announces, in the permanence of stone under the neon on the base of the sign, that Harrah's Cherokee Casino is run for and by the Eastern Band of Cherokee Indians. The parking lots are vast, and Harrah's runs small shuttles to bring people all the way up to the casino itself, reminiscent of any large theme park. The brick and mortar of the casino is designed in the style of a generic Indian lodge. Faux wood and faux stone create a portico large enough to accommodate the huge buses filled with tourists from North Carolina, South Carolina, Tennessee, Georgia, Alabama, Virginia, and Kentucky. All of these are within 200 miles of the Boundary and near three major interstates—I-40 (east-west) and I-81 and I-75 (north-south)—and bring the preponderance of tourists to the casino. Many others come from even further away.

When one enters the casino, the sound, light, and color moving all together create a remarkable impression. Whether it is because one is impressed or shocked, the scene takes one's breath away. The soaring cathedral open-beamed ceilings rise to at least 40 feet at the apex. Waves of neon wings, images of water, flash by every few seconds. One is greeted by uniformed Harrah's personnel with smiles and "Enjoy your stay" or "Have a great day." I have been there several times for different reasons with different groups of people. I went to the grand opening, and since I was working at Tsali Manor, I went for "Senior's Day," also with Tsali Manor. I went on my own to take field notes.

I also went with family and friends who wanted to see what I had described to them.

The music played throughout the gaming area changes from day to day. Sometimes, especially on the occasions when the EBCI members were being introduced to the casino, generic American Indian music was played, such as flutes and drums. I have also heard country music and 1950s and 1960s rock and roll. So far, I haven't been greeted by hip-hop or rap. This is a little surprising, since the teenagers of Cherokee and their friends really love that genre. In addition, there are always special promotions going on, and the music is generally geared to them.

The Gambling Area

The center of the huge building is the heart of the gambling operations. The bargain the EBCI struck with the state of North Carolina, the U.S. government, and Harrah's, in accordance with the Indian Gaming Regulatory Act, stipulated that all gaming would be computerized. And it is not just the slot machines. All the games available to play—Blackjack, Poker, Roulette, and so forth—are jazzed-up video games. There are virtual cards, virtual roulette wheels, and not a single dealer to "play" one-on-one with the people gaming. In theory, this lack of the human element keeps the chances of organized crime down. It also ensures, again in theory, that the gamers have equal chances of winning because of the computerized randomness. It would also allegedly take away the chance of gamers cheating the house. After all, one cannot stash a virtual ace up one's sleeve.

In row after row there are hundreds of slots to be played from 5 cents to $20. There are dozens of poker and blackjack tables and several roulette tables. Unlike other casino venues, where I have lost my obligatory $20 in change at the slots, at Harrah's Cherokee Casino one cannot just sit down and "feed a machine." An element of control is imposed on gamblers here to keep up with everyone; that is, everyone who gambles must obtain a card on a leash. Each person is signed in through an ATM-style card that one must not lose in order to play. In the 1990s, each time I was at the casino nearly every machine or table was in use.

Here, as at almost every other casino, drinks are free. However, the Boundary is dry (alcohol-free), so gamers can only get soft drinks, water, coffee, tea, or juice. Since there is no alcohol on the premises, players don't get drunk (at least not in the casino) and therefore don't have that extra push toward reckless spending. Certainly, many gamblers go far beyond their means, but not because they can become inebriated in Cherokee. The alcohol-free atmosphere initially allowed Harrah's Cherokee Casino to offer a children's area, but that lasted only for the first few seasons. There was a large room of video games, televisions, and play apparatus where parents could "park" their children while the adults gambled. This was done, at least in part, to quell some anxiety over having the "wrong kind" of tourists come to the Boundary, since the rest of the tourist venues and attractions in town are still geared toward family-style tourism (Abram 1997; Hipps 1998; Cherokee Tribal Travel and Promotion 1997). Because of liability issues for minors, however, child care was eliminated from the casino on July 1, 2001.

Restaurants: Something for Everyone

Beyond the gaming area are several restaurants of various price ranges. These vary from a coffee shop with pastries to an expensive steakhouse. A medium-priced cafeteria-style area is a favorite of the Cherokee people with whom I visited the casino. Cherokees like to have plenty of choices when they eat at a restaurant, and all of the popular eating establishments on the rest of the Boundary are set up in buffet style. The casino's priciest restaurant is called Seven Sisters. I have not eaten there, partially because of the price and partially because the Cherokee people think of it as particularly touristy and avoid it. There are exceptions, of course. As of this writing there are six food venues inside the casino, from Club Cappuccino for coffee to Truffles and Stuff for dessert.

Mythic female Cherokees figure prominently in the design of the casino's eating establishments. I find it interesting that here, amidst what may be the epitome of capitalism, the images of the clan mothers and Selu, the corn mother, are so blithely used. J. Anthony Paredes pointed out to me that "Indian gaming 'capitalism' is a kind of perverse economic transmogrification of capitalism to become 'socialized capitalism' wherein all the members of the tribe are also share holders in the capitalist venture [and get the benefit of per capita checks, for example]. . . . In that sense acknowledgment of Selu in the casino context isn't odd at all . . . it is the continued viability of the Eastern Cherokee as a federally recognized tribe that makes it all possible and in turn that viability depends in part on cultural continuity despite massive change from previous generations" (personal communication 2007). For whose benefit were these decisions made? For the Cherokee or for the tourists? The former rarely use these restaurants. The latter are given no explanation of the names, so they have no recognition of the intrinsic and cultural value of the archetypal feminine in Cherokee myth.

The casino has a smallish gift shop that is a kind of hybrid. A few displays offer authentic Cherokee arts and crafts for sale, but there is also a plethora of souvenirs by which to remember one's Harrah's experience. From dice and playing cards to dream catchers and wind-whirlers, everything is marked "Harrah's." There are blocks of complimentary tickets for enrolled members, and, as is the norm for all places in Cherokee, residents get a "local discount" for everything available at the casino. All of this adds to the theme-park atmosphere. And it is growing. A new 15-story hotel—the tallest building in Cherokee—was added in 2002 to accommodate more and more tourists. There are attempts at packaging Harrah's with other venues. However, attendance at most Cherokee tourist venues has yet to bounce back to the levels of the 1960s through 1980s, even after they were updated for the twenty-first century.

For the tourist, Cherokee-as-destination is quite a package. But how does this package affect Cherokee people themselves? Are there commonalities between the packaging of Cherokee and other tourist havens in the United States and around the world where indigenous populations are involved? The following chapter will present the views of both scholars and everyday Cherokees on the effects of mass tourism and the ongoing colonial presence that the tourism industry represents. Further, I will discuss the continuing ability of Cherokees to adapt and make choices that maximize tourism's economic benefits for themselves.

6
Mass Tourism's Effects on Indigenous Communities

Throughout this book I have been considering the following questions: How has the past century of mass tourism affected indigenous peoples, specifically, the Eastern Cherokee? What happens to the traditions and familial relationships of those who are constantly under the tourist gaze? Is tourism a benign entity that seeks to give the tourist an outlet, something to do during precious "down time" from the chaos of consumerism, commercialism, and capitalism that the economics of the world at large run on? Does mass tourism perpetuate the implicit cultural imperatives of racism and exoticism, the "us" versus "them" mind-set that continues to be taught to American children through public education? Or is tourism in the business of educating the public about unique indigenous histories? Finally, are the lifeways of autochthonous peoples altered so quickly by mass tourism, once it settles on an area, that they have difficulty with the changes that result?

To answer these questions, I will make reference to Dean MacCannell's work on tourism and anthropology. In his review of the film *Cannibal Tours,* MacCannell writes that "there is so much mutual complicity in the overall definition of the interaction between the postmodern tourist and the ex-primitive that the system comes close to producing the impossible economic ideal. The performing primitives claim to be exploited, but in so doing they take great care not to develop this claim to the point where their value as 'primitive' attraction is diminished. In short, they must appear as almost noble savages, authentic except for a few changes forced on them by others. . . . They gain sympathy from the tourist based on the conditions of their relationship to the tourist" (1990:16). MacCannell implies that the "ex-primitive" is in collusion with the forces that make up the tourist trade in order to gain economically from it. As I have shown in earlier chapters, the Eastern Cherokee have capitalized on mass tourism since the mid-twentieth century. However, *collusion* with the tourist industry suggests a secretive, illegal, or "underhanded" cooperation to bilk the unsuspecting tourist. If I apply this aspect of MacCannell's analysis, collusion would be seen by fellow enrolled members as destructive to one's personal relationships with the community at large in the context of living on the Boundary. While there are some strident objections and criticisms of tourism, tourists, and the outsiders who make up that population, in my experience of the Boundary, outright collusion is not acceptable, nor is it aspired to, for Cherokee residents.

CULTURAL CONTINUITY: THE PRIVATE CHEROKEE

The use of tourism as a tool for tribal and personal independence during the past hundred years *by* Eastern Cherokee people to survive and, in many cases, thrive, is analogous to the Cherokee ability to adapt to changes in lifeways since the time of early contact and trading (Perdue 1998). This malleability to influences outside Cherokee society for their apparent good, as well as the opposite Cherokee tendency to maintain an outward semblance of the harmony ethic toward non-Cherokees, have, after a century of tourism, led some to hypothesize that the Eastern Cherokee have not maintained the smallest semblance of continuity within their own community traditions. However, I found this far from the actual reality.

The most visible uses of tourism on the Boundary, artisanship and chiefing, are marked in specific ways for women and for men. Although a number of men work as artisans, very few women work at the chiefing business. Perhaps one out of ten Eastern Cherokees actually makes artisanship her or his sole livelihood. In fact, the percentage of Cherokee artisans among the total enrolled members is quite small. Women engage in basket and pottery making, finger weaving, and beadwork, while men carve wood and stone. The items they produce end up for sale in the Qualla Co-op or in what Cherokees consider a reputable local gift shop (R. M. Abram, personal correspondence 2003; Sharpe 1998). A majority of the full-time artisans are women, and artisanship is nearly always gender-specific by craft, with only a few crossing over. For the most part, women's artisanship allows them—or makes it necessary for them—to stay on the Boundary. This, along with the fact that one of women's traditional pre-constitutional roles was to tend to the business of daily life, both in the home and in the village, has been a major factor in the observable continuation of many matrilocal and matrifocal lifeways (Brown 1999; Fogelson 1992; French 1998; Jackson 1975; Mankiller 1993; Perdue 1985, 1995, 1998; Reed 1993). Likewise, this continuation of tradition has led those women who are not interested in working for tourists into community-based careers such as education (preschool to community college), nursing and related medical professions, myriad jobs within the tribal government (e.g., paralegals, clerical workers, archivists, administrators, social workers, accountants, cooks, court recorders), as well as homemakers and volunteers. Since I did my initial fieldwork in 1997 and 1998, this type of cultural continuity has been further strengthened and deepened and has pulled more and more men into those roles as well.

The men who continue chiefing stand for hours in the heat or cold to have their picture taken with tourists for a few dollars each. Some have sent their children to college, law school, or medical school on this income. Chiefing has been highly criticized by Cherokees from other nations, tribes, and bands, by non-Cherokee Indians, and by some people on the Boundary itself. However, the "chiefs" know that they are performing for the tourists' imagination and that a vast majority of tourists neither realize nor care that they are being given the same preexisting image to take home that they came to the Boundary with in the first place. At the same time, chiefing is for some the only viable option in a tourist industry mostly interested in conserving the image of the stereotypical Indian. While one can be an artisan almost entirely in the privacy of one's home, chiefing happens under the gaze of every tourist who comes through the Boundary. Because of this permanence of the tourist gaze, "chiefs" by definition have to fit the phenotypical stereotype. Most Eastern Cherokees do not fit this stereotype and therefore do not become involved in chiefing. The result is that less than 0.2 percent of the total population is involved in chiefing at any given time.[1]

The CHA venues also base employment of both women and men on the phenotypical stereotype, further reducing the numbers of those who might otherwise engage in chiefing. But from the 1950s through the 1990s the CHA jobs were few and far between and thereby employed a small number of the overall population. Since a limited number of jobs are available on the Boundary, men are more likely to go off of the Boundary for their work or careers and return home nightly, weekly, monthly, or upon retirement. Although many men work in the tribal government, their jobs are quite different from women's (e.g., bus drivers, carpentry and related trades, police officers). A few men still make their living at the difficult work of logging, which is also in step with the pre-constitution Cherokee division of labor (S. H. Hill 1997; Perdue 1998).

The gambling industry remains a sore point among many Cherokee. To illustrate, I turn to the small membership of the Yellowhill Baptist Church. Their leader in 1997 and 1998 was Denny Crowe. A lay Baptist preacher by persuasion, Crowe began preaching against the casino in the mid-1990s when the facility was fairly limited and was located across the street from the Cherokee High School. A growing number of people across the Boundary joined this resistance group, and by 1998 about one hundred people had signed waivers to both protest and reject the per capita checks that are given to enrolled members as a result of the casino's success (Martin 1998l). While this may seem like a small number, only about 1 percent of the population of the Boundary, it is still significant because this 1 percent represents a wide section of the communities, community clubs, and churches that have joined this cause.

Crowe's moral objections to gambling and casinos, which match those of a number of other fundamentalist Protestant groups nationwide, include a strong statement about what it means to be Cherokee. Interestingly, Crowe conflates Cherokee-ness with a certain type of tourism. Of his many arguments against Harrah's, the most forceful is the concern that the casino will change the kind of tourist that comes to the Boundary. He sees the presence of more and more gamblers as a deterrent and hindrance to the advancement of family tourism. He fears that people who come primarily to gamble will not be interested in the cultural venues and events that have made Cherokee a popular destination for nearly a century. According to Crowe's way of conceptualizing the tourist gambling population, being Cherokee and expressing that identity for the tourist population will be negated, and the economic base for a great many enrolled members will disappear (Loy 1997). If tourists aren't interested in attending *Unto These Hills,* going to Oconaluftee Indian Village, and buying authentic Cherokee craft items, this could very well be the result.

Some people have become quite wealthy from the tourist industry, since Harrah's Cherokee Casino and related motels, other motels, restaurants, and craft shops stand on their families' property and they collect the rents on land leases. Others live in poverty with abuse and alcoholism in the coves and "hollers" of the remote parts of the Boundary. Dirt roads lead to ramshackle cabins that bear no indication of the arrival of the twenty-first century. Yet, some of these people would rather stay in the mountains and live in the "old ways" than have the burden of technology, government, or tourism on their backs. These people are generally 40 years of age or more, from traditional or conservative families.

It is the children of the contiguous Boundary, isolated Snowbird excluded, who face the most acculturation and assimilation. This has always been the case in the United States, with Pratt's nineteenth-century boarding school system as a primary example, but in some ways it is just as pronounced today (Lesiak and Jones 1991). The Cherokee school system endeavors to immerse children in a specifically Cherokee cultural system that includes artisanship, family and community, and language use and comprehension, in particular. However, these children, like their parents (who had little in school to foster a specific Cherokee identity), must still have English as their first language. They are constantly exposed to capitalism and consumerism and to the ongoing, centuries-old disease of racism and exoticism. Still, the Eastern Cherokee continue to live their own cultural system and allow tourists to remain ignorant of them as private Cherokees. The cultural systems of the Cherokee will continue to shift, just as in other places of mass tourism, to accommodate both the taste of the tourist and the needs of the people. Past generations are more traditional than those presently in their early twenties to thirties. Younger generations—those who are just coming into the school system and are in the hands of Cherokee people who are determined to teach and maintain the culture through them—may have more of a tendency to turn that pattern around and be more traditional. Some individuals, families, and communities will continue to carry on traditional Cherokee lifeways. However, tourism has consequences for all people on the Boundary. To illustrate, I will present a piece of local humor circulated in the 1990s and brought to my attention by another researcher, Mike Zogry, titled "Dr. I. M. Uneg."

"DR. I. M. UNEG: TRACING YOUR HYSTERICAL ROOTS"

This piece is Cherokee satire at its best. After talking with so many people, I can say that Cherokees understand the fact that almost every "Indian ancestry" claim that is made is "I'm a Cherokee." We must keep in mind, however, that books and videos on how to trace one's Cherokee ancestry have been available for years (Blankenship 1992, 1994). Most of the Cherokees I've had this discussion with don't have a lot of respect for people who suddenly "discover" their "Cherokee-ness" late in life. Why, since the above-cited ancestry books are published by a Cherokee press? I would point out that I also have a hint of Cherokee ancestry. Yet, the Cherokee people whom I came to work closely with and whom I still call my friends don't care about that. The difference is that, for many, "white" people have "come out of the woodwork" in the past 15 to 20 years to join the group, some group, of Cherokee. Many of them want per capita checks, tuition reimbursement, and free health care. They are all about a BIA card for their own benefit, not about traditions and learning, reviving language or arts. The disdain for this behavior is clearly evident in the "Dr. I. M. Uneg" piece.

First, the name of the author is pure satire, as *uneg* is the word Cherokees use for the very worst characteristics about white people. The "Brief Forward [*sic*]" includes a biography of "Dr. Uneg":

He has a B.S. degree from college and recently discovered his Cherokee roots during a visit to the Cherokee Indian Reservation in Cherokee, North Carolina. While visiting the local craft shops on the reservations, Dr. Uneg was surprised to discover how many people that walked through the door that [*sic*] were Cherokee. He began to understand

that there was a side of the Cherokee people that "whites" knew nothing about. He learned that there was an entire system of monarchy here
on the reservation before the removal. This was plainly obvious because
so many of the people who said they were Cherokee stated that their
great-great-grandmothers were "full blood Cherokee princesses." This
was when Uneg discovered that there used to be Cherokee Princes and
a whole lot of Cherokee Princesses. In fact, based on what people said,
Uneg calculated that there were at least 100 Cherokee Princesses for
every Cherokee Prince. Thus, because there were so many more Cherokee Princesses than men, the women were forced into the arms of Europeans. Based on his calculations, Dr. Uneg has discovered there are well
over 550,000 Cherokee people living in the United States today.

The article covers every annoying, irritating, and infuriating thing about white
people who come onto the Boundary. A list of 28 questions will, according to
"Dr. Uneg," help you find out if you are "Real Cherokee." I heard every one of
these claims or criteria either in laughter at the "stupidity of *unegs*" or in anger
at them. Prior to beginning the list of questions, "Dr. Uneg" states that there
are several "hallmark" signs of being Cherokee and suggests keeping track as
you go through the list to make sure you find out your "true" ancestry. "He"
also points out that if you discover that you do have Cherokee heritage, there
is a form to fill out and send in at the end of the survey. Here are five of my
personal favorites, which go a long way toward communicating—through sarcasm and caustic humor—how Eastern Cherokees feel about their ongoing,
institutionalized position of being exoticized:

1. First and foremost, let us begin with the largest common denominator—
   skin color. We know the Great Creator has made people of many flavors,
   some chocolate, some lemon, some vanilla, and so on. We have also been
   told that to "walk in beauty" we must never judge a book by its cover.
   However, in this case, we must be forced to look at skin color. Are you
   pasty and extremely white? For instance, when you wear shorts are other
   people compelled to put on sunglasses? If you answered "yes" to this question, then you may be Cherokee.
15. Have you started to grow your feathers yet? (We keep it a secret as to just
    what age Indians actually being [*sic*] to grow their feathers at). If you think
    you are about to grow your feathers, then you may well be an Indian.
25. Are you convinced that we hold our Indian Ceremonies in secret here on
    the reservation? Do you have knowledge that we hold right [*sic*] of pas-
    sage ceremonies where we light a big bonfire, dance around it while wear-

ing full Western regalia, and that sometimes (just sometimes) we adopt a white into the tribe and give him his Indian name? You could only know this if you were Cherokee!

27. Last but not least, do you have absolutely no proof whatsoever that anybody in your inbred family tree was ever even remotely near an Indian at any time in the past let alone romantically involved with a Cherokee Princess? If you answered "yes" then you have only one question left to answer!

28. Are you convinced that you can prove your Cherokee ancestry through a blood test? If you answered "yes" then you are a full-blood!

The sarcasm and anger evident in this "article," which has no hint as to its actual author or publisher, combined with the fact that it was circulated among those considered "Real Cherokee" in the population with whom I worked, further validates the internal rancor that the Eastern Cherokee carry against the "white" people. When faced with Euro-American inscrutability, Cherokees inevitably turn to humor to soften the racism.

CHANGING WITH THE TIMES:
CHEROKEES AS TOURISTS

From the beginning of contact with the British in the late seventeenth and early eighteenth centuries, Cherokees have not only been visited and exoticized but have also traveled to the place of the European "other." Mooney told of the first Cherokee excursion to Europe:

> In 1730, to further fix the Cherokee in the English interest, Sir Alexander Cuming was dispatched on a secret mission to that tribe, which was again smarting under grievances and almost ready to join with the Creeks in an alliance with the French. Proceeding to the ancient town of Nequassee (Nîkwâsî, at the present Franklin, North Carolina), he so impressed the chiefs by his bold bearing that they conceded without question all his demands, submitting themselves and their people for the second time to the English dominion and designating Moytoy, of Tellico, to act as their "emperor" and to represent the Nation in all transactions with the whites. Seven chiefs were selected to visit England, where, in the palace at Whitehall, they solemnly renewed the treaty, acknowledging the sovereignty of England and binding themselves to have no trade or alliance with any other nation, not to allow any other white people to settle among them, and to deliver up any fugitive slaves who might seek refuge with them. To confirm their words they delivered a "crown," five

eagle-tails, and four scalps, which they had brought with them. In return they received the usual glittering promises of love and perpetual friendship, together with a substantial quantity of guns, ammunition, and red paint. The treaty being concluded in September, they took the ship for Carolina, where they arrived, as we are told by the governor, "in good health and mightily well satisfied with His Majesty's bounty to them." (1982 [1891]:35–36)

While Moytoy and his party were certainly not tourists in the modern sense of the word, they did travel and participate in a cultural system that was "exotic" and "other" than their own.

The Eastern Cherokee elders are regular travelers as well. Not only did they venture out as early as the eighteenth century to see and discover as travelers, but they have been a constant presence in the U.S. military since the late nineteenth century. They mostly travel to other parts of the United States in the well-appointed EBCI charter buses. Between 1996 and 1998 they went to Myrtle Beach, South Carolina, to Amish country in Pennsylvania, and on various short trips within a day's bus ride of the Boundary. According to the stories I heard from the elders, they thoroughly enjoy these trips and look forward to seeing the "silly white people and what they do" out in the world. The Cherokee sense of humor is always at work on these trips, and it can be wicked, as the following story exemplifies.

While touring Pennsylvania Amish country, the bus passed a group of farmers trying to dig a huge oak stump out of a field. It was early in the morning. After touring, sightseeing, and dining, they passed the same way late that same day on their way back to their hotel, and the Amish men were still hard at work on the same stump. One of the Cherokee men asked the tour guide about it and learned that the Amish won't use "modern conveniences." He was surprised, to say the least. After all, I was told, white people have been making us "be like them" for hundreds of years! He finally said, "Man, somebody ought to tell those guys to throw a stick of dynamite in that stump so they can get on with it!" Even years after the event, howls of laughter ensued at Tsali Manor, and the topic of conversation for the rest of the day was about the white men who don't even use their own inventions.

RELATIONSHIPS TO THE ACADEMY

Let me reiterate the points I consider most important in this work. First, the tourist industry is always already a double-edged sword. While it brings on rapid cultural change that some communities find it difficult, and sometimes impossible, to keep pace with, it is simultaneously often the impetus for craft and "traditional" culture revitalization movements. Without these movements over the course of the twentieth century and into the twenty-first, indigenous cultural variety and particularity might have been lost.

The other important point relates to the concept of public and private spaces of daily lived experience for Eastern Cherokee people. Women and men have always shared both public and private space in Cherokee society, as in most other indigenous societies in North America (S. H. Hill 1997; Perdue 1998). However, the performative aspects of the public personas specifically for tourism differ greatly between women and men. Women tend to gravitate toward and be employed through the cultural heritage venues, which portray "traditional" pre-removal Cherokee lifeways, while men tend to portray the "generalized Indian" for the tourist masses by way of chiefing. Aspects of life that are specifically Cherokee and private are deliberately kept away from the tourist gaze, whether it is the schoolchildren at play or the Cherokee Indian Fair. Within the private space of "being Cherokee," gender roles continue to be defined in a specific way. There is considerable primary source material concerning the Cherokee from the seventeenth century to the time of removal in the early nineteenth century, and cultural continuity is apparent. For instance, women generally have been the purveyors of "traditional" knowledge, such as where the best ramp patches are found in the deep mountains, and matrifocality can still be observed.

This work has brought to the fore many new questions and lines of inquiry. Among the many possibilities, I choose to address two specific areas that I would like to personally follow up on with future research or which I would like to see the scholarly community take up in a systematic and critical way: tourism and gender, and tourism in the context of American Indian and Native studies. I will briefly discuss each of these areas to suggest how this project begins these inquiries and how these lines of inquiry might be furthered in future research.

Tourism and gender is not a new line of inquiry. However, the ways in which gender has been considered within the tourist literature, both at the academic and the policy-making levels, have generally eschewed a native perspective. This discussion is usually from the perspective of the tourist industry, in whatever form it takes. A preponderance of the discussion currently taking place concerning gender is preoccupied with hospitality services and the ways in which tourists, usually male, usually "foreign," *use* those "services," usually female, usually "native" to the area being toured (Kinnaird and Hall 1994; Williams 2002). These concerns are, more often than not, at the center of the inquiries about gender. Gender, then, in most cases, is considered to be nearly entirely about women, and sometimes children. This is a vital part of the discussion and must be continued in both the academic and policy-making arenas to stem the tide of violence against women and children. However, to come to a better understanding of how societies both allow and either intentionally or unintentionally condone the practices of subjugation among their most vulnerable citizens, attention must be paid to specific gender roles in specific societies in terms of the tourist onslaught (Bolles 1997). Second, more research is needed on specifically indigenous societies—which are always within the borders of a nation-state—that may be dealing with violence against women, perpetrated by men in private life, but who are not subjected to outright prostitution. For instance, little has been said about the roles of "native" men in societal situations where mass tourism has become the dominant economic system. "Native" male roles and their juxtaposition to female roles continue to be unmarked and therefore unproblematized.

There are some obvious exceptions. Barbara Babcock's "Mudwomen and Whitemen" centers on the experience and voice of Pueblo "mudwomen" potters. However, within her narrative, one "mudwoman," Helen Cordero, who first made Storyteller dolls in 1964, unsettles a gendered notion of Pueblo peoples that remains popular in the minds of many. Babcock writes: "When I first encountered a Storyteller figure, I read it as female and as a powerful image of generativity, of reproductive power. I soon learned that this was not simply another image of a Pueblo mother, of which Helen herself has made several, but a male figure: 'It's my grandfather. He's giving me these. He had lots of stories and lots of grandchildren, and we're all in there, in the clay'" (1994:190). She notes that "in studying these grandfather Storytellers, which are also images of cultural reproduction, I have discovered that synchronic essentialism and significations of stability in Pueblo art and culture are not entirely a matter of Anglo projection" (1994:190). This is an important point, since Helen Cordero, a Pueblo artisan, consciously chose to make a statement in clay about the passing on of a traditional story to the grandchildren by an elder male. There is important information here about gendered relationships and gender roles in the private Pueblo community.

Babcock was careful to point out that this construction and understanding of relationships was not merely a "matter of Anglo perception" but was "traditional" and came directly from the Pueblo point of view. Her article had a major influence on my discussion throughout this volume on native perspectives of gender roles as well as how the tourist industry acts on a given society and encourages, or perhaps forces, acculturation and cultural change. To bring this point back to the Cherokee, I present a short discussion of primary Cherokee attitudes toward the work of the late Robert Thomas as it appears in *Cherokees at the Crossroads,* long considered the baseline ethnography and community study of the Eastern Cherokee (Raymond D. Fogelson, personal communication 1999; Gulick 1960; White 2001). Thomas, an Oklahoma Cherokee and a University of Chicago–trained anthropologist, worked on the University of North Carolina's Institute for Research in Social Science ethnographic project in Cherokee, North Carolina, from 1955 to 1959. This project was also the training ground for many other students of American Indian anthropology.[2] Thomas's work specifically addresses a "classification of sub-cultural types (or 'value systems')" among the Eastern Cherokee. Thomas found four value systems in operation in the late 1950s: "Conservative, Generalized Indian, 'Rural-White' Indian, and Middle Class Indian" (quoted in Gulick 1960:127). In my own work I found that these value systems still obtain. Thomas's explanations for the four systems, in brief, are as follows:

> The Conservative conceives of himself as a different order of man from the rest of the world. . . . His distinction is, of course, that he is a "true Indian." Insofar as aboriginal personality traits and values remain, it is the Conservative who retains them most consistently.
>
> The Generalized Indian very definitely conceives of himself as being an Indian, but he also conceives of himself as being a part of the larger culture. This is perhaps the decisive difference between the Generalized Indian and the Conservative; and its most clear-cut indication may well be the fact that though the Generalized Indian may know the Cherokee language, he does not use it by preference.
>
> The "Rural-White" Indians on the reservation are very much like Southern rural whites in all respects. . . . These people usually have a minimal degree of Indian inheritance, within the 1/32 limit, and most of them have few, if any, Indian physical features.
>
> The Middle Class values system reveals itself primarily in participation in non-agricultural business enterprise and office work, hence the label. Those who have made this adjustment appear, however, to have come from two origins: Generalized Indian and "Rural-White" Indian. These people have a tendency to associate socially with non-Indians who are comparable to them in occupational orientation. (quoted in Gulick 1960:128–129)

The struggle for Eastern Cherokees, in the 1950s and in the early twenty-first century, involves the relationship between their own cultural system and the "standard" American one. The difficulties inherent in those relationships result from the "'submerged' aspects of culture" (Gulick 1958:21). Gulick argues that most people cannot perceive these submerged aspects, or implicit cultural patterns, and that these elements create problems in both perception and communication between groups. When we are speaking of people squarely within the dominant cultural system, that may very well be true; however, for peoples who live in the shadow of the dominant culture, understanding the dominant other is a vital part of living one's life. In the context of the Cherokee and mass tourism, this means being both a "public Indian" (to satisfy the economic base) and a "private Cherokee" (to satisfy and maintain a palpable sense of cultural continuity).

There is no question of the economic importance of tourism for American Indian and Native communities. My central argument is that although tourism acts as the primary acculturative agent in these communities, a sense of continuity of tradition, whether storytelling or eating your own food, remains intact. As such, it is vital to go even further with research and analysis of this type, specifically, research that centers the American Indian and native perspectives and attitudes *toward* a tourist economy. While some studies have addressed this, the great majority of American Indian and Alaska and Hawaiian Native literature still gives the tourist industry a backseat.[3] When tourism is mentioned, there is a tendency to concentrate on the tourists themselves and on the industry venues in relationship to the tourists. There is relatively little in the literature about the often contradictory and conflicting stances that autochthonous communities adopt toward tourism or on the continuing acculturative processes at work on indigenous peoples (Chambers 1997).

While doing my fieldwork I attempted to address in some practical ways some basic methodological difficulties that have been critiqued by American Indians and Alaska and Hawaiian Natives over much of the twentieth century (Biolsi and Zimmerman 1997; Deloria 1997; King 1979b). Primarily, I began and ended my fieldwork with an elder population, those who attended Tsali Manor on a regular basis. By acknowledging both the memory and wisdom of the Cherokee elders and the high regard in which Cherokee tradition holds them, I was able to tap into both empirical facts for analysis and into the wider web of relationships that those elders represented. Because of my associations with the elders, I was able to meet children, grandchildren, and great-grandchildren who were willing to talk with me because "granny" had done so. I also found that within specific age groups, the stories and memories of the lifeways tended to be consistent. I found the same for memories about the tourist industry. From its early genesis, or "exploration phase," of the 1930s, through the mature, or "stagnation phase," of the 1990s, age-group stories tended to be about the same types of pieces of the overall puzzle (Butler 1980). As a result of beginning with the elders, the research has a depth and longevity that adds to the palimpsest of knowledge about the contemporary Eastern Cherokee.

The Eastern Cherokee appreciate and understand their situation. As with the Booger Dance and the Miss Pretty Legs contest, Cherokee humor turns what is impossible to deal with on its head in order to create a joke. This atmosphere, which is specifically kept within the accepted Cherokee realm, is part of the harmony ethic that Thomas wrote about in the 1960s. However, as I have shown, the facade of harmony is a delicate cloth that conceals the real anger and resentment that most Eastern Cherokee live with on a day-to-day basis. Whether this anger is over historical events that cannot be changed or over daily occurrences with tourists, white employers, or each other, the Eastern Cherokee find themselves walking a balance beam between their specific cultural system and the mainstream America that would and could easily devour them.

Epilogue
An Eastern Cherokee Renaissance

In 2006, ten years after starting my fieldwork in Cherokee, I returned to renew friendships, refresh my memory, and see how things had changed in the ensuing decade. I had been back since 1996, as I make regular trips to Gatlinburg, Tennessee, to visit my parents, who are artists and own a studio/shop in that very touristy city just over the mountain from Cherokee. I had been watching the new hotels rise from the remains of 50-year-old gas stations and country markets throughout the early 2000s. I had seen the new and elaborate stone entrance billboard announcing the driver's arrival to the Eastern Tribe of Cherokee Indians from the Great Smoky Mountains National Park side, replete with dancing water fountains that are running as long as the temperature is warm enough. I had seen the total revamping of the ceremonial grounds and the giant white sail that offers, for the first time, welcome shade to the also revamped, much improved grandstand that hosts all the big events on the Boundary. I had seen all of this happening, and I had even talked about the changes with a few of my friends who own shops in Cherokee, but all of that was fairly superficial. From where did all this change come? And whence the "boomtown" atmosphere, when tourism is down overall in the South? What was going on in the wonderful world of Cherokee? To find out, I decided to talk to old contacts and make some new ones. While I cannot discuss every aspect of the present tourist industry in Cherokee, I will take up some points I discussed earlier to identify the changes in the new millennium.

A NEW PROSPERITY

The area around Harrah's Cherokee Casino had multiplied over the last decade with hotels, restaurants, big-name entertainers, and a constant influx of money. Many Cherokee parents I spoke with were concerned that their young children would not know how to handle the responsibility that comes with the

7.1. Ceremonial grounds with tented bleachers, Cherokee, North Carolina, 2006 (Author's photo)

amount of money they are accruing through per capita checks. EBCI children born today will inherit million-dollar trust funds when they reach the age of 18. To help alleviate some of those anxieties, the tribal government, with support from Western Carolina University, set in place new programs to train people in managing money. Some enrolled members live, not from paycheck to paycheck, but from "per cap to per cap," and this only exacerbates the condition of those on the Boundary who are poor (Williamson 2006). However, the bright side to the influx of funds is the tribal government's ability to improve every aspect of infrastructure: roads and bridges, parks and water/sewer systems, and education.

One of these improvements that was currently in the building stages was a new Cherokee Elementary School. It is being built on the flat river-bottom plain just before one enters the Big Cove community. This facility promises to be state-of-the-art, and it is hoped that most Cherokee children will attend. Programs are also being implemented that will improve the use of the Cherokee language among the next generation of enrolled members. Juanita Wilson is the deputy officer in charge of the language and cultural programs for the EBCI. Of the many programs she has under her watch, she seems passionate about the language immersion piece of the puzzle. This newest form of an idea that started in the 1990s begins with preschool children *and* their par-

7.2. Entrance to Harrah's Cherokee Casino, Cherokee, North Carolina, 2006 (Author's photo)

ents. When parents sign a waiting list for their toddlers to get into these (already overflowing) classes, they must make a commitment to attend Cherokee language classes as well. It is well established that in order for a language to become second nature, it must be heard in all of the places where people speak to each other. If children in an immersion program learn to say simple sentences in Cherokee and use that language throughout the day in school, they must be able to go on speaking Cherokee with their parents and siblings once home from the classroom. The goal is to make parents more a part of the day-to-day learning with this program.

Along with producing teachers who have their teaching credentials in Cherokee (through a Western Carolina University program in Cherokee Studies) and a commitment to extending community outreach to work with families with children in the immersion program, there is promise that the Cherokee language will continue its revival. Here is an anecdote of my own about the language. One morning, I was sitting in Peter's Pancakes waiting for my breakfast when, at the table behind me, there was a conversation proceeding *in Cherokee*. In my 40-year-long relationship with the Smoky Mountains and the town of Cherokee, this was the first time I had experienced that in a public setting. As I recall, it was a youngish woman with a toddler and another woman, who appeared to be the child's grandmother. They were just having breakfast, chatting and showing the child objects on the table and their corresponding words, all in Cherokee. Lovely. Something is working.

The new millennium has seen Cherokees reclaim those parts of the tourist industry that had been, for more than half a century, controlled almost exclusively by non-Cherokee interests from the seven-county western North Carolina region. As John Finger wrote in 1991 in *Cherokee Americans:* "The CHA was clearly a white-dominated organization. Harry E. Buchanan was chairman and Joe Jennings, the Cherokee agent, was treasurer. Jennings was one of the most enthusiastic proponents of the pageant [*Unto These Hills*] and a necessary liaison between the association and the Band. Mollie Blankenship [Arneach], the association's secretary, was the only member of the Band holding an administrative position" (1991:115). As I mentioned in chapter 2, while some Cherokees were involved with the beginnings of the CHA, the majority of participants were white businessmen and promoters. In 2004, that changed.

REPRESENTATIONS OF CHEROKEES: REPRISE

Change is seldom easy, and the changes in the cultural representations of Cherokees and of Cherokee, North Carolina, are no exception. As mentioned in chapter 2, the Cherokee Historical Association was founded by a mostly white group of entrepreneurs from the counties surrounding the Boundary. While there was always a Cherokee presence on the CHA's executive board (usually between one and three people at a time), nearly every decision taken— from the Drama to the Village to who was hired for each—was made by non-Cherokees. Probably the biggest coup in the history of the tourist industry in Cherokee was accomplished in 2004 with the takeover of the CHA Executive Board. This was at the behest of many enrolled members on the Boundary, all of whom wanted to see drastic changes made to *Unto These Hills*.

James Bradley, the CHA's director in 2006, told me about the drastic changes made to the board and, soon thereafter, to *Unto These Hills*. The old executive board was quite large, and its members, once appointed, held the position for life. In 2004 that old board was disbanded, and a new one was formed with a new structure and complexion. The new structure—nine members with three-year rotations each—was designed to continually infuse the board with new ideas and fresh perspectives. The other drastic change was that the first new board was made up entirely of enrolled members of the EBCI. This was the first time since the CHA's founding that the organization was run entirely by Eastern Cherokees. Bradley was the vice-chair of this first incarnation of the revamped structure. In that capacity he came into the CHA offices and put in all new equipment: a phone system with voicemail, online ticket sales for the Drama, and new computers with updated systems for the twenty-first century (they had been working with MS-DOS programs from the early 1990s).

The next task was to do something about the declining interest in *Unto These Hills*. The former version of the play had lasted from its opening in 1950 until 2004 (when it closed because of poor attendance and a failing box office) with few variations from the original play, score, and choreography. In fact, attendance had fallen from 80,000 to 90,000 in the late 1980s to early 1990s to about 40,000 in 2000. Enrolled members were even telling tourists not to go to the Drama and weren't taking friends and family because, according to Bradley, "It's not *us* up there, just white ideas of us." In November 2005 the new CHA board decided to dump the original version of the show in favor of a new one, and staff members were told that there would be a complete revamping for 2006, meaning that everyone's job from props manager to the director would be reexamined and rethought.

REMODELING *UNTO THESE HILLS* FOR THE FUTURE

The new board had two main directives: first, to get Cherokee people out of the crowd scenes and into vital speaking roles; and second, to repair and replace errors in the original interpretation of the story and make it more culturally accurate. Once the staff was told about the changes that were coming, they in turn told the players that they would not be asked back automatically as had been done for a very long time. Here are two anecdotes that Bradley shared with me:

> The actors seemed to be mostly interested in having a homecoming every summer with friends. They thought of the dorm housing as theirs. That meant that every Saturday night after the performance of *Unto These Hills* there would be late-night parties with illegal substances. [Even beer is illegal to sell on the Boundary.] No one checked IDs and no one looked out for underage Cherokees. When I took over and told them they couldn't do that anymore, I got the retort, "This is our place. Tell the Chief to put an ad in the *One Feather* that says Cherokees should not go up to the dorms and backstage on Saturday nights." I cannot, will not, tell enrolled members that they can't go to a part of *their* land because some white people want to party! (Bradley 2006)

But that was not the only problems with the old staff and the takeover. Bradley also told me about the old-style auditions:

> At audition calls for the new version [which premiered in May 2006], most of the former players wouldn't come and try out for the new and some of the former roles. Since the play was changed and the staff was changed, they wanted nothing to do with it. In the old way of doing

it, there had been two different audition times set: one for a Cherokee "cattle-call" and one for the actual speaking roles. Save for a few who *knew* that, most Cherokees never even had the chance to use their actual talent. As family number two or family number seven, they were moved where the director wanted them to be by having their numbers called out. They didn't even use their names, just numbers. It's the Trail all over again! (Bradley 2006)

Bradley knew all of this firsthand because he had been one of those few who knew when to show up. He had been a dancer in the show for a long time before college.

The EBCN primarily wanted six points to be addressed in the new *Unto These Hills:*

1. To tell the story in a Cherokee storytelling tradition instead of as a linear series of vignettes.
2. To add dialogue and songs in the Cherokee language wherever possible.
3. To add actual Cherokee dances and the corresponding chants/songs, and to eliminate the anglicized versions.
4. To replace the key staff positions with Cherokees, where possible, and with other American Indian tribal members everywhere else.
5. To hold only one set of auditions so that all interested Cherokees could audition.
6. To have a Community Review Committee play a large part in the overhaul.

As far as I could tell, in just a year the CHA achieved these six goals. Regarding the fifth, at the first open audition (in 2005) more than 125 enrolled members showed up. In 2006's cast nearly 70 percent were Cherokee—a vast difference from the days when only about 20 percent of the cast was Cherokee and of those only a few had speaking roles (Duncan 2006).

After my interview with Bradley, I purchased a ticket and went to the 8 p.m. performance. On this evening I was in the general audience with all the other tourists who had bought tickets. A disturbing event took place with a tourist family prior to the opening of the show. They were sitting directly behind me and were jovial, trying to keep their young children from kicking the backs of the chair in front of them before any action started onstage. The kids were asking a thousand questions, as kids are wont to do, among which was, "Are the Indians real, Mommy?" The mother answered, "No, they are white people in makeup, just like the movies!" Well, I'm thinking that maybe Mom is going on previous knowledge of the show, when over 80 percent of the cast *was* white people in makeup. Toward giving some good news and enlightening a set of tourists on the progress of the Cherokee, I spoke to them and told them that this year, and from now on, the people playing Cherokee Indians *are* Cherokee Indians. Mom, however, insisted that they were white. So I introduced myself, a little more formally, as doing research and assured her that they are Cherokee. This woman went ballistic. She screamed at me that if her children believed that there were "real Indians" onstage, they would be scared to death! She finished, "Don't you get it?!" I replied that I not only didn't "get it," but I wondered what she meant by "real Indians"? What on earth, in 2006, was she teaching her children about American indigenous populations?

Then it hit me. For those few moments, I think I *felt* what it is like to be a Cherokee living with millions of tourists, day after day, week after week, year after year. I was dumbfounded by the racism and stereotyping with which I was angrily being confronted. I gave up, but I felt profoundly sad for that family, those children. I let them be in their strange little world.

The "drama" is no longer a drama. True to the promise of change, Bradley and the new CHA board have a show that is nonlinear and musical. It is much more "native," especially with the choreographic influence of Hanay Geiogamah (Kiowa, Delaware), one of the founders of the American Indian Dance Theatre, and the addition of specifically Cherokee characters. The seven clans are represented as masked ancestors. Ka'na'ti, the great hunter, and Selu, the corn mother, have been added and given the role of narrators or storytellers for the whole show. It is a very new entity, this new *Unto These Hills,* that still gives credit to the original author, Kermit Hunter, and goes on to be something completely unique. Having seen the former drama on numerous occasions, I found the new show very refreshing. It was remarkable to hear the Cherokee language spoken onstage by Cherokee performers. Gone from the old version is the overwhelming sense of morbidity and defeat. While portraying the historical facts surrounding the Trail of Tears, this show depicts the reunion of the Eastern Cherokee and the Cherokee Nation of Oklahoma at Red Clay, Georgia, in 1984.

OCONALUFTEE INDIAN VILLAGE

Many improvements are planned for the Oconaluftee Indian Village, another CHA enterprise and a major player in Cherokee tourism. Among them are new costumes, renovations to the Village's 50-year-old infrastructure, and updated material for each craft station. When I went on a tour of the Village in the summer of 2006, I found it enlivened with younger people in all of the stations alongside elders who had been there for, in some cases, decades. Every station was buzzing with activity, something I had not found in years past, and two busloads of tourists—one in front of the group I was with, one behind—were enjoying the tour and watching skilled Cherokee artisans make everything from beadwork and belts to baskets and pottery, to blowguns and darts and carved masks of the seven clans.

THE MUSEUM OF THE CHEROKEE INDIAN: SOME WELCOME ADDITIONS

I also returned to the museum to take the tour again and see if anything had changed there. I hadn't expected that it would have changed much, since the museum went through a radical remodeling in 1998 (discussed in chapter 5). The permanent collection is unchanged. However, I was pleased to see that the museum's directors have made additions that addressed some of the very critiques that I and numerous others had of the museum. There are now five new permanent exhibits at the end of the maze where everything stopped before. In the order in which they are encountered, they are:

- Boarding schools: This is one of the most tragic and delicate topics for American Indians. This exhibit has some explanations from the Eastern Cherokee viewpoint and a picture from the Carlisle Boarding School in Pennsylvania.
- Seven clans: This new display describes the known matrilineal clans of the Cherokee with paintings and words. While this is an excellent addition to the permanent collection, there is so much more to say about the clan system and its continued cultural importance.
- Stickball: This display offers a good explanation of the importance of *anetso* in the late nineteenth and early twentieth centuries. A photograph from that era is also available for viewing on the museum's website. Little is said about how the game is being played today.
- Dance: This display tells the visitor about numerous types of Cherokee dances, especially the Booger Dance. Eleven masks are on display to show the many representations of European Americans, African Americans, diseases, and satire that were conveyed through art and dance.
- Cherokee women: The role of women in Cherokee society from time immemorial to the present day is shown, with explanations of War Women and Beloved Women. Former principal chief Joyce Dugan, the first woman principal chief of the EBCN, is discussed.

These displays have some elements that change occasionally, and at least one person related having recently seen a display about tourism on the Bound-

7.3. Renovated entrance to Museum of the Cherokee Indian, Cherokee, North Carolina, 2006 (Author's photo)

ary. Beyond these much-needed displays, the museum is reaching out with special exhibitions. These represent a move toward making the museum a destination for traveling shows from across the nation. This alone will afford the people of the Boundary opportunities for education and aesthetic appreciation that they have not had before. In addition to the display floor, the museum is now offering classes in Cherokee language and Cherokee history and culture in connection with Western Carolina University's Cherokee Studies program.

BILLBOARDS: DRASTIC CHANGES
FOR AN OLD INSTITUTION

Another element discussed in chapter 2 was the change in billboard advertising that took place between 1996 and 1998, a period that marked the opening of Harrah's Cherokee Casino. Nothing points to changes that the ensuing decade has brought to the revitalization and renaissance of Cherokee lifeways more than these billboards. In the 1990s, some of the billboards hadn't been changed on the Boundary since at least the 1960s, and those that were new offered stereotypical representations of the touristic image of the "public Indian." In

2006, some of the old billboards for Oconaluftee Indian Village were still in place, but the advertisements were brand new. Bigger-than-life-size images of the new Cherokee dance troupe, the Warriors of AniKituhwa, are everywhere within a 100-mile radius of the Boundary. These dancers are depicted performing the Cherokee War Dance and the Eagle Tail Dance, in bright-red full-body paint. These pictures are at first startling, then intriguing. They invite the tourist into "Indian country" or "Cherokee country" to experience the real culture and people. The Warriors of AniKituhwa are one of the Museum of the Cherokee Indian's new community-outreach programs. The EBCN has designated the Warriors as their official cultural ambassadors (Duncan 2006), so it is appropriate that they should be the harbingers for a renaissance among their people.

CHIEFING REVISITED

While a whirlwind of change continues on the Boundary, one aspect of the tourist industry that is the most visible to the most tourists at any given time is chiefing. In June 2006 I spoke with four Cherokee men who were out early one day, even though it was a weekday and the weekday traffic for family and cultural tourism is very light. The most famous of these four men was Henry Lambert. I spoke with him about conditions for the work he had been involved in for the last 56 years.

> I started chiefin' at the age of 15 in 1950. It was easy back then, but I'll probably retire after the 2007 season because of my health. The biggest changes that happened here that have to do with chiefin' were in the 1980s. They [the BIA] instituted a trader's license, a vendor's license, for everyone who wanted to be a street chief. That was because too many people from other tribes were coming in to chief. They didn't know anything about chiefin' or about how to tell people directions to places. The tourist business has gone downhill. The heyday was the 1950s to the 1970s. Cars were bumper to bumper through the whole town from May to October. Now, look at it. Hardly anything. There just isn't anything for kids and teenagers of this generation to do. (Lambert 2006)

One of the other chiefs I spoke with that day, Chief Red Hawk (née Taylor), spoke eloquently about the current state of chiefing:

> I've been doing this for 10 years now. The biggest problem on the Boundary right now is from people switching tribal affiliation to Cherokee to get per cap checks. Maybe they were, I don't know, a Kiowa dad and

7.4. Still chiefing after all these years: "Chief" Henry Lambert, Cherokee, North Carolina, 2006 (Author's photo)

a Cherokee mom and had spent their whole life on a western rez, but now they go and switch over to Cherokee. It's legal. Hmmpph. As far as chiefin' goes, some non-Cherokee Indians are here dancing and chiefin' illegally. You know we have to have a license? Well, some don't and it takes away income from the legal chiefs and dancers. Until this season [2006] the BIA issued the license. Now, the tribe just took it over and the price quadrupled this year! (Taylor 2006)

As soon as a group of kids came out of the store that Chief Red Hawk was working in front of, he was no longer telling me about problems. He was, in an instant, a great entertainer. The kids asked questions rapid-fire: Do you go hunting? Do you live in a teepee? Are you a real Indian? He answered their questions one at a time and ended up with a little lesson in Cherokee history. "To be a Cherokee is great! Now, we never did live in teepees. That house is out west where they had to travel around a lot. We stayed here, in the mountains. We have seven clans: Wolf, Blue, Paint, Wild Potato, Long Hair, Bird, and Deer. Now, the clans are tied to the women, so when any of us boys get married, we have to make sure we're outside of our mother's clans" (Taylor 2006). The kids were amazed. They all had their picture taken with Chief Red Hawk before spotting another chief down the road in front of a huge teepee. The last thing we heard as they were walking away was, "Well, I bet that one isn't as good as Chief Red Hawk! Anyway, Cherokees don't live in teepees!" He looked very pleased.

LIFT CULTURE HOUSE AND
TRIBAL GROUNDS COFFEE SHOP

Perhaps the most innovative of the changes in the tourist scene is a spot named Tribal Grounds, which includes LIFT Culture House. Owned by enrolled member Natalie Smith and her partner, Leon Grodski, this establishment is in the building that was formerly the TeePee Restaurant. Natalie and Leon acquired the building when the proprietors of the TeePee let the lease lapse. Now, Tribal Grounds makes the best coffee in town, maybe the region, and brings contemporary, cutting-edge art to the Eastern Cherokee.

I interviewed Natalie and Leon on what turned out to be a very busy afternoon. While waiting for them, I sat in the room that had been the TeePee's large dining room. At the table next to me, a group of adult students from the Museum of the Cherokee Indian's language class were having coffee and playing Yahtzee—*in Cherokee*. Again, this trip is the first time in all these years that I heard the Cherokee language spoken casually outside a classroom in Cherokee, North Carolina. When Natalie and Leon finally joined me, they acknowledged that some people on the Boundary do not like the direction they are taking art. Those people think that "culture always means the 1800s or just baskets, pots, and carving." But, says Leon, "this is a revolutionary idea for this place." The opening art show for LIFT Culture House was an international show titled *FLIGHT*, which featured Yoko Ono's work. Leon went on to say that the first show "went as well as it could have gone," since the idea of a contemporary art gallery is very foreign to most Cherokees. But, this premiere and the following show, which featured Davy Arch, a well-respected local Cherokee woodcarver, enabled them to legitimize their business and themselves in the community. They see their space as a place for "everyday culture." And it is a real café. Their objective is to provide a place where people can "sit and chill and hang out . . . where no one is pushing you, no wait staff hovering for your table."

Natalie was born on the Boundary and studied art at Western Carolina University and Eastern Carolina University. Her goals for LIFT include becoming an institution of the tribe and being a transitional place for tourists to think about contemporary Cherokee lifeways; perhaps most importantly, however, she wants a public way to use her degree in art education. "I want to have workshops, hands-on stuff, for the entire community. I want this to be a place our people can be at home in public." Judging by the reviews LIFT has received, she appears to be on the way to achieving that goal.

A PAUSE, NOT A CONCLUSION

One might think that after 500 years of contact, forced removal, and being in sunder for 150 years, forcibly separated from language and tradition, and 100 years of someone else's economic plan, the Eastern Cherokee would be a downtrodden lot. The reality is, however, that they are thriving, bringing back their language, and keeping their cultural traditions alive. Because I haven't done so up to now, I offer the reader this view of the Great Smoky Mountains, beloved by the Eastern Cherokee.

The Great Smokies, at the southernmost end of the Appalachian range of mountains, are lush and verdant. Here are millions of acres of wilderness. These are places where cars cannot go, only creatures on foot or wing, as it has been since before humans found their way to this green place. There is a rhythm to life here in the mountains. It is unlike anything or anywhere else. The cyclical year dictates life patterns for the inhabitants of these mountains, both Cherokee and non-Cherokee, human and other, permanent and transient.

It is deep summer. Trees, as far as the eye can see, stretch out in every direction. Trees, from seedlings of evergreen pine and spruce, fir and cedar and mountain magnolia to virgin deciduous groves of huge poplars, giant red oaks and maple, are the medium used to paint every nuance of this landscape. Undulating hills fold upon each other so that each swell seems to repeat the one before and after it, like some ancient ocean frozen for a moment. Everything, everywhere, in the summer of the year, is green. From the mile-high tops of the evergreen-spiked peaks to those deciduous valley floors, the mountains roll from one green wave to the next. There is a hush in the Smoky Mountains that is unlike anywhere else. But the summer hush is not silence. Birds are constant in the vigilant watch over nest and young. Squealing black bear cubs and their ever-observant mothers slide down muddy embankments for the clear wa-

7.5. Natalie Smith and Leon Grodski, owners of LIFT Culture House and Tribal Grounds coffee shop, Cherokee, North Carolina, 2006 (Author's photo)

ter in the stream falling—sometimes with a roar—through rocks below them. Squirrels, chipmunks, rabbits, whitetail deer, wild turkeys, foxes, to name but a few, raise their young in their own voices in this secluded world.

When a crisp autumn chill rolls down into the valley floor around the first of October, though sometimes as early as late August, the annual spectacle of color is triggered. Like Dorothy's entry from the black-and-white world of Kansas into the multi-jeweled tones of Oz, green gives way to golds, reds, and oranges that appear lit from within. As summer yields to autumn, the sinuous waves of every shade of green become flames pouring up and down, over the mountains. Green stays, however. But only in the evergreen peaks and then only waiting for the snow and hoarfrost that will lay down a blanket from late November to mid-April. The darkness of the changing season comes on the mountains, a blanket that tells the hibernating creatures to gather up, grow fat, and turn in for the cold. Summer birds fly south, winter birds begin to arrive.

The mountains in winter are silent. Cold and icy, blue-white light reflects off of ice and snow. The stark figures of the sleeping hardwoods accentuate the silence. The only sounds are the occasional winter bird and that constant rush of water that comes off of the Appalachian heights. But even the water, so raucous throughout the year, is slowed by the chill of the short days and long starry nights. Some secluded valleys never see the sun in the season of darkness, and everything is in a state of repose. Huge boulders and rifted peaks are cleared of the multi-hued overcoat of the rest of the year, and it is possible to witness the sheer force of the earth's pushing up these mountains only to wear them away again over eons of wind and rain. Of the mammalian inhabitants that are not in hibernation, many have retreated far into the wilderness.

Then, with an inevitability as sure as the sunrise and the moonrise, spring comes on. The frozen water begins to drip in the lengthening sunlight of the new year. Snow melts to fuel the gushing streams and call to life trout that have been at rest in frigid, limpid pools. Summer birds begin their returns and the song of spring echoes with nest building and courtship. Spring brings yet another spectacle of color. This one is pink, white, yellow, purple, and the fresh new green of awakening plant life. Even the solid green of the pines, spruce, and cedar are enlivened as new growth in limey shades pushes through the verdant old growth. Black bears reappear with newborns and last year's cubs in tow. Graceful whitetail does peek out into burgeoning grassy meadows to watch for any danger as the bambies frolic and get their wobbly legs beneath them. Then, the cycle is complete. Once again, back to summer.

I'll end with the same Cherokee voice with whom I began. Freeman Owle is now an elder-in-residence at Western Carolina University with the Cherokee Studies program. He is a carver and a regular lecturer on Cherokee culture in the Southeast. When we met up in 2006, the first time we had talked at length since 1998, he said to me, "Welcome home." That meant more than I can find words to describe. On looking back at his comments from nearly a decade before, even he was surprised how correct he had been. So, I asked Freeman to comment on the here and now, circa 2006. "The Eastern Cherokee people have survived as a nation despite the cheating and deception of a European-based government. They [U.S. government] could only slow the drumbeats. Even while the language and culture was beaten out of us in the boarding schools, the beat of the drum, our Cherokee heartbeat, remained a constant. We have always valued a harmony ethic. That is something to live by, to take aggression and turn it into love. Many things are changing, for the better, and we have the chance to renew harmony, renew the *gadugi*, fix the balance and be true to ourselves and to our ancestors."

Notes

CHAPTER 1

1. For an exceptional discussion of the Trout Farm and fishing in general on the Boundary, see *Eastern Cherokee Fishing* by Heidi Altman (2006).

2. Currently, the "grease" is either lard or vegetable oil, although in pre-contact times it was bear grease.

3. I audited a Cherokee language class with Laura Pinnix, a Cherokee enrolled member, native, speaker, and teacher, through Western Carolina University.

4. The Cherokee term *uneg* means "white man" with every unpleasant connotation.

CHAPTER 2

1. Valene L. Smith's edited volume *Hosts and Guests* is generally considered the baseline study in anthropological tourism research. Originally published in 1977, its second edition was published in 1989 with an updated introduction.

2. The use of the word *tradition* here is in contrast to my references to "conservative" Cherokee lifeways, as defined by numerous authors (Finger 1991, 1995; French and Hornbuckle 1981; Gulick 1960; Leftwich 1970; Stucki 1981). I use *tradition* to describe cultural change, especially in the ways it shifts and changes from one generation to the next, as in Hobsbawm and Ranger (1983).

3. Archaeological records suggest a much longer occupation of peoples related to the Cherokee as well as occupations prior to the time of the Cherokee (Keel 1976).

4. An in-depth analysis of the reasons why the A-ni-Yu-n-wi-ya people accepted and took on the misnomer *Cherokee* has yet to be attempted. I suspect that colonialism, invasion, decimation by disease, and European intermarriage all worked together to turn the A-ni-Yu-n-wi-ya into the Cherokee.

5. In this section I haven't tried to separate the voices of the Welch sisters as they talked all at once, as family members are prone to do. The audiotape (archived in the Museum of the Cherokee Indian and the Cherokee Heritage Museum) bears this out well.

6. This will be discussed in chapter 4.

7. I make this statement because I cannot find the paper in any collection, published or unpublished. The author, at the time of our meeting a fit, fully cognizant 90-year-old, did not recall this particular paper.

8. For more detail see King 1979b; Finger 1984, 1991, 1995.

9. For the full account see Connor 1982; King 1979b; and Umberger 1970.

10. For many years there was also a venue called the Cyclorama in Painttown on Highway 19, the major east-west route through the Boundary. Although it had been closed for several years at the time of my fieldwork, the Cyclorama was a popular attraction from the 1960s to the 1980s.

11. Taking non-enrolled guests is an entitlement that enrolled members are extended by the Eastern Cherokee government. It meant a great deal to me that Lisa wanted to take me through the Village as her guest. We also attended the Drama this way.

12. Quotations here and below are from the official tour guide script used by employees of the Oconaluftee Indian Village. According to guides and workers, this script has been used since the Village opened in 1955.

13. Bull thistle, *Cirsium vulgare Tenore,* is an Eurasian weed that was accidentally introduced to the United States from Europe during the 1800s. It spread through North Carolina by airborne seed or by transport of seed-contaminated hay. A native North American example is often simply called prairie thistle; Flodman's thistle is found throughout North Dakota. Plants found in the northeastern—and presumably, the southeastern—United States have been introduced (McDonald 2002; Native Wildflowers of the North Dakota Grassland 2002).

14. For a complete explanation of the dyes, see Duggan 2005; S. H. Hill 1997; and Ruehl 1994.

15. Flint knapping is the means of producing stone arrowheads or spearheads. It involves chiseling or hammering something such as a stone so that it breaks into flakes (Soukhanov 1999:996).

16. "Traditional" arts and crafts are taught in the Cherokee school system in grades K–12. The young woman mentioned by Bushyhead might have been a weaver for a dozen years already by age 16 or 17.

17. I will discuss some of these venues and attractions at length in chapters 3 and 5.

CHAPTER 3

1. I will engage Patsy West's (1981, 1998) description of Seminole tourism later in this chapter.

2. See the front cover photograph of Matthew and the "chiefs."

3. The earliest mention of "domestic dependent nations" status was in the 1831 lawsuit *Cherokee Nation v. Georgia,* the outcome of which legally blocked the removal of the Cherokee from their lands in the Southeast to Indian Territory west of the Mississippi. President Andrew Jackson ignored the Supreme Court in this case.

4. Gordon Gray (University of North Carolina), Joffre Coe (University of North

Carolina, Charlotte), T. M. N. Lewis (University of Tennessee, Knoxville), Madeline Kneberg (University of Tennessee, Knoxville), and A. R. Kelly (University of Georgia) were the anthropologists, historians, and archaeologists who were involved in the Tsali Institute of Cherokee Research from the beginning of the Village project.

CHAPTER 4

1. For comprehensive ethnohistoric examinations of women's basket making and marketing on the Qualla Boundary see Speck 1920; S. H. Hill 1997; and Duggan 2005.

2. Some of those same baskets would now have a price tag of $900 or more (for doublewoven rivercane).

3. See Dickins (1976:25, Figure 10) for comparisons with contemporary pottery decoration.

4. I have chosen the term that Ruth Behar coined because of the delicate position I found myself in with the Eastern Cherokee. I was, indeed, a "vulnerable observer" as I was observed throughout my first six-week stay in North Carolina.

CHAPTER 5

1. In the epilogue I discuss the five cases that have been added to the permanent exhibit since my initial trips in the late 1990s.

2. Harrah's as a gambling business entity has 25 major casinos, at least one in every U.S. state where gambling is permitted (Harrah's 2001). In 2007 Harrah's was reportedly selling the casino to another gambling enterprise. This had not happened as of 2008.

CHAPTER 6

1. There are never more than twenty chiefs working the tourist strip. With twelve thousand or so inhabitants of the Boundary, this is less than 0.2 percent.

2. Other students included E. Pendleton Banks, Hester A. Davis, Raymond D. Fogelson, Annie Cofield Gardner, John L. Grant, Charles H. Holzinger, Harriet J. Kupferer, R. Paul Kutsche Jr., and J. Earl Somers.

3. See especially Babcock 1994; Chambers 2000; Desmond 1999; Hill 2001; Johnson and Underiner 2001; and P. West 1998.

Bibliography

Abram, Christa

1998   Personal interview with the author, April.

Abram, R. Michael

1998   Personal interview with the author, March.

2003   Personal interview with the author, December.

Abram, Susan M.

1997   Going for Broke: Jackpot or Craps? The Cherokee Casino and Effect of
        the Community of Cherokee, North Carolina. n.d. Independent Study/AN
        481-02 directed by Dr. Anne Rogers.

1998   Personal interview with the author, March.

Adair, James

1775   *The History of the American Indians.* Edward and Charles Dilly, London.

Adams, Kathleen M.

1995   Making-Up the Toraja? The Appropriation of Tourism, Anthropology, and
        Museums for Politics in Upland Sulawesi, Indonesia. *Ethnology* 34(2):143–153.

Albers, Patricia, and William James

1983   Tourism and the Changing Photographic Image of the Great Lakes Indians.
        Annals of Tourism Research 10:123–148.

Allison, Sally

1998   Personal interview with the author, March.

Altman, Heidi

2006   *Eastern Cherokee Fishing.* University of Alabama Press, Tuscaloosa.

Anderson, David G., and Kenneth E. Sassaman (editors)

1996   *The Paleoindian and Early Archaic Southeast.* University of Alabama Press,
        Tuscaloosa.

Arch, Davy

2006   Personal interview with the author, October.

Asheville Citizen-Times

1950   Editorial: "On 'Unto These Hills.'" 30 May:12.

1997   Dugan's Overcome Odds to Lead Tribe to New Heights. 10 November:A1.

Babcock, Barbara

1990   "A New Mexican Rebecca": Imaging Pueblo Women. *Journal of the Southwest* 32(4):400–437.

1994   Mudwomen and Whitemen. In *Discovered Country: Tourism and Survival in the American West*, edited by Scott Norris, pp. 180–195. Stone Ladder Press, Albuquerque.

Bartram, William

1955   *Travels of William Bartram.* Edited by Mark Van Doren. Dover, New York.
[1791]

Baudrillard, Jean

1988   *America.* Translated by Chris Turner. Verso, London.

Behar, Ruth

1996   *The Vulnerable Observer: Anthropology That Breaks Your Heart.* Beacon Press, Boston.

Bender, Margaret

1996   Reading Culture: The Cherokee Syllabary and the Eastern Cherokees, 1993–1995. Dissertation presented to the Graduate School, University of Chicago.

Berkhofer, Robert F., Jr.

1978   *The White Man's Indian: Images of the American Indian from Columbus to the Present.* Knopf, New York.

Berman, Tressa

2003   *Circle of Goods: Women, Work, and Welfare in a Reservation Community.* SUNY Press, Albany, New York.

Besculides, Antonia, Martha E. Lee, and Peter J. McCormick

2002   Residents' Perceptions of the Cultural Benefits of Tourism. *Annals of Tourism Research* 29:303–319.

Biolsi, Thomas, and Larry J. Zimmerman (editors)

1997   *Indians and Anthropologists: Vine Deloria Jr. and the Critique of Anthropology.* University of Arizona Press, Tucson.

Bird, James

1998   More on Language Immersion. *Cherokee One Feather* 16 July:4.

Blankenship, Bob

1992   *Cherokee Roots.* 2 vols. 2nd ed. Cherokee Roots Publishing, Cherokee, North Carolina.

1994   *Dawes Role Plus of the Cherokee Nation.* Cherokee Roots Publishing, Cherokee, North Carolina.

Blankenship, Mollie

1987   History. In *Contemporary Artists and Craftsmen of the Eastern Band of Cherokee Indians: Promotional Exhibitions, 1969–1985*, pp. i–ii. Organized by the Indian Arts and Crafts Board in cooperation with Qualla Arts and Crafts Mutual, Cherokee, North Carolina.

Bolles, A. Lynn

1997   Women as a Category of Analysis in Scholarship on Tourism: Jamaican Women and Tourism Employment. In *Tourism and Culture: An Ap-*

plied Perspective, edited by Erve Chambers, pp. 77–92. SUNY Press, Albany, New York.

Bone, Dakota

1997a   Dear Editor. *Cherokee One Feather* 10 September:2.

1997b   Letter to the Editor: Very Frustrated. *Cherokee One Feather* 27 August:2.

Bowden, Charles

1994   A Wave of the Hand. In *Discovered Country: Tourism and Survival in the American West,* edited by Scott Norris, pp. 227–247. Stone Ladder Press, Albuquerque.

Bradley, James

2006   Personal interview with the author, June.

Brewer, T. F., and J. Baillie

1991   The Journal of George Pawley's 1746 Agency to the Cherokee. *Journal of Cherokee Studies* 16:2–22.

Brown, Jane L.

1999   Steadfast and Changing: The Apparent Paradox of Cherokee Kinship. *Journal of Cherokee Studies* 20:28–49.

Bruner, Edward M., and Barbara Kirshenblatt-Gimblett

1994   Maasai on the Lawn: Tourist Realism in East Africa. *Cultural Anthropology* 9(4):435–470.

Bryman, Alan

2004   *The Disneyization of Society.* Sage, London.

Burt, Jesse, and Robert B. Ferguson

1973   *Indians of the Southeast: Then and Now.* Abingdon Press, Nashville and New York.

Bushyhead, Shana

1998   Personal interview with the author, July.

Butler, R. W.

1980   The Concept of a Tourist Area Cycle of Evolution: Implications for Management of Resources. *Canadian Geographer* 24:5–12.

Capone, Patricia

1998   The Wright Collection of Southwestern Pottery: Perspectives on Pottery Making and Collecting. In *Makers and Markets: The Wright Collection of Twentieth-Century Native American Art,* edited by Penelope Ballard Drooker, pp. 35–84. Peabody Museum Press, Harvard University, Cambridge.

Carter, Kevin

2002   Cherokee Keeps Culture, Expands Horizons. *Mountain Travel Guide,* published by *Asheville Citizen-Times,* Spring/Summer Edition:8.

Caton, J. L.

1937   *The Cher. Indians of the Qualla Reservation, Cherokee, NC.* Knoxville.

1937   *The Eastern Cherokee: Their History and How They Live Today.* Knoxville.

Chambers, Erve

2000   *Native Tours: The Anthropology of Travel and Tourism.* Waveland Press, Prospect Heights, Illinois.

Chambers, Erve (editor)

1997 *Tourism and Culture: An Applied Perspective.* SUNY Press, Albany, New York.

Chapman, Jefferson

1985 *Tellico Archaeology: 12,000 Years of Native American History.* University of Tennessee Press, Knoxville.

Cherokee Indian Fair Committee

1998 *86th Annual Cherokee Indian Fair, October 6–9, 1998.* Cherokee Indian Fair Committee, Cherokee, North Carolina.

Cherokee Nation v. Georgia

1831 30 U.S. (5 Pet.) 1, 17.

Cherokee One Feather

1997a Cherokee People Celebrate Return to Mound. 8 October:1.

1997b Casino Opens November 13, No Later. 3 September:1.

1997c Smokies July Travel Sets New Record. 20 August:1

1997d Park Visitation Down for June. 30 July:1.

1997e Granite Trough Donated to Museum. 7 May:3, 14.

1998 Gambling Money to Help Restore Cherokee Language. 25 June:3.

Cherokee Trails Newsletter

2000 Electronic document, http://rosecity.net/cherokee_trails_newsletter/october_2000.html, accessed June 2002.

Cherokee Tribal Travel and Promotion

1991 *Cherokee Indian Reservation, North Carolina: Official Vacation Guide and Directory.* Cherokee Tribal Travel and Promotion, Cherokee, North Carolina.

1992 *Cherokee Indian Reservation, North Carolina: Official Vacation Guide and Directory.* Cherokee Tribal Travel and Promotion, Cherokee, North Carolina.

1993 *Cherokee Indian Reservation, North Carolina: Official Vacation Guide and Directory.* Cherokee Tribal Travel and Promotion, Cherokee, North Carolina.

1994 *Cherokee Indian Reservation, North Carolina: Official Vacation Guide and Directory.* Cherokee Tribal Travel and Promotion, Cherokee, North Carolina.

1996 *Cherokee Indian Reservation.* Tourist newspaper. Cherokee Tribal Travel and Promotion, Cherokee, North Carolina.

1997 *Cherokee Indian Reservation, North Carolina: Official Vacation Guide and Directory.* Cherokee Tribal Travel and Promotion, Cherokee, North Carolina.

Chhabra, Deepak, Robert Healy, and Erin Sills

2003 Staged Authenticity and Heritage Tourism. *Annals of Tourism Research* 30:702–719.

Chiltoskey, G. B.

1996 Personal interview with the author, January.

Chiltoskey, Mary Ulmer

1972 *Cherokee Words with Pictures.* Self-published by Mary Ulmer and G. B. Chiltoskey, Cherokee, North Carolina.

1995 *Cherokee Fair and Festival: A History thru 1978.* Gilbert Printing, Asheville, North Carolina.

Chiltoskey, Mary Ulmer (guest editor)

1986   *Now and Then: Cherokees.* Center for Appalachian Studies and Services/
        Institute for Appalachian Affairs. East Tennessee State University, Johnson
        City, Tennessee 3(3).

Chiltoskey, Mary Ulmer, and Samuel E. Beck (editors)

1951   *Cherokee Cooklore: To Make My Bread.* Self-published by Mary Ulmer and
        G. B. Chiltoskey, Cherokee, North Carolina.

Chiltoskie, Bertha

1998   Personal interview with the author, March.

Clifford, James

1997   *Routes: Travel and Translation in the Late Twentieth Century.* Harvard Uni-
        versity Press, Cambridge.

Coin, Owen

1998   Smoky Mountain Host Renews Partnerships in Western North Carolina.
        Cherokee One Feather 10 June:2.

Colonial Williamsburg

1997   Colonial Williamsburg. Electronic document, http://www.history.org,
        accessed September 2007.

Connor, William P., Jr.

1982   *History of Cherokee Historical Association, 1946–1982.* Cherokee Historical
        Society, Cherokee, North Carolina.

Cucumber, Ariane

1998   Personal interview with the author, May.

Cypher, Jennifer, and Eric Higgs

1999   Journey into the Imagination. Electronic document, http://www.ethics.ubc.
        ca/papers/invited/cypher-higgs.html. University of British Columbia, Van-
        couver, accessed October 2006.

Davis, Tracy, and Sandy Wall

1997   Casino Draws Big Money, Big Dreams: Cherokee Gambling Complex
        to Bring Jobs, Tourists, Questions. *Asheville Citizen-Times* 26 October:1,
        8–9.

Debo, Angie

1966   *And Still the Waters Run.* Gordian Press, New York.

Deitch, Lewis I.

1977   The Impact of Tourism upon the Art and Crafts of the Indians of the
        Southwestern United States. In *Hosts and Guests: The Anthropology of Tour-
        ism,* edited by Valene L. Smith, pp. 223–236. University of Pennsylvania
        Press, Philadelphia.

Deloria, Vine, Jr.

1992   American Indians. In *Multiculturalism in the United States: A Comparative
        Guide to Acculturation and Ethnicity,* edited by John D. Buenker and Lorman
        A. Ratner, pp. 31–52. Greenwood Press, Westport, Connecticut.

1997   Conclusion: Anthros, Indians, and Planetary Reality. In *Indians and Anthro-
        pologists: Vine Deloria Jr. and the Critique of Anthropology,* edited by Thomas

Biolsi and Larry J. Zimmerman, pp. 209–222. University of Arizona Press, Tucson.

Desmond, Jane
1999   *Staging Tourism: Bodies on Display from Waikiki to Sea World.* University of Chicago Press, Chicago.

Dickins, Roy S.
1976   *Cherokee Prehistory: The Pisgah Phase in the Appalachian Summit Region.* University of Tennessee Press, Knoxville.

Digance, Justine
2003   Pilgrimage at Contested Sites. *Annals of Tourism Research* 30:143–159.

Divisekera, Sarath
2003   A Model of Demand for International Tourism. *Annals of Tourism Research* 30:31–49.

Dominguez, Virginia
1986   *White by Definition: Social Classification in Creole Louisiana.* Rutgers University Press, New Brunswick, New Jersey.

Dorwin, Pat
1997   Gamblers: Casino Is Entertainment. *The Mountain Press* 30 October:1–2. Gatlinburg, Tennessee.

Douthit, Margie E.
1998   Personal interview with the author, February.

Dugan, Joyce Conseen
1997   Return Home: Reclamations of Our Heritage at Kituwah Mound. *Cherokee One Feather* 15 October:1.

Duggan, Betty J.
1997   Tourism, Cultural Authenticity, and the Native Crafts Cooperative: The Eastern Cherokee Experience. In *Tourism and Culture: An Applied Perspective,* edited by Erve Chambers, pp. 31–57. SUNY Press, Albany, New York.

1998   Being Cherokee in a White World: The Ethnic Persistence of a Post-Removal American Indian Enclave. Ph.D. dissertation, University of Tennessee, Knoxville.

2002a   Voices from the Periphery: Reconstructing and Interpreting Post-Removal Histories of the Duck Town Cherokees. In *Southern Indians and Anthropologists: Culture, Politics, and Identity,* edited by Lisa J. Lefler and Frederic W. Gleach, pp. 43–68. University of Georgia, Athens.

2002b   The Eastern Cherokees in Southern Appalachia: Principal People, Persistent People. In *Appalachia: Social Context Past and Present,* edited by Phillip J. Overmiller and Michael E. Maloney, pp. 80–100. 4th ed. Kendall/Hunt, Dubuque, Iowa.

2005   Baskets of the Southeast. In *By Native Hands: Woven Treasures from the Lauren Rogers Museum of Art,* edited by Jill R. Chancey, pp. 26–75. Lauren Rogers Museum of Art, Laurel, Mississippi.

Duggan, Betty J., and Brett H. Riggs
1991   Cherokee Basketry: An Evolving Tradition. In *Studies in Cherokee Basketry,*

edited by B. J. Duggan and B. H. Riggs, pp. 1–10. Frank H. McClung Museum, University of Tennessee, Knoxville.

Duncan, Barbara R.

2006   Personal interview with the author, June.

Duncan, Barbara R. (compiler and editor)

1998   *Living Stories of the Cherokee: With Stories Told by Davey Arch, Robert Bushyhead, Edna Chekelelee, Marie Junaluska, Kathi Smith Littlejohn, and Freeman Owle.* University of North Carolina Press, Chapel Hill.

Duncan, Dolores

1998   Coyote . . . *Cherokee One Feather* 4 January:2.

Dykeman, Wilma, and Stokely Dykeman

1978   *Appalachian Mountains.* Illustrated by Clyde H. Smith. Graphic Arts Center, Portland.

Echtner, Charlotte M., and Pushkala Prasad

2003   The Context of Third World Tourism Marketing. *Annals of Tourism Research* 30:660–683.

Ellison, Quinton

1997   Cherokee Betting on Harrah's History, Industry Record. *Asheville Citizen-Times* 26 October:8.

Errington, Frederick, and Deborah Gewertz

1989   Tourism and Anthropology in a Post-Modern World. *Oceania* 60:37–55.

1991   *Twisted Histories, Altered Contexts: Representing the Chambri in a World System.* Cambridge University Press, Cambridge and New York.

Finger, John R.

1983   Introduction. In *The Cherokees of the Smoky Mountains* [1936] Horace Kephart, [no press given] Cherokee, North Carolina.

1984   *The Eastern Band of Cherokees, 1819–1900.* University of Tennessee Press, Knoxville.

1991   *Cherokee Americans: The Eastern Band of Cherokees in the Twentieth Century.* University of Nebraska Press, Lincoln.

1995   Cherokee Accommodation and Persistence in the Southern Appalachians. In *Appalachia in the Making,* edited by Mary Beth Pudup, Dwight B. Billings, and Altina L Waller, pp. 21–38. University of North Carolina Press, Chapel Hill.

2001   *Tennessee Frontiers: Three Regions in Transition.* Indiana University Press, Bloomington.

Fogelson, Raymond D.

1960   Change, Persistence, and Accommodation in Cherokee Medico-Magical Beliefs. In *Symposium on Cherokee and Iroquois Culture,* edited by William N. Fenton and John Gulick, pp. 213–226. Smithsonian Institution Bureau of American Ethnology, Bulletin 180, Washington, D.C.

1962   The Cherokee Ball Game: A Study in Southeastern Ethnology. Unpublished Ph.D. dissertation, University of Pennsylvania.

1977   Cherokee Notions of Power. In *The Anthropology of Power: Ethnographic*

Studies from Asia, Oceania, and the New World, edited by Raymond D. Fogelson and Richard N. Adams, pp. 185–194. Academic Press, New York.

1983   Cherokee Booger Mask Tradition. In *The Power of Symbols: Masks and Masquerade in the Americas,* edited by N. Ross Crumrine and Marjorie Halpin, pp. 70–83. University of British Columbia Press, Vancouver.

1992   On the "Petticoat Government" of the Eighteenth Century Cherokee. In *Personality and the Cultural Construction of Society: Papers in Honor of Melford E. Spiro,* edited by D. K. Jordan and M. J. Swartz, pp. 161–181. University of Alabama Press, Tuscaloosa.

1998   Perspectives on Native American Identity. In *Studying Native America: Problems and Prospects,* edited by Russell Thornton, pp. 40–59. University of Wisconsin Press, Madison.

2001   Foreword. In *Anthropologists and Indians in the New South,* edited by Rachel A. Bonney and J. Anthony Paredes, pp. ix–x. University of Alabama Press, Tuscaloosa.

Fogelson, Raymond, and Paul Kutsche
1961   Cherokee Economic Cooperatives: The Gadugi. In *Symposium on Cherokee and Iroquois Culture,* edited by William N. Fenton and John Gulick, pp. 83–124. Smithsonian Institution Bureau of American Ethnology, Bulletin 180, Washington, D.C.

Foght, Harold
1935   Letter to John Collier, January 10, 1935. In Records of the Bureau of Indian Affairs, Record Group 75, Cherokee Agency, Series 6, Box 9 of 89 Boxes. U.S. Federal Records Center, East Point, Georgia.

Foster, Martha Harroun
1995   Lost Women of the Matriarch: Iroquois Women in the Historical Literature. *American Indian Culture and Research Journal* 19(3):121–140.

Frankenburg, Ruth
1993   *White Women, Race Matters: The Social Construction of Whiteness.* University of Minnesota Press, Minneapolis.

French, Laurence A.
1998   *The Qualla Cherokee: Surviving in Two Worlds.* Edwin Mellen Press, Lewiston, New York.

French, Laurence A., and Jim Hornbuckle
1981   *The Cherokee Perspective.* Appalachian Consortium Press, Boone, North Carolina.

Friday, Susan
1998   Saving Grace: Father-Daughter Team Work to Preserve Cherokee Dialect. Reprinted from *Southern Living Magazine. Cherokee One Feather* 1 April:1, 3.

Frome, Michael
1980   *Strangers in High Places: The Story of the Great Smoky Mountains.* 1966. University of Tennessee Press, Knoxville.

Fusco, Coco
1995   The Other History of Intercultural Performance. In *English Is Broken*

Here: Notes on Cultural Fusion in the Americas, pp. 37–64. New Press, New York.

Giese, Paula

1996 Bandolier Bags. Electronic document, http://www.kstrom.net/isk/art/beads/bando1.html, accessed March 2004.

Gómez, Arthur R.

1994 *Quest for the Golden Circle: The Four Corners and the Metropolitan West: 1945–1970.* University of New Mexico Press, Albuquerque.

Goodwin, Gary

1977 *Cherokees in Transition.* University of Chicago, Department of Geography, Chicago.

Graburn, Nelson H. H.

1977 Tourism: The Sacred Journey. In *Hosts and Guests: The Anthropology of Tourism,* edited by Valene L. Smith, pp. 21–36. University of Pennsylvania Press, Philadelphia.

1980 Teaching the Anthropology of Tourism. *International Social Science Journal* 32:56–68.

1983 The Anthropology of Tourism. *Annals of Tourism Research* 10:9–33.

Great Smoky Mountains National Park

2002 Rod's Guide to the North Carolina and Tennessee Smoky Mountains. Electronic document, http://www.rodsguide.com/cherokee_ocona.html, accessed June 2002.

Greenbaum, Susan

1991 What's in a Label? Identity Problems of Southern Indian Tribes. *Journal of Ethnic Studies* 19(2):107–126.

Grodski, Leon

2006 Personal interview with the author, October.

Grünewald, Rodrigo de Azeredo

2002 Tourism and Cultural Revival. *Annals of Tourism Research* 29:1004–1021.

Gulick, John

1958 Problems of Cultural Communication: The Eastern Cherokees. *American Indian* 8(1):20–30.

1960 *Cherokees at the Crossroads.* Institute for Research in Social Science, University of North Carolina Press, Chapel Hill.

Hamel, Paul B., and Mary U. Chiltoskey

1975 *Cherokee Plants and Their Uses: A 400-Year History.* Self-published, Cherokee, North Carolina.

Harlan, Birdie Lynne

1998 Personal interview with the author, April.

Harrah's

2001 Harrah's Casino homepage. Electronic document, http://www.harrahs.com/home_flash/index2.html, accessed October 2003.

2002 Harrah's Cherokee Casino homepage. Electronic document, http://www.harrahs.com/our_casinos/che/index.html, accessed October 2003.

Hatley, Thomas

1991   Cherokee Women Farmers Hold Their Ground. In *Appalachian Frontiers: Settlement, Society and Development in the Preindustrial Era,* edited by Robert D. Mitchell, pp. 37–54. University Press of Kentucky, Lexington.

Haywood, John

1973   *Natural and Aboriginal History of Tennessee, up to the First Settlement Therein*
[1823]   *by the White People, in the Year 1768.* F. M. Hill Books, Nashville.

Hickman, Bryan

1992   Cherokee Stomp Dance. Electronic document, http://www.manataka.org/page612.html, accessed January 2004.

Hill, Sarah H.

1997   *Weaving New Worlds: Southeastern Cherokee Women and Their Basketry.* University of North Carolina Press, Chapel Hill.

2001   Marketing Traditions: Cherokee Basketry and Tourist Economics. In *Selling the Indian: Commercializing and Appropriating American Indian Cultures,* edited by Carter Jones Meyer and Diana Royer, pp. 212–235. University of Arizona Press, Tucson.

Hill, Thomas

1997   Taking Business Elsewhere. *Cherokee One Feather* 23 April:2.

Hipps, Barry

1998   Personal interview with the author, February.

Hobsbawm, Eric, and Terence Ranger

1983   *The Invention of Tradition.* Cambridge University Press, Cambridge.

Hollinshead, Keith

1991   "White" Gaze, "Red" People: Shadow Visions: The Disidentification of "Indians" in Cultural Tourism. *Leisure Studies* 11(1):43–64.

Hornbuckle, Molly

1998   Personal interview with the author, May.

Indian Health Service

2001   Press Package. Department of Health and Human Services, Washington, D.C.

Isikoff, Michael, and Evan Thomas

1998   Clinton and the Intern. *Newsweek* February 2:18.

Jackson, Gilliam

1975   Cultural Identity for the Modern Cherokees. *Appalachian Journal* 2:280–83.

Jacobs, Harvey

1997   Reactions. *Cherokee One Feather* 24 September:2.

[Jennifer]

1998   Personal interview with the author, April.

Johnson, Katie N., and Tamara Underiner

2001   Command Performances: Staging Native Americans at Tillicum Village. In *Selling the Indian: Commercializing and Appropriating American Indian Cultures,* edited by Carter Jones Meyer and Diana Royer, pp. 44–61. University of Arizona Press, Tucson.

Johnson, Sir William

1757   Journal of Sir William Johnson's Proceedings with the Indians, 31 July–20
        September, 1757. Box 7, volume 4, William Johnson Papers, New York State
        Library.

1768   Proceedings of Sir William Johnson with the Indians, 4–12 March, 1786.
        Box 35, volume 26, William Johnson Papers, New York State Library.

Kafka, Franz

1983   A Report to an Academy. In *The Complete Stories and Parables,* edited by
        Nabum N. Glatzer, pp. 250–259. Quality Paperback Book Club, New York.

Kaplan, Caren

1996   *Questions of Travel: Postmodern Discourses of Displacement.* Duke University
        Press, Durham, North Carolina.

Keel, Bennie C.

1976   *Cherokee Archaeology: A Study of the Appalachian Summit.* University of Ten-
        nessee Press, Knoxville.

Kehoe, Alice Beck

1983   The Shackles of Tradition. In *The Hidden Half: Studies of Plains Indian
        Women,* edited by Patricia Albers and Beatrice Medicine, pp. 48–64. Uni-
        versity Press of America, Lanham, Maryland.

1995   Blackfoot Persons. In *Women and Power in Native North America,* edited by
        Laura Klein and Lillian Ackerman, pp. 113–125. University of Oklahoma
        Press, Norman.

2002   *America before the European Invasions.* Longman Press, New York.

2005   *The Kensington Runestone: Approaching a Research Question Holistically.*
        Waveland Press, Long Grove, Illinois.

Kephart, Horace

1983   *The Cherokees of the Smoky Mountains: A Little Band That Has Stood against
[1936]   the White Tide for Three Hundred Years.* New introduction by John R. Finger.
        N.p., Cherokee, North Carolina.

King, Duane H.

1977   Lessons in Cherokee Ethnology from the "Captivity of Joseph Brown,
        1788–1789." *Journal of the Cherokee Indian* 2(2):219–229.

1979a   Introduction. In *The Cherokee Indian Nation: A Troubled History,* edited by
        Duane H. King, pp. ix–xix. University of Tennessee Press, Knoxville.

1979b   The Origin of the Eastern Cherokees as a Social and Political Entity. In
        The Cherokee Indian Nation: A Troubled History, edited by Duane H. King,
        pp. 164–180. University of Tennessee Press, Knoxville.

Kinnaird, Vivian, and Derek Hall (editors)

1994   *Tourism: A Gender Analysis.* Wiley, Chichester.

Klein, Herbert S., and Daniel C. Schiffner

2003   The Current Debate about the Origins of the Paleoindians of America.
        Journal of Social History 37(2):483–494.

Knight, Vernon James

2008   Moundville Archaeological Park. Electronic document, http://www.ua.edu/
        academic/museums/moundville/home.html, accessed April 9, 2008.

Kupferer, Harriet Jane

1961   The "Principal People," 1960: A Study of Cultural and Social Groups of the
        Eastern Cherokee. Smithsonian Institution, Bureau of American Ethnology
        Bulletin 196, Papers 78, pp. 215–325. Government Printing Office, Wash-
        ington, D.C.

1968   The Isolated Eastern Cherokee. In The American Indian Today, edited by
        Stuart Levine and Nancy Oestreich Lurie, pp. 66–78. Everett Edwards,
        Deland, Florida.

Kurtz, Paul

1995   The Disneyfication of America. Free Inquiry 15(4):5–9.

Lambert, Henry

2006   Personal interview with the author, October.

Leftwich, Rodney L.

1970   Arts and Crafts of the Cherokee. Cherokee Publications, Cherokee, North
        Carolina.

Lesiak, Christine, and Matthew Jones (producers)

1991   In the White Man's Image. Produced for The American Experience series, PBS.

Lett, James W.

1987   The Human Enterprise: A Critical Introduction to Anthropological Theory.
        Westview Press, Boulder, Colorado.

Lewis, T. M. N., and Madeline Kneberg

1954   Oconaluftee Indian Village: An Interpretation of a Cherokee Community of 1750.
        Cherokee Historical Association, Cherokee, North Carolina.

Littlejohn, Jonathon Dwight

1997   Authoritarian and Totalitarianism. Cherokee One Feather 1 October:2.

1998   Experiencing Challenge. Cherokee One Feather 7 October:2.

Littlejohn, Kathi Smith

1998   Stories. In Living Stories of the Cherokee: With Stories Told by Davey Arch,
        Robert Bushyhead, Edna Chekelelee, Marie Junaluska, Kathi Smith Littlejohn,
        and Freeman Owle, compiled and edited by Barbara R. Duncan, pp. 4–6.
        University of North Carolina Press, Chapel Hill.

Living History Farms

2007   Travel through 300 Years of Iowa's Agricultural Heritage. Electronic docu-
        ment, http://www.lhf.org.

Long, Nancy R. [Old Nancy Longtongue]

1998a   Response to McCoy. Cherokee One Feather 7 October:2.

1998b   Second Class Citizens. Cherokee One Feather 25 June:2.

Lossiah, Donna Toineeta

1998   Personal interview with the author, May.

Loy, Wesley

1997   The Gamble. Knoxville News Sentinel, final edition, October 26:1, 12–13.

MacCannell, Dean

1973   Nonviolent Action as Theater: A Dramaturgical Analysis of 146 Demonstrations.
        Nonviolent Action Research Project of the Center for Nonviolent Conflict
        Resolution. Haverford College, Haverford, Pennsylvania.

1976   *The Tourist: A New Theory of the Leisure Class.* Macmillan, London.

1984   Reconstructed Ethnicity: Tourism and Cultural Identity in Third World Communities. *Annals of Tourism Research* 11:375–391.

1990   Cannibal Tours. *Society for Visual Anthropology Review* 6(2):14–24.

1992   *Empty Meeting Grounds: The Tourist Papers.* Routledge Press, New York.

1994   Tradition's Next Step. In *Discovered Country: Tourism and Survival in the American West,* edited by Scott Norris, pp. 161–179. Stone Ladder Press, Albuquerque.

Macionis, John J.

2002   *Society: The Basics.* 6th ed. Annotated instructors ed. Prentice Hall, Upper Saddle River, New Jersey.

Maney, Arnessa

1998   Personal interview with the author, March.

Mani, Lata, and Ruth Frankenberg

1985   The Challenge of Orientalism. *Economy and Society* 14(2):174–194.

Mankiller, Wilma

1993   *Mankiller: A Chief and Her People, An Autobiography by the Principal Chief of the Cherokee Nation.* With Michael Wallis. St. Martin's Press, New York.

Markwick, Marion

2001   Postcards from Malta: Image, Consumption, Context. *Annals of Tourism Research* 28:417–438.

Martin, Joseph

1996a   Opposing State Recognition. *Cherokee One Feather* 9 October:2.

1996b   Tribes Oppose State Recognition. *Cherokee One Feather* 9 October:1.

1997a   Tribe's Affairs Are Tribe's Business. *Cherokee One Feather* 29 October:2.

1997b   Do Experts Know Better? *Cherokee One Feather* 27 August:2.

1997c   The Dreaded Indian "S" Word. *Cherokee One Feather* 18 June:2.

1997d   Casino Ads, Legal or Not? *Cherokee One Feather* 2 April:2.

1998a   Enrollment Requirements Questioned in Council. *Cherokee One Feather* 16 September:1.

1998b   Tribe Markets Bottled Water. *Cherokee One Feather* 9 September:1.

1998c   Cultural Youth Dance Group: "Cherokee Dancers of Fire" Created by the Wildcats. *Cherokee One Feather* 22 July:3.

1998d   New Parkway Interpretive Station. *Cherokee One Feather* 22 July:11.

1998e   "Unto These Hills" Comes to Harrah's Cherokee. [Photo and short story] *Cherokee One Feather* 1 July:3.

1998f   Spring in the Smokies Attracts More Visitors. *Cherokee One Feather* 1 July:4.

1998g   Bigmeat-Maney Honored by State Folk Heritage Award Ceremony. *Cherokee One Feather* 10 June:1.

1998h   "Unto These Hills" Opens for 49th Summer Season. *Cherokee One Feather* 10 June:1.

1998i   Museum Visitors to See New Renovations. [Photo] *Cherokee One Feather* 10 June:3.

1998j   We Built It, Let Them Come. [Photo] *Cherokee One Feather* 10 June:8.

1998k   Museum Renovation. *Cherokee One Feather* 10 June:10.

1998l   Two Check Per Capita Passes: 18-Year-Olds Must Graduate or Wait until 21. *Cherokee One Feather* 3 June:1.

1998m   Appreciation for Locals. *Cherokee One Feather* 3 June:3.

1998n   Professional Boxing Comes to Cherokee. *Cherokee One Feather* 18 March:1.

1998o   Reporting Casino Revenues. *Cherokee One Feather* 18 March:2.

1998p   Government Functions Are No Place for Violence. *Cherokee One Feather* 18 February:2.

1998q   Indian Perspective Needed in Race Initiative. *Cherokee One Feather* 4 February:2.

1998r   Erwin's Controversy Continues. *Cherokee One Feather* 14 January:2.

Martini, Don

1989   *Inside the Smokies.* Covenant House Books, New York.

Mata, Ruth

1997a   To the Tribe. *Cherokee One Feather* 17 September:2.

1997b   To the Tribe. *Cherokee One Feather* 3 September:2.

1997c   To the Public. *Cherokee One Feather* 2 April:2.

Maybury-Lewis, David

2001   The Cultural Survival of Indigenous Peoples: Theoretical Problems and Practical Dilemmas. In *PLENARY: Indigenous Rights and Conflicts.* 2001 AES/CASCA/SCA Meetings, Montréal, Quebec, Canada. MS.

McCoy, Teresa

2006   Personal interview with the author, October.

McDonald, Richard

2002   Biological Control of the Bull Thistle, NCDA Plant Industry Division. Electronic document, http://ipmwww.ncsu.edu/ncda/bcbull.html, accessed June 2002.

McKie, Scott

1998a   Smokey Mountains Rumble II. *Cherokee One Feather* 18 November:1.

1998b   Miss Cherokee and Miss Teen Contestants Honored. *Cherokee One Feather* 7 October:1, 3.

McLaughlin, Renissa

1998   Language Class Needs Space. *Cherokee One Feather* 5 August:2.

McLoughlin, William G.

1986   *Cherokee Renascence in the New Republic.* Princeton University Press, Princeton.

Medicine, Beatrice

1978   *The Native American Woman: A Perspective.* National Educational Laboratory Publishers, Austin.

1980   Indian Women: Tribal Identity as Status Quo. In *Woman's Nature: Rationalizations of Inequality,* edited by Marian Lowe and Ruth Hubbard, pp. 63–74. The Athene Series, Pergamon Press, New York.

2001a   North American Indigenous Women and Cultural Domination. [1993]. In *Learning to Be an Anthropologist and Remaining "Native": Selected Writings,* edited by Beatrice Medicine with Sue-Ellen Jacobs, pp. 153–160. University of Illinois Press, Urbana and Chicago.

2001b   *Learning to Be an Anthropologist and Remaining "Native": Selected Writings.*
        Edited with Sue-Ellen Jacobs. University of Illinois Press, Urbana and
        Chicago.

Medina, Laurie Kroshus
2003   Commoditizing Culture: Tourism and Mayan Identity. *Annals of Tourism
        Research* 30:353–368.

Mihesuah, Devon A.
1995   *American Indians: Stereotypes and Realities.* Clarity Press, Atlanta.
1996   Commonality of Difference: American Indian Women and History.
        American Indian Quarterly 20(1):15–28.

Milner, George R.
2004   *The Moundbuilders: Ancient Peoples of Eastern North America.* Thames and
        Hudson, London.

Minnick, Nathaniel.
2006   Disney's Lands in the History of Colonial Displays of the Exotic. Unpub-
        lished paper, University of Michigan.

Mooney, James
1932   *The Swimmer Manuscript: Cherokee Sacred Formulas and Medicinal Prescrip-
        tions.* Revised, completed, and edited by Frans M. Olbrechts, Bureau of
        American Ethnology Bulletin 99, Washington, D.C.
1982   *Myths of the Cherokees and Sacred Formulas of the Cherokees.* Elder Booksellers,
[1891] Nashville, Tennessee.

Moore, David
1999   Cherokee Archaeology. North Carolina Archaeological Society. Electronic
        document, http://www.arch.dcr.state.nc.us/cherokee.htm, accessed March
        2001.

Moreno, Josephine, and Mary Ann Littrell
2001   Negotiating Tradition: Tourism Retailers in Guatemala. *Annals of Tourism
        Research* 28:658–685.

Museum of the Cherokee Indian
1999   Museum of the Cherokee Indian homepage. Electronic document,
        http://www.cherokeemuseum.org, accessed March 2000.

Narayan, Kirin
1996   How Native Is a "Native" Anthropologist? *American Anthropologist*
        95(3):671–687.

Nash, Dennison
1977   Tourism as a Form of Imperialism. In *Hosts and Guests: The Anthropology of
        Tourism,* edited by Valene L. Smith, pp. 37–54. University of Pennsylvania
        Press, Philadelphia.
1996   On Anthropologists and Tourists. *Annals of Tourism Research* 23:691–94.
2001   On Travelers, Ethnographers and Tourists. *Annals of Tourism Research*
        28:493–496.

National Park Service
1997   Outline of Prehistory and History, Southeastern North America and the

Caribbean. Southeast Archaeological Center, Washington, D.C. Electronic document, http://www.nps.gov/history/seac/misslate.htm, accessed April 2008.

2001a Paleoindian Archaeology. Electronic document, http://www.cr.nps.gov/seac/paleoind.htm, accessed March 2001.

2001b Archaic Indian Archaeology. Electronic document, http://www.cr.nps.gov/seac/archaic.htm, accessed March 2001.

2002 Great Smoky Mountains National Park Fishing. Electronic document, http://www.main.nc.us/gsmnp/fishing, accessed September 2003.

Nations, Vida

1998 Personal interview with the author, May.

Native American Chronological Timeline

2001 Electronic document, http://www.channel-e-philadelphia.com/natchronology.html, accessed March 2001.

NativeTech

2002a Finger Weaving. Electronic document, http://www.nativetech.org/finger/belts.html, accessed March 2002.

2002b Woven Wampum Beadwork: History and Background. Electronic document, http://www.nativetech.org/wampum/wamphist.html, accessed March 2002.

Native Wildflowers of the North Dakota Grassland

2002 USGS–Northern Prairie Wildlife Research Center. Electronic document, http://www.npwrc.usgs.gov/resource/literatr/wildflwr/species/cirsflod.htm, accessed June 2002.

Neely, Sharlotte

1979 Acculturation and Persistence among North Carolina's Eastern Band of Cherokee Indians. In *Southeastern Indians since the Removal Era,* edited by Walter L. Williams, pp. 201–230. University of Georgia Press, Athens.

1980 Forced Acculturation in the Eastern Cherokee Bureau of Indian Affairs Schools, 1892–1933. In *Contemporary Political Organizations of Native North America,* edited by Ernest L. Schuskey, pp. 85–106. University Press of America, Washington, D.C.

1991 *Snowbird Cherokee: People of Persistence.* University of Tennessee Press, Knoxville.

Norman, Geoffrey

1995 Two Nations, One People: The Cherokee. *National Geographic* 187(5):72–97.

Norris, Scott (editor)

1994 *Discovered Country: Tourism and Survival in the American West.* Stone Ladder Press, Albuquerque.

Nuñez, Theron

1977 Touristic Studies in Anthropological Perspective. In *Hosts and Guests: The Anthropology of Tourism,* edited by Valene L. Smith, pp. 265–274. University of Pennsylvania Press, Philadelphia.

Oconaluftee Indian Village

2000   Cherokee Tourist Attractions. Electronic document, http://www.cherokee-nc.com/Press%20Releases/oconaluftee_indian_village.htm, accessed June 2000.

O'Rourke, Dennis (producer and director)

1987   *Cannibal Tours.* Distributed by Direct Cinema, Los Angeles.

Orr, Eric

2003   Booger Dance. Electronic document, http://www.chattogariver.org/index.php?req=index&quart=F2003, accessed April 2006.

Owle, Freeman

1998a   Personal interview with the author, March.

1998b   The Earth. In *Living Stories of the Cherokee: With Stories Told by Davey Arch, Robert Bushyhead, Edna Chekelelee, Marie Junaluska, Kathi Smith Littlejohn, and Freeman Owle,* compiled and edited by Barbara R. Duncan, p. 75. University of North Carolina Press, Chapel Hill.

2006   Personal interview with the author, June.

Perdue, Theda

1979   *Slavery and the Evolution of Cherokee Society, 1540–1866.* University of Tennessee Press, Knoxville.

1983   *Cherokee Editor: The Writings of Elias Boudinot.* University of Tennessee Press, Knoxville.

1985   Southern Indians and the Cult of True Womanhood. In *The Web of Southern Social Relations: Women, Family, and Education,* edited by W. J. Fraser Jr., R. F. Saunders Jr., and J. L. Wakelyn, pp. 35–51. University of Georgia Press, Athens.

1995   Women, Men and American Indian Policy: The Cherokee Response to "Civilization." In *Negotiators of Change: Historical Perspectives on Native American Women,* edited by Nancy Shoemaker, pp. 91–114. Routledge, New York.

1998   *Cherokee Women: Gender and Culture Change, 1700–1835.* University of Nebraska Press, Lincoln.

Persico, V. Richard, Jr.

1979   Early Nineteenth-Century Cherokee Political Organization. In *The Cherokee Indian Nation: A Troubled History,* edited by Duane H. King, pp. 92–109. University of Tennessee Press, Knoxville.

Pierce, Daniel S.

2000   *The Great Smokies: From Natural Habitat to National Park.* University of Tennessee Press, Knoxville.

Pinnix, Laura

1998   Personal interview with the author, April.

Plane, Ann Marie

1996   Putting a Face on Colonization: Factionalism and Gender Politics in the Life History of Awashunkes, the "Squaw Sachem" of Saconnet. In *North-*

eastern Indian Lives, 1632–1816, edited by Robert S. Grumet, pp. 140–165. University of Massachusetts Press, Amherst.

Poria, Yaniv, Richard Butler, and David Airey

2003   The Core of Heritage Tourism. *Annals of Tourism Research* 30:238–254.

Povinelli, Elizabeth A.

1991   Organizing Women: Rhetoric, Economy, and Politics in Process among Australian Aborigines. In *Gender at the Crossroads of Knowledge: Feminist Anthropology in the Postmodern Era,* edited by Micaela di Leonardo, pp. 235–256. University of California Press, Berkeley.

Pretes, Michael

2003   Tourism and Nationalism. *Annals of Tourism Research* 30:125–142.

Price, Mark

2003   A Drama Threatened. *Charlotte Observer* June 22:1A.

Rajotte, Freda, and Ron Crocombe (editors)

1980   *Pacific Tourism: As Islanders See It.* The Institute of Pacific Studies of the University of the South Pacific in Association with the South Pacific Social Sciences Association, Honolulu.

Redfield, Robert

1989   *The Little Community.* University of Chicago Press, Chicago.
[1956]

Redman, David

1998   Personal interview with the author, March.

Reed, Marcelina

1993   *Seven Clans of the Cherokee Society.* Illustrated by William Taylor. Cherokee Publications, Cherokee, North Carolina.

Richmond, Stephen

1987   Introduction. In *Contemporary Artists and Craftsmen of the Eastern Band of Cherokee Indians: Promotional Exhibitions, 1969–1985,* pp. 1–7. Organized by the Indian Arts and Crafts Board in cooperation with Qualla Arts and Crafts Mutual, Cherokee, North Carolina.

Riggs, Brett H.

1997   The Significance of Kituwah Mound Site to the Eastern Band of Cherokee Indians. *Cherokee One Feather* 15 October:1, 5.

1999   Removal Period Cherokee Households in Southwestern North Carolina: Material Perspectives on Ethnicity and Cultural Differentiation. Unpublished Ph.D. dissertation, University of Tennessee, Knoxville.

Riggs, Brett H., and Chris Rodning

2002   Cherokee Ceramic Traditions of Southwestern North Carolina, ca. A.D. 1400–2002: A Preface to "The Last of the Iroquois Potters." *North Carolina Archaeology* 51:34–54.

Riggs, Brett H., and M. Scott Shumate

2003a   Archaeological Investigations at the Lemmons Branch Site (31SW365), a Probable Post-Removal Cherokee Farmstead in Swain County, North Carolina. Research Laboratories of Archaeology, Chapel Hill, North

Carolina. Submitted to the Tennessee Valley Authority, Norris, Tennessee.

2003b   Archaeological Testing at Kituhwa. Research Laboratories of Archaeology, Chapel Hill, North Carolina. Submitted to the Eastern Band of Cherokee Indians Cultural Resources Program.

[Robert]

2006   Personal interview with the author, June.

Rodriguez, Sylvia

1994   Art, Tourism, and Race Relations in Taos. *Discovered Country: Tourism and Survival in the American West,* edited by Scott Norris, pp. 143–160. Stone Ladder Press, Albuquerque.

Rojek, Chris, and John Urry

1997   *Touring Cultures: Transformations of Travel and Theory.* Routledge Press, London.

Romans, Van

1999   Introduction: Museum of the Cherokee Indian. Electronic document, http://www.cherokeemuseum.org, accessed March 2003.

Rose, Wendy

1992   The Great Pretenders: Further Reflections on Whiteshamanism. In *The State of Native America: Genocide, Colonization, and Resistance,* edited by M. Annette Jaimes, pp. 403–420. South End Press, Boston.

Rossel, Pierre

1988   Tourism and Cultural Minorities: Double Marginalisation and Survival Strategies. In *Tourism: Manufacturing the Exotic,* edited by Pierre Rossel, pp. 23–48. International Work Group for Indigenous Affairs, Copenhagen.

Rowell, Rosalie

1997   Racism Hurts Tourism. *Cherokee One Feather* 21 May:2.

Royce, Charles C.

1887   "The Cherokee Nation of Indians: A Narrative of Their Official Relations with the Colonial and Federal Government." *U.S. Bureau of American Ethnology. Fifth Annual Report, 1883–84,* pp. 121–378, plates VII–IX (maps). Washington, D.C.

Ruehl, Ronald (director)

1994   *The Qualla Arts and Crafts Cooperative: The Basket Weavers.* Produced in conjunction with The Eastern Band of Cherokee Indians, Cherokee, North Carolina.

1995   *The Qualla Arts and Crafts Cooperative: The Wood Carvers.* Produced in conjunction with The Eastern Band of Cherokee Indians, Cherokee, North Carolina.

1996   *The Qualla Arts and Crafts Cooperative: The Potters.* Produced in conjunction with The Eastern Band of Cherokee Indians, Cherokee, North Carolina.

1998   *The Eastern Band of Cherokee Indians. Narrated by Wes Studi.* Produced in conjunction with The Eastern Band of Cherokee Indians and South Carolina Public Television.

Ryan, Chris, and Jeremy Huyton
   2002   Tourists and Aboriginal People. *Annals of Tourism Research* 29:631–647.
Sahlins, Marshall
   1995   *How Natives Think: About Captain Cook, for Example.* University of Chicago Press, Chicago.
Said, Edward
   2000   Commencement Speech: American University of Beirut. June 28, 2000. Electronic document, http://www.aub.edu.lb/activities/public/graduation/ed-said.html, accessed September 2003.
Sampson, Tyson
   1997a   Indigo Girls Rock Qualla Boundary. *Cherokee One Feather* 24 September:1, 10.
   1997b   First Campout to Enhance Cultural Experiences. *Cherokee One Feather* 3 September:1.
Sarris, Greg
   1993   *Keeping Slug Woman Alive: A Holistic Approach to American Indian Texts.* University of California Press, Berkeley.
Saunooke, Josh
   1998   Personal interview with the author, April.
Schulte-Tenckhoff, Isabelle
   1988   Potlatch and Totem: The Attraction of America's Northwest Coast. In *Tourism: Manufacturing the Exotic,* edited by Pierre Rossel, pp. 124–140. International Work Group for Indigenous Affairs, Copenhagen.
Sears, John F.
   1989   *Sacred Places: American Tourist Attractions in the Nineteenth Century.* Oxford University Press, New York.
Seiler-Baldinger, Annemarie
   1988   Tourism in the Upper Amazon and Its Effects on the Indigenous Population. In *Tourism: Manufacturing the Exotic,* edited by Pierre Rossel, pp. 177–193. International Work Group for Indigenous Affairs, Copenhagen.
Sharpe, Kay
   1998   Personal interview with the author, February.
   2003   Personal interview with the author, December.
Silverstein, Michael
   1996   The Secret Life of Texts. In *Natural Histories of Discourse,* edited by Michael Silverstein and Greg Urban, pp. 81–105. University of Chicago Press, Chicago.
Simpson, George L., and Harriet L. Herring
   1956   *Western North Carolina Communities.* Pamphlet. N.p.
Smith, Betty Anderson
   1979   Distribution of Eighteenth-Century Cherokee Settlements. In *The Cherokee Indian Nation: A Troubled History,* edited by Duane H. King, pp. 46–60. University of Tennessee Press, Knoxville.

Smith, Jan
1998   Personal interview with the author, March.
Smith, M. Estellie
1997   Hegemony and Elite Capital: The Tools of Tourism. In *Tourism and Culture: An Applied Perspective,* edited by Erve Chambers, pp. 199–214. SUNY Press, Albany, New York.
Smith, Natalie
2006   Personal interview with the author, October.
Smith, Valene L.
1989   Eskimo Tourism: Micro-Models and Marginal Men. In *Hosts and Guests: The Anthropology of Tourism,* edited by V. L. Smith, pp. 55–82. 2nd ed. University of Pennsylvania Press, Philadelphia.
Smith, Valene L. (editor)
1989   *Hosts and Guests: The Anthropology of Tourism.* 2nd ed. University of Pennsylvania Press, Philadelphia.
Sofaer, Anna (scriptwriter/consultant)
2000   *The Mystery of Chaco Canyon.* Produced in conjunction with The Solstice Project and Robert Redford Productions. PBS/WGBH, Boston.
Soukhanov, Anne H.
1999   *Encarta World English Dictionary.* St. Martin's Press, New York.
Southern Highlands Attractions
1998   *Oconaluftee Indian Village.* Southern Highlands Attractions, Asheville, North Carolina.
Speck, Frank G.
1920   *Decorative Art and Basketry of the Cherokee.* Published by the Order of the Trustees, Milwaukee.
Speck, Frank G., and Leonard Broom
1951   *Cherokee Dance and Drama.* University of California Press, Berkeley.
Squirrel, John A.
1997a   To Whom It May Concern. *Cherokee One Feather* 29 October:2.
1997b   Trail of Broken Promises. *Cherokee One Feather* 27 August:2.
Staleup, Anthony (interviewer)
1981   Foxfire Interview Control Sheet Interview #A-81-28: GoingBack Chiltoskey. Subject of Interview: Profile of GoingBack.
Stannard, David E.
1993   *American Holocaust: The Conquest of the New World.* Oxford University Press, Oxford.
Storm, Christopher
1997   Preserving Cherokee Heritage by Preserving Cherokee Language. *Cherokee One Feather* 30 July:3.
Stronza, Amanda
2001   Anthropology of Tourism: Forging New Ground for Ecotourism and Other Alternatives. *Annual Review of Anthropology* 30:261–283.

Stucki, Larry R.

1981   Will the "Real" Indian Survive? Tourism and Affluence at Cherokee, N.C. *Proceedings of the American Ethnological Society,* Washington, D.C.

Sturm, Circe

2002   *Blood Politics: Race, Culture, and Identity in the Cherokee Nation of Oklahoma.* University of California Press, Berkeley.

Sutter, Paul

2002   *Driven Wild: How the Fight against Automobiles Launched the First Modern Wilderness Movement.* University of Washington Press, Seattle.

Swanton, John R.

1946   *The Indians of the Southeastern United States.* Bureau of American Ethnology Bulletin 137. Government Printing Office, Washington, D.C.

Swedenburg, Ted, and Smadar Lavie

1996   *Displacement, Diaspora, and Geographies of Identity.* Duke University Press, Durham, North Carolina.

Sweet, Jill

1989   Burlesquing "The Other" in Pueblo Performance. *Annals of Tourism Research* 16:63–75.

Swimmer, Amanda

1998   Personal interview with the author, April.

Takaki, Ronald

1993   *A Different Mirror: A History of Multicultural America.* Back Bay Books, Little, Brown, New York.

Taylor, Charlotte

1998   Personal interview with the author, May.

Taylor [Chief Red Hawk]

2006   Personal interview with the author, October.

Taylor, Christina M. [Christina T. Beard-Moose]

1998   Representations of American Indian Women: The Case of Nancy Ward. *disClosure: A Journal of Social Theory* 7:63–84.

Taylor, Maryjane

1998   Personal interview with the author, May.

Taylor, Robert

1997   Open Letter to the People. *Cherokee One Feather* 2 April:2.

Teo, Peggy, and Lim Hiong Li

2003   Global and Local Interactions in Tourism. *Annals of Tourism Research* 30:287–306.

Thomas, David H.

2000   *Exploring Native North America.* Oxford University Press, New York.

Thomas, Robert

1958   Cherokee Values and Worldview. Unpublished typescript, Institute for Research in Social Science, University of North Carolina.

Thompson, Caroline

1998   Personal interview with the author, May.

Thompson, Tiney B.
1998   Personal interview with the author, March.

Thomson, Jennifer L.
1998   Personal interview with the author, May.

Thornton, Russell
1990   *The Cherokees: A Population History.* University of Nebraska Press, Lincoln.
1998   The Demography of Colonialism and "Old" and "New" Native Americans. In *Studying Native America: Problems and Prospects,* edited by Russell Thornton, pp. 17–39. University of Wisconsin Press, Madison.

Tiller, Veronica E. (compiler and editor)
1996   *American Indian Reservation and Trust Areas.* Economic Development Administration, U.S. Department of Commerce, Washington, D.C.

Timberlake, Henry
1765   The Memoirs of Lieut. Henry Timberlake: (who accompanied the three Cherokee Indians to England in the year 1762). Printed for the author, London.

Tsali Institute of Cherokee Research, Inc.
1951   Certificate of Incorporation.

Two Eagles, Bruce [Cree/Chippewa], Don Merzlak [Blackfoot/Sioux], and Issac Welch [Cherokee]
1997   White Lies: Broken Promises. *Cherokee One Feather* 18 June:2.

Umberger, Wallace R.
1970   A History of *Unto These Hills,* 1941 to 1968. Ph.D. dissertation, Tulane University, University Microfilms, Ann Arbor.

Underwood, Tom
1998   Personal interview with the author, February.

The Unknown Author
1932   *America's First Big Parade.* David L. Cooley, Little Rock, Arkansas.

Unto These Hills
1960   Drama program. Cherokee Historical Association, Cherokee, North Carolina.
1996   Drama program. Cherokee Historical Association, Cherokee, North Carolina.
1997   Drama program. Cherokee Historical Association, Cherokee, North Carolina.

Urry, John
1990   *The Tourist Gaze: Leisure and Travel in Contemporary Societies.* Sage, New York.
1995   *Consuming Places.* Routledge, London.

Volkman, T.
1990   Visions and Revisions: Toraja Culture and the Tourist Gaze. *American Ethnologist* 17(1):91–110.

Walker, Amy
1998   Personal interview with the author, March.

Wallace, Anthony F. C.
1999   *Jefferson and the Indians: The Tragic Fate of the First Americans.* Belknap Press
        of Harvard University Press, Cambridge.
West, Debbie
1998   Personal interview with the author, May.
West, Patsy
1981   The Miami Indian Tourist Attractions: A History and Analysis of a
        Transitional Mikasuki Seminole Environment. *Florida Anthropologist*
        34(4):200–224.
1998   *The Enduring Seminoles: From Alligator Wrestling to Ecotourism.* University
        Press of Florida, Gainesville.
White, Max E.
2001   Anthropologists and the Eastern Cherokees. In *Anthropologists and Indi-
        ans in the New South,* edited by Rachel A. Bonney and J. Anthony Paredes,
        pp. 12–25. University of Alabama Press, Tuscaloosa.
Wiggins, Kayce Crowe
1998   Personal interview with the author, March.
Wiggins, Richard
1998   Personal interview with the author, March.
Wike, Clarence
1998   Personal interview with the author, April.
Williams, Mariama
2002   Tourism Liberalization, Gender and the GATS. Occasional Paper, Eco-
        nomic Literacy Series: General Agreement on Trade in Services, Inter-
        national Gender and Trade Network.
Williamson, Teresa
2006   Personal interview with the author, June.
Wilson, Alexander
1994   The View from the Road: Recreation and Tourism. In *Discovered Country:
        Tourism and Survival in the American West,* edited by Scott Norris, pp. 3–22.
        Stone Ladder Press, Albuquerque.
Wilson, Juanita
2006   Personal interview with the author, June.
Witthoft, John
1946   The Cherokee Green Corn Festival and the Green Corn Medicine. *Journal
        of the Washington Academy of Science* 36:213–219.
1979   Observations on Social Change among the Eastern Cherokees. In *The
        Cherokee Indian Nation: A Troubled History,* edited by Duane H. King,
        pp. 202–222. University of Tennessee Press, Knoxville.
Woodhead, Henry (series editor)
1994   *The American Indians: Tribes of the Southern Woodlands.* Raymond D. Fogel-
        son, Michael D. Green, and Frederick E. Hoxie, general consultants, and
        Duane King, special consultant. Time-Life Books, Alexandria, Virginia.

Wright, Ronald

1992   *Stolen Continents: The "New World" through Indian Eyes.* Houghton Mifflin,
        Boston.

Youngbird, Myrtle

1998   Personal interview with the author, May.

Zogry, Michael J.

2003   Playing or Praying? The Cherokee Anetso Ceremonial Complex. Unpub-
        lished Ph.D. dissertation, University of California, Santa Barbara.

2005   Ball Games: North American Indian Ballgames. In *The Encyclopedia of Reli-
        gion,* p. 238. Rev. ed. Macmillan, New York.

Index